Trials of Modernity:
Europe Since 1500

Stacy Burton

Dennis Dworkin

SIMON & SCHUSTER
CUSTOM PUBLISHING

SIMON & SCHUSTER CUSTOM PUBLISHING
160 Gould Street/Needham Heights, MA 02194
Simon & Schuster Education Group

Acknowledgments

Grateful acknowledgment is made to the following sources for permission to reprint material copyrighted or controlled by them:

"Ten Colloquies," by Desiderius Erasmus, reprinted from *Charon*, The Bobbs-Merrill Company, Inc., 1957.

"Nathan the Wise," by Gotthold Ephraim Lessing, reprinted from *Laocoön, Nathan the Wise, Minna von Barnhelm*, edited by William A. Steel, J. M. Dent & Sons, Ltd., 1930.

"What is the Third Estate?" by Emmanuel Sieyès, reprinted from *A Documentary Survey of the French Revolution*, edited by John Hall Stewart, Macmillan Publishing Company, 1951.

"Toward a Critique of Political Economy: Preface (1859)," by Karl Marx, reprinted from *Marx Selections*, edited by Allen W. Wood, Macmillan Publishing Company, 1970.

Excerpt from *Marinetti: Selected Writings* by Filippo Tommaso Marinetti, edited by R. W. Flint. English translation copyright © 1971, 1972 by Farrar, Straus & Giroux, Inc. Reprinted by permission of Farrar, Straus & Giroux, Inc.

"Dulce Et Decorum Est," by Wilfred Owen, from *The Collected Poems of Wilfred Owen*. Copyright © 1963 by Chatto & Windus, Ltd. Reprinted by permission of New Directions Publishing Corp.

"The Second Coming," reprinted with the permission of Simon & Schuster from *The Poems of W. B. Yeats: A New Edition*, edited by Richard J. Finneran. Copyright © 1924 by Macmillan Publishing Company, renewed 1952 by Bertha George Yeats.

"Women and Wages" by Rebecca West, reprinted from *The Young Rebecca: Writings of Rebecca West 1911-1917*. Reprinted by permission of the Peters Fraser & Dunlop Group Ltd.

"The Buddhist Priest's Wife," by Olive Schreiner, reprinted from *An Olive Schreiner Reader: Writings on Women and South Africa*, Pandora, 1987.

Excerpt from *A Room of One's Own* by Virginia Woolf. Copyright © 1929 by Harcourt Brace Jovanovich, renewed 1957 by Leonard Woolf.

Contents

Introduction

There are many ways that the readings in this book of original sources in European cultural history can be interpreted. In our view, one of the principal threads is the exploration of the modern experience. On the cover is Edvard Munch's 1893 painting, *The Scream*. The painting, according to the artist, is autobiographical.

> I was tired and ill—I stood looking out across the fjord—the sun was setting—the clouds were colored red—like blood—I felt as though a scream went through nature—I thought I heard a scream—I painted the picture—painted the clouds like real blood. The colors were screaming.

The artist suggests that the painting is about his inner life; and indeed most viewers have emphasized its subjective and psychological qualities as well. It has been interpreted as being about the individual's isolation from others and the world, the fragmentation of the self, and a feeling of anguish about the human condition. *The Scream is* most often thought of as being part of "modern art." This is in part because of when and how it was painted, but also because it captures the anxieties, fears, and apprehensions that many have felt about the world in which we live. We have chosen it because it visually represents the title of this volume: *Trials of Modernity.*

At the same time, the "trials of modernity" are not exhausted by the qualities found in Munch's painting. What modernity is, when it came into existence, and indeed whether it still exists are all questions that resist easy answers. Nor is the nature of the intellectual and cultural movements that have grown up in response to this modern world—modern thought or, more recently, 'modernism'—any easier to define. There have been those like Munch who appear anxious and fearful about this world. Frequently this has been accompanied by nostalgia or longing for an unrecoverable past. Yet there have been others who view modernity as being synonymous with 'progress' and look forward eagerly to an even better future. Both responses seem characteristic. As the critic Marshall Berman writes: "To be modern is to find ourselves in an environment that promises us adventure, power, joy, growth, transformation of ourselves and the world—and, at the same time, that threatens to destroy everything we have, everything we know, everything we are." Whether Berman's definition is useful is an open question. We hope that the readings we've selected will allow readers to make up their own minds.

Yet the readings are not about modernity in general. As the subtitle suggests—and in our view it is as important as the title—the book is about European culture since 1500. Because some now question why we still need to know about Europe, it seems appropriate to give our own views on the subject. First, it is impossible to understand fully the meaning of American identities without coming to grips with the European traditions which have been so important in shaping them. European society should not be studied instead of other cultures that have shaped the American way of life but in conjunction with them. Second, if we are interested in understanding the modern world there is no better place to start than Europe, where the terms to define this experience were originally established. Given that the process of modernization has been nearly universal, what happened in Europe and how Europeans reacted to it is of great interest.

As we've suggested, 'modernity' is not the only theme that runs through the readings in this book. Texts that we've chosen can be interpreted from numerous perspectives. Some of the readings address the question: What is human nature? Are human beings naturally good, or naturally evil? Are they controlled by fate, or responsible for their own destiny? Another dimension of the readings involves the relationship between an individual and his or her society. Here we might ask the questions: What makes a good society? What responsibilities do individuals have to societies, and societies to individuals? Several of the readings explore the relations between men and women. When considering these readings, we might ask: What are—and what could or should be—the relations (social, economic, intellectual, sexual) between men and women? Do women and men differ inherently, or are apparent gender differences socially-constructed? If so, what significance should we attach to differences? Why have women traditionally been treated very differently from men? In more than one section, readings explore Europe's connections with other cultures. Several issues are relevant here. Why do human cultures differ and conflict? What are or should be the intellectual, economic, and social relationships between differing cultures? What does it mean to be 'civilized' or 'enlightened,' to be 'barbaric' or 'primitive'? Why are barbaric acts sometimes perpetrated by apparently civilized societies? The numerous questions that have been asked here are by no means the only possible ones. Students and instructors will certainly come up with their own.

The date given for each text is in almost all cases the date of first publication. Selecting the most representative dates can be difficult, since some texts were written years, even decades, before they were published. William Blake's "Mock on, mock on," for example, comes from a manuscript notebook he kept from about 1790 to 1810, and Olive Schreiner's story "The Buddhist Priest's Wife" was first published thirty years after it was written. We have chosen to use dates of publication since they best reflect when the text entered into public discussion.

This book could not have been produced without the generous contributions of the Western Traditions faculty. We thank Scott Casper for reading drafts of the introduction and Martha Hildreth and Bruce Moran for reading section introductions and suggesting readings for inclusion. Several other faculty members have suggested texts to us or commented on the first draft of the table of contents: Deborah Achtenberg, Viktoria Hertling, Louis Marvick, Gaye McCollum, Thomas Nickles, and Margaret Urie. We thank them all. We would also like to express our gratitude to Phillip Boardman, chair of the Western Traditions program, who has supported our efforts since the project's inception. Finally, we would like to acknowledge the help of Jonathan Conley who helped us read the proofs.

Stacy Burton
Dennis Dworkin
University of Nevada, Reno

I. Early Modern Europe: The Reformation and the Emergence of Science

The modern world did not suddenly appear during a specific year, at a particular time, and at a precise place. Nor did medieval society suddenly cease to exist. Indeed, the transition from a medieval world to a modern one took place over centuries, and it is only with hindsight that we can understand it in these terms. The pace of change was unevenly distributed: different parts of Europe were affected by it at different rates. And the experience of this transition was neither uniform nor homogeneous. Indeed, there was not even a uniform set of signs indicating the arrival of modernity. Yet beginning in the sixteenth and seventeenth centuries—and according to some historians perhaps even earlier—it is possible to detect social, economic, political, and cultural developments that would re-shape European society and consciousness. In retrospect, we can see that these represented the first glimmers of the modern world.

The readings in this chapter explore two of these developments: the Protestant Reformation and the Scientific Revolution. The immediate event that triggered the Protestant Reformation—the first successful attempt in Western European history to break the monopoly power of the Roman Catholic Church—was the attempt by Pope Leo X to raise money to build St. Peter's Cathedral in Rome by granting papal indulgences, or pardons of sin, in return for appropriate donations to the Church. (The practice of granting indulgences was not new, and there had been objections before.) When in 1517, a papal agent, a Dominican friar named John Tetzel, attempted to raise money through the granting of indulgences in central Germany, Martin Luther (1483–1546), a professor in old testament studies at the University of Wittenberg, responded by posting a list of ninety-five theses or propositions on the Castle Church protesting (what he perceived as) a mockery of religious practice. Although it was Luther's response to a specific abuse of church authority that originally provoked the Reformation, the substance of his critique had much wider implications.

This is made clear in Luther's "An Open Letter to the Christian Nobility of the German Nation Concerning the Reform of the Christian Estate, 1520," a sweeping condemnation of the entire foundation of Roman Catholic authority. Inspired by his reading of St. Paul and St. Augustine, Luther held that original sin was inescapable: salvation was unattainable through individual action or "works"; it was a gift freely given by God to those who lived a life of faith. Luther in effect dismissed the need for a Roman Catholic Church, for he rejected the idea (central to Catholicism) that an ordained priesthood's administration of the sacraments was necessary for an individual's salvation. Luther supplanted the idea of a priestly hierarchy with a priesthood of all believers, an emphasis on individual responsibility that became a central tenet of the Protestant revolution in religious thought. Just as important, he regarded the Roman Church's meddling in affairs of sovereign states as unjustified; the implications of his thought were as much political as religious.

As a result of his attack on the early sixteenth-century Church, Luther left the Catholic fold. In contrast, Desiderius Erasmus (1466–1536), a reformer who had many of the same misgivings, chose to reform the Church from within and remained a Catholic his entire life. A humanist and scholar, Erasmus was one of the most prolific and influential authors of his time. One of his main projects was to revive Christian piety by creating reliable editions of the Bible and the writings of the church fathers and providing commentary upon them. Much of his writing involved fostering Christianity as a practice, one which combined piety, faith, and learning. Yet it is as a satirist that Erasmus is best known; and one of his greatest works in this genre was his *Colloquia* from which the selection "Charon" is drawn. The original intent of the *Colloquia* was to teach students correct conversational and written Latin through the reading of dialogues, but as they evolved Erasmus used them to express informally his views on such things as current affairs, ideas, and customs. "Charon" is an excellent introduction to Erasmus's satire. The most blatant target is the warfare of the sixteenth century, yet Erasmus also makes jibes at Luther and his followers. He agrees with many of Luther's criticisms of the Church, and is impatient with those of Luther's critics who dismiss him without reading him, but he thinks that Luther and his supporters are intransigent and holds them responsible for the turmoil and conflict that the Reformation sets in motion.

The second subject of this section—the Scientific Revolution—does not at first glance seem to have much to do with the birth of Protestantism. What possibly could Copernicus's heliocentric view of the universe (the view that the earth revolves around the sun) and Luther's struggle against the Catholic church have in common? But if we think about it, despite the very different nature of the concerns of religious reformers and astronomers, they both challenged the received wisdom of the past—the world view which had held together medieval life. Religious reformers challenged the infallibility of the papacy and the viability of the Roman Catholic Church. Astronomers and the creators of modern physics challenged the medieval view of the universe, the Ptolemaic or geocentric view which held that the earth was the center of the universe. Most important, the pioneers of the new science were more concerned with discovering the underlying laws governing the motion of the heavens than with understanding what the ultimate purpose of the heavens was. They were interested in learning about the "how" rather than the "why" of the natural world. Speculation about divine purpose disappeared from proper scientific inquiry.

The nature of the emerging scientific method is the subject of the selections drawn from the writings of two Englishmen—Francis Bacon (1561–1626) and Isaac Newton (1642–1727). Bacon combined the dual role of statesman and philosopher. As a statesman, Bacon was a leading government official during the reign of James I: he was solicitor general, attorney general, privy counsellor, Lord Keeper, and Lord Chancellor. He was also convicted of accepting bribes from office suitors and was fined, imprisoned, and banished from parliament and the court. As a thinker, he is best known as one of the major forces in developing the inductive method in the sciences, the view that scientific understanding can only come from careful and ongoing observation of specific occurrences. Bacon discusses this idea in the "New Organon," a series of aphorisms which were part of a larger work, *Great Renewal*. Bacon saw *Great Renewal* as representing a "total reconstruction of the sciences, arts, and all human knowledge."

Bacon has sometimes been referred to as the "prophet of the scientific revolution." If he is its prophet, Isaac Newton is its consummation. Newton was an eccentric and remote individual who was as interested in mysticism and the occult as he was in modern science. His *The Mathematical Principles of Natural Philosophy*, in which he sets forth the theory of the universal gravitation, is among the most original and path breaking works in the history of science. The importance of the book is that Newton is able to explain the movement of bodies in both heaven and earth on the basis of a universal set of laws, three involving their motion and one their attraction towards each other. Yet if Newton's mechanics was path breaking, it is also a culmination of over two-hundred years of scientific exploration, building on the labors of scientists such as Nicolaus Copernicus, Tycho Brahe, Johannes Kepler, and Galileo. Similarly, Newton's description of the scientific method in *The Mathematical Principles of Natural Philosophy* builds on the work of thinkers such as Bacon, while offering an extension of these ideas as well.

We have suggested that the Protestant Reformation and the Scientific Revolution represent different expressions of the same revolt against received authority. But they did not always inhabit separate spheres. A thinker who bridges these two worlds is Thomas Hobbes (1558-1679), one of the first modern political philosophers and one of the founders of the emerging field of political science. Hobbes embraced the scientific method and was an admirer of approaches drawn from pure mathematics. In his major work, *Leviathan*, Hobbes's political vision—an argument for the necessity of a strong ruler and state—was shaped by his living through the seventeenth-century English Revolution, an event whose origins are in part attributable to the Reformation in England a hundred years before. Because of his aristocratic associations, Hobbes was forced to flee England and live in Paris, where he tutored the exiled, future king of England, Charles II, in mathematics. Hobbes's experience of decades of violence and bloodshed helped shape his ideas about the proper role of government and the state.

Martin Luther

from An Open Letter to the Christian Nobility of the German Nation Concerning the Reform of the Christian Estate (1520)

To His Most Illustrious and Mighty Imperial Majesty,
and to the Christian Nobility of the German Nation,

Grace and power from God, Most illustrious Majesty, and most gracious and dear Lords.

It is not out of sheer forwardness or rashness that I, a single, poor man, have undertaken to address your worships. The distress and oppression which weigh down all the Estate of Christendom, especially of Germany, and which move not me alone, but everyone to cry out time and again, and to pray for help, have forced me even now to cry aloud that God may inspire some one with His Spirit to lend this suffering nation a helping hand. Ofttimes the councils have made some pretence at reformation, but their attempts have been cleverly hindered by the guile of certain men and things have gone from bad to worse. I now intend, by the help of God, to throw some light upon the wiles and wickedness of these men, to the end that when they are known, they may not henceforth be so hurtful and so great a hindrance. God has given us a noble youth to be our head and thereby has awakened great hopes of good in many hearts; wherefore it is meet that we should do our part and profitably use this time of grace.

In this whole matter the first and most important thing is that we take earnest heed not to enter on it trusting in great might or in human reason, even though all power in the world were ours; for God cannot and will not suffer a good work to be begun with trust in our own power or reason. Such works He crushes ruthlessly to earth, as it is written in the xxxiii Psalm, "There is no king saved by the multitude of an host; a mighty man is not delivered by much strength." On this account, I fear, it came to pass of old that the good Emperors Frederick I and II, and many other German emperors were shamefully oppressed and trodden under foot by the popes, although all the world feared them. It may be that they relied on their own might more than on God, and therefore they had to fall. In our own times, too, what was it that raised the blood-thirsty Julius II to such heights? Nothing else, I fear, except that France, the Germans, and Venice relied upon themselves. The children of Benjamin slew forty-two thousand Israelites because the latter relied on their own strength.

That it may not so fare with us and our noble young Emperor Charles, we must be sure that in this matter we are dealing not with men, but with the princes of hell, who can fill the world with war and bloodshed, but whom war and bloodshed do not overcome. We must go at this work despairing of physical force and humbly trusting God; we must seek God's help with earnest prayer, and fix our minds on nothing else than the misery and distress of suffering Christendom, without regard to the deserts of evil men. Otherwise we may start the game with great prospect of success, but when we get well into it the evil spirits will stir up such confusion that the whole world will swim in blood, and yet nothing will come of it. Let us act wisely, therefore, and in the fear of God. The more force we use, the greater our disaster if we do not act humbly and in God's fear. The popes and the Romans have hitherto been able, by the devil's help, to set kings at odds with one another, and they may well be able to do it again, if we proceed by our own might and cunning, without God's help.

I. The Three Walls of the Romanists

The Romanists, with great adroitness, have built three walls about them, behind which they have hitherto defended themselves in such wise that no one has been able to reform them; and this has been the cause of terrible corruption throughout all Christendom.

First, when pressed by the temporal power, they have made decrees and said that the temporal power has no jurisdiction over them, but, on the other hand, that the spiritual is above the temporal power. Second, when the attempt is made to reprove them out of the Scriptures, they raise the objection that the interpretation of the Scriptures belongs to no one except the pope. Third, if threatened with a council, they answer with the fable that no one can call a council but the pope. . . .

Against the first wall we will direct our first attack.

It is pure invention that pope, bishops, priests and monks are to be called the "spiritual estate"; princes, lords, artisans, and farmers the "temporal estate." That is indeed a fine bit of lying and hypocrisy. Yet no one should be frightened by it; and for this reason—*viz.*, that all Christians are truly of the "spiritual estate," and there is among them no difference at all but that of office, as Paul says in I Corinthians xii, We are all one body, yet every member has its own work, whereby it serves every other, all because we have one baptism, one Gospel, one faith, and are all alike Christians; for baptism, Gospel and faith alone make us "spiritual" and a Christian people. . . .

To make it still clearer. If a little group of pious Christian laymen were taken captive and set down in a wilderness, and had among them no priest consecrated by a bishop, and if there in the wilderness they were to agree in choosing one of themselves, married or unmarried, and were to charge him with the office of baptizing, saying mass, absolving and preaching, such a man would be as truly a priest as though all bishops and popes had consecrated him. That is why in cases of necessity any one can baptize and give absolution, which would be impossible unless we were all priests. This great grace and power of baptism and of the Christian Estate they have well-nigh destroyed and caused us to forget through the canon law. It was in the manner aforesaid that Christians in olden days chose from their number bishops and priests, who were afterwards confirmed by other bishops, without all the show which now obtains. It was thus that Sts. Augustine, Ambrose, and Cyprian became bishops. . . .

From all this it follows that there is really no difference between laymen and priests, princes and bishops, "spirituals" and "temporals," as they call them, except that of office and work, but not of "estate"; for they are all of the same estate,—true priests, bishops, and popes,—though they are not all engaged in the same work, just as all priests and monks have not the same work. This is the teaching of St. Paul in Romans xii and I Corinthians xii, and of St. Peter in I Peter ii, as I have said above, *viz.*, that we are only one body of Christ, the Head, all members one of another. Christ has not two different bodies, one "temporal," the other "spiritual." He is one Head, and He has one body. . . .

See, now, how Christian is the decree which says that the temporal power is not above the "spiritual estate" and may not punish it. That is as much as to say that the hand shall lend no aid when the eye is suffering. Is it not unnatural, not to say unchristian, that one member should not help another and prevent its destruction? Verily, the more honorable the member, the more should the others help. I say then, since the temporal power is ordained of God to punish evildoers and to protect them that do well, it should therefore be left free to perform its office without hindrance through the whole body of Christendom without respect of persons, whether it affect pope, bishops, priests, monks, nuns or anybody else. For if the mere fact that the temporal power has a smaller place among the Christian offices than has the office of preachers or confessors, or of the clergy, then the tailors, cobblers, masons, carpenters, potboys, tapsters, farmers, and all the secular tradesmen, should also be prevented from providing pope, bishops, priests and monks with shoes, clothing, houses, meat and drink, and from paying them tribute. But if these laymen are allowed to do their work unhindered, what do the Roman scribes mean by their laws, with which they withdraw themselves from the jurisdiction of the temporal Christian power, only so that they may be free to do evil and to fulfill what St. Peter has said: "There shall be false teachers among you, and through covetousness shall they with feigned words make merchandise of you."

On this account the Christian temporal power should exercise its office without let or hindrance, regardless whether it be pope, bishop, or priest whom it affects; whoever is guilty, let him suffer. All that the canon law has said to the contrary is sheer invention of Roman presumption. . . .

The second wall is still more flimsy and worthless. They wish to be the only Masters of the Holy Scriptures, even though in all their lives they learn nothing from them. They assume for themselves sole authority, and with insolent juggling of words they would persuade us that the pope, whether he be a bad man or a good man, cannot err in matters of faith; and yet they cannot prove a single letter of it. Hence it comes that so many heretical and unchristian, nay, even unnatural ordinances have a place in the canon law, of which, however, there is no present need to speak. For since they think that the Holy Spirit never leaves them, be they ever so unlearned and wicked, they make bold to decree whatever they will. And if it were true, where would be the need or use of the Holy Scriptures? Let us burn them, and be satisfied with the unlearned lords at Rome, who are possessed of the Holy Spirit,—although He can possess only pious hearts! Unless I had read it myself, I could not have believed that the devil would make such clumsy pretensions at Rome, and find a following.

But, not to fight them with mere words, we will quote the Scriptures. St. Paul says in I Corinthians xiv: "If to anyone something better is revealed, though he be sitting and listening to another in God's Word, then the first, who is speaking, shall hold his peace and give place." What would be the use of this commandment, if we were only to believe him who does the talking or who has the highest seat? Christ also says in John vi, that all Christians shall be taught of God. Thus it may well happen that the pope and his followers are wicked men, and no true Christians, not taught of God, not having true understanding. On the other hand, an ordinary man may have true understanding; why then should we not follow him? Has not the pope erred many times? Who would help Christendom when the pope errs, if we were not to believe another, who had the Scriptures on his side, more than the pope? . . .

Besides, if we are all priests, as was said above, and all have one faith, one Gospel, one sacrament, why should we not also have the power to test and judge what is correct or incorrect in matters of faith? What becomes of the words of Paul in I Corinthians ii: "He that is spiritual judgeth all things, yet he himself is judged of no man," and in II Corinthians iv: "We have all the same Spirit of faith"? Why, then, should not we perceive what squares with faith and what does not, as well as does an unbelieving pope? . . .

The third wall falls of itself when the first two are down. For when the pope acts contrary to the Scriptures, it is our duty to stand by the Scriptures, to reprove him, and to constrain him, according to the word of Christ in Matthew xviii:

> If thy brother sin against thee, go and tell it him between thee and him alone; if he hear thee not, then take with thee one or two more; if he hear them not, tell it to the Church; if he hear not the Church, consider him a heathen.

They have no basis in Scripture for their contention that it belongs to the pope alone to call a council or confirm its actions; for this is based merely upon their own laws, which are valid only in so far as they are not injurious to Christendom or contrary to the laws of God. When the Pope deserves punishment, such laws go out of force, since it is injurious to Christendom not to punish him by means of a council. . . .

Therefore, when necessity demands, and the pope is an offence to Christendom, the first man who is able should, as a faithful member of the whole body, do what he can to bring about a truly free council. No one can do this so well as the temporal authorities, especially since now they also are fellow-Christians, fellow-priests, "fellow-spirituals" fellow-lords over all things, and whenever it is needful or profitable, they should give free course to the office and work in which God has put them above every man. Would it not be an unnatural thing, if a fire broke out in a city, and every body were to stand by and let it burn on and on and consume everything that could burn, for the sole reason that nobody had the authority of the burgomaster, or because, perhaps, the fire broke out in the burgomaster's house? In such case is it not the duty of every citizen to arouse and call the rest? How much more should this be done in the spiritual city of Christ, if a fire of offence breaks out, whether in the papal government, or anywhere else? In the same way, if the enemy attacks a city, he who first rouses the others deserves honour and thanks; why then should he not deserve honour who makes known the presence of the enemy from hell, and awakens the Christians, and calls them together? . . .

Thus I hope that the false, lying terror with which the Romans have this long time made our conscience timid and stupid, has been allayed. They, like all of us, are subject to the temporal sword; they have no power to interpret the Scriptures by mere authority, without learning; they have no authority to prevent a council or, in sheer wantonness, to pledge it, bind it, or take away its liberty; but if they do this, they are in truth in the communion of Antichrist and of the devil, and have nothing at all of Christ except the name.

II. Abuses to be Discussed in Councils

We shall now look at the matters which should be discussed in the councils, and with which popes, cardinals, bishops, and all the scholars ought properly to be occupied day and night if they love Christ and His Church. . . .

1. It is a horrible and frightful thing that the ruler of Christendom who boasts himself vicar of Christ and successor of St. Peter, lives in such worldly splendor that in this regard no king nor emperor can equal or approach him, and that he who claims the title of "most holy" and "most spiritual" is more worldly than the world itself. He wears a triple crown, when the greatest kings wear but a single crown; if that is like the poverty of Christ and of St. Peter, then it is a new kind of likeness. When a word is said against it, they cry out "Heresy!" but that is because they do not wish to hear how unchristian and ungodly such a practice is. I think, however, that if the pope were with tears to pray to God he would have to lay aside these crowns, for our God can suffer no pride, and his office is nothing else than this,—daily to weep and pray for Christendom, and to set an example of all humility. . . .

2. What is the use in Christendom of these people who are called the cardinals? I shall tell you. Italy and Germany have many rich monasteries, foundations, benefices, and livings. No better way has been discovered to bring all these to Rome than by creating cardinals and giving them the bishoprics, monasteries, and prelacies, and so overthrowing the worship of God. For this reason we now see Italy a very wilderness—monasteries in ruins, bishoprics devoured, the prelacies and the revenues of all the churches drawn to Rome, cities decayed, land and people laid waste, because there is no more worship or preaching. Why? The cardinals must have the income. No Turk could have so devastated Italy and suppressed the worship of God.

Now that Italy is sucked dry, they come into Germany, and begin oh so gently. But let us beware, or Germany will soon become like Italy. Already we have some cardinals; what the Romans seek by that the "drunken Germans" are not to understand until we have not a bishopric, a monastery, a living, a benefice, *a heller* or a *pfennig* left. Antichrist must take the treasures of the earth, as it was prophesied. . . .

I advise, however, that the number of cardinals be reduced, or that the pope be made to keep them at his own expense. Twelve of them would be more than enough, and each of them might have an income of a thousand *gulden* a year. How comes it that we Germans must put up with such robbery and such extortion of our property, at the hands of the pope? . . .

3. If ninety-nine parts of the papal court were done away and only the hundredth part allowed to remain, it would still be large enough to give decisions in matters of faith. Now, however, there is such a swarm of vermin yonder in Rome, all boasting that they are "pa-

pal," that there was nothing like it in Babylon. These are more than three thousand papal secretaries alone; who will count the other offices, when they are so many that they scarcely can be counted? And they all lie in wait for the prebends and benefices of Germany as wolves lie in wait for the sheep. I believe that Germany now gives much more to the pope at Rome than it gave in former times to the emperors. Indeed, some estimate that every year more than three hundred thousand *gulden* find their way from Germany to Rome, quite uselessly and fruitlessly; we get nothing for it but scorn and contempt. And yet we wonder that princes, nobles, cities, endowments, land, and people are impoverished! We should rather wonder that we still have anything to eat!

ERASMUS

from Ten Colloquies (1529)

Charon

Charon, The Spirit Alastor

Charon. Why the hustle and bustle, Alastor?

Alastor. Well met, Charon! I was speeding to you.

Charon. What's new?

Alastor. I bring news that will delight you and Proserpina.[1]

Charon. Out with it, then. Unload it.

Alastor. The Furies have done their work with as much zeal as success. Not a corner of the earth have they left unravaged by their hellish dissensions—wars, robberies, plagues: so much so that now, with their snakes let loose, they're completely bald.[2] Drained of poisons, they roam about, looking for whatever vipers and asps they can find, since they're as smooth-headed as an egg—not a hair on their crowns, nor a drop of good poison in their breasts. So get your boat and oars ready, for there'll soon be such a crowd of shades coming that I fear you can't ferry them all.

Charon. No news to me.

Alastor. Where did you learn it?

Charon. Ossa[3] brought it more than two days ago.

Alastor. Can't get ahead of that goddess! But why are you loitering here without your boat, then?

Charon. Business trip: I came here to get a good, strong trireme ready. My galley's so rotten with age and so patched up that it won't do for this job, if what Ossa told me is true. Though what need was there of Ossa? The plain fact of the matter demands it: I've had a shipwreck.

Alastor. You *are* dripping wet, undoubtedly. I thought you were coming back from a bath.

Charon. Oh, no, I've been swimming out of the Stygian swamp.

Alastor. Where have you left the shades?

Charon. Swimming with the frogs.

Alastor. But what did Ossa report?

Charon. That the three rulers of the world, in deadly hatred, clash to their mutual destruction.[4] No part of Christendom is safe from the ravages of war, for those three have

10

dragged all the rest into alliance. They're all in such a mood that none of them is willing to yield to another. Neither Dane nor Pole nor Scot nor Turk,[5] in fact, is at peace; catastrophes are building up; the plague rages everywhere, in Spain, Britain, Italy, France. In addition, there's a new epidemic,[6] born of difference of opinion. It has so corrupted everybody's mind that sincere friendship exists nowhere, but brother distrusts brother, and husband and wife disagree. I have hopes of a splendid slaughter in the near future, too, if the war of tongues and pens come to actual blows.

Alastor. Ossa reported all this quite correctly, for I've seen more than this with my own eyes; I, the constant attendant and assistant of the Furies, who have never shown themselves more deserving of their name.

Charon. But there's danger that some devil may turn up and preach peace all of a sudden—and mortal minds are fickle. I hear there's a certain Polygraphus[7] up there who's incessantly attacking war with his pen and urging men to peace.

Alastor. He's sung to deaf ears this long while. He once wrote a "Complaint of Peace O'erthrown"; now he's written the epitaph of peace dead and buried. On the other hand, there are some who are as helpful to our cause as the Furies themselves.

Charon. Who are those?

Alastor. Certain creatures in black and white cloaks and ash gray tunics, adorned with plumage of various kinds.[8] They never leave the courts of princes. They instill into their ears a love of war; they incite rulers and populace alike; they proclaim in their evangelical sermons that war is just, holy, and right. And—to make you marvel more at the audacity of the fellows—they proclaim the very same thing on both sides. To the French they preach that God is on the French side: he who has God to protect him cannot be conquered! To the English and Spanish they declare this war is not the emperor's but God's: only let them show themselves valiant men and victory is certain! But if anyone *does* get killed, he doesn't perish utterly but flies straight up to heaven, armed just as he was.

Charon. And people believe these men?

Alastor. What can a pretense of religion not achieve? Youth, inexperience, thirst for glory, anger, and natural human inclination swallow this whole. People are easily imposed upon. And it's not hard to upset a cart that's ready to collapse of its own accord.

Charon. I'll be glad to reward these creatures!

Alastor. Give them a fine dinner. They like nothing better.

Charon. A dinner of mallows, lupines, and leeks. That's the only fare we have, as you know.

Alastor. Oh, no, it must be partridges, capons, and pheasants if you wish to be an acceptable host.

Charon. But what makes them such warmongers? Or what advantage are they afraid of losing?

Alastor. They make more profit from the dying than from the living. There are wills, masses for kinsmen, bulls, and many other sources of revenue not to be despised. In short, they prefer to buzz in camp rather than in their own hives. War spawns many bishops who in peacetime weren't worth a penny.

Charon. They're smart.

Alastor. But why do you need a trireme?

Charon. I don't, if I want to be shipwrecked in the middle of the swamp again.

Alastor. On account of the crowd?

Charon. Of course.

Alastor. But you haul shades, not bodies. Just how light are shades?

Charon. They may be water skippers, but enough water skippers could sink a boat. Then, you know, the boat is unsubstantial, too.

Alastor. But sometimes, I remember, when there was a crowd so large the boat couldn't hold them all, I saw three thousand shades hanging from your rudder, and you didn't feel any weight.

Charon. I grant there are such souls, which departed little by little from bodies worn away by consumption or hectic fever. But those plucked on the sudden from heavy bodies bring a good deal of bodily substance along with them. Apoplexy, quinsy, plague, but especially war, send this kind.

Alastor. Frenchmen or Spaniards don't weigh much, I suppose.

Charon. Much less than others, though even their souls are not exactly featherweight. But from well-fed Britons and Germans such shades come at times that lately I've hardly dared to ferry even ten, and unless I'd thrown them overboard I'd have gone down along with boat, rowers, and passage money.

Alastor. A terrible risk!

Charon. Meanwhile what do you think is going to happen when heavy lords, Thrasos, and swashbucklers come along?

Alastor. None of those who die in a just war[9] come to you, I believe. For these, they say, fly straight to heaven.

Charon. Where they may fly to, I don't know. I do know one thing: that whenever a war's on, so many come to me wounded and cut up that I'd be surprised if any had been left on earth. They come loaded not only with debauchery and gluttony but even with bulls, benefices, and many other things.

Alastor. But they don't bring these along with them. The souls come to you naked.

Charon. True, but newcomers bring along dreams of such things.

Alastor. So dreams are heavy?

Charon. They weigh down my boat. Weigh down, did I say? They've already sunk it! Finally, do you imagine so many obols weigh nothing?

Alastor. Well, I suppose they *are* heavy if they're copper ones.

Charon. So I've decided to look out for a vessel strong enough for the load.

Alastor. Lucky you!

Charon. How so?

Alastor. Because you'll soon grow rich.

Charon. From a lot of shades?

Alastor. Of course.

Charon. If only they'd bring their riches with them! As it is, those in the boat who lament the kingdoms, prelacies, abbacies, and countless talents of gold they left up there bring me nothing but an obol. And so everything I've scraped together in three thousand years has to be laid out for one trireme.

Alastor. If you want to make money, you have to spend money.

Charon. Yet mortals, as I hear, do business better: with Mercury's help they grow rich within three years.

Alastor. But sometimes those same mortals go broke. Your profit is less, but it's more certain.

Charon. How certain I can't tell. If some god should turn up now and settle the affairs of princes, my whole fortune would be lost.

Alastor. Don't give the matter a thought; just leave it to me. You've no reason to fear a peace within ten whole years.[10] Only the Roman pontiff is zealous in urging peace, but his efforts are wasted. Cities, too, weary of their troubles, complain bitterly. People—I don't know who they are—mutter that it's outrageous for human affairs to be turned topsy-turvy on account of the personal grudges or ambitions of two or three men. But the Furies, believe me, will defeat counsel, no matter how good it is.—Yet what need was there for you to ask this favor of those above? Haven't we workmen of our own? We have Vulcan, surely.

Charon. Fine—if I wanted a bronze ship.

Alastor. Labor's cheap.

Charon. Yes, but we're short of timber.

Alastor. What, aren't there any forests here?

Charon. Even the groves in the Elysian fields have been used up.

Alastor. What for?

Charon. For burning shades of heretics. So that we've been forced of late to mine coal from the depths of the earth.

Alastor. What, can't those shades be punished at less expense?

Charon. This was the decision of Rhadamanthus.[11]

Alastor. When you've bought your trireme, where will you get rowers?

Charon. My job is to hold the tiller; the shades must row if they want passage.

Alastor. But some haven't learned how to handle an oar.

Charon. No distinction of persons with me: monarchs row and cardinals row, each in their turn, no less than common folk, whether they've learned or not.

Alastor. Good luck in getting a trireme at a bargain! I won't hold you up any longer. I'll take the good news to Orcus.[12] But say, Charon—

Charon. What?

Alastor. Hurry back, so the crowd won't quickly overwhelm you.

Charon. Oh, you'll meet over two hundred thousand on the bank already, besides those swimming in the swamp. But I'll hurry as much as I can. Tell 'em I'll be there right away.

Notes

1. Queen of the underworld.
2. The Furies had poisonous snakes for hair. These they sent to torment the consciences of the wicked.
3. In Homer, the goddess Rumor.
4. The passage refers to the recent course of the Italian wars. The three rulers are Charles V, Holy Roman Emperor, Francis I, king of France, and Henry VIII, king of England. Francis had been captured at the battle of Pavia (1525). When the Treaty of Madrid was signed and Francis

released by the Spanish, he immediately joined with Milan, Venice, Florence, and the papacy in a league against Charles. England supported the league unofficially. In the Italian campaigns that followed, the fighting mostly favored the Imperial forces. It culminated in the Sack of Rome by undisciplined Imperial forces in May, 1527, the most spectacular disaster suffered by the papacy in centuries. Henry VIII had now joined Francis, and gave the war his active assistance. A new Italian campaign opened, but after six months the pope, warned by Imperial successes, began efforts to make peace. Charles rejected the terms, and the war went on until August, 1529. By that time the Empire had won control of Italy.

5. The Turks had crushed the Hungarian army in the battle of Mohacs, August, 1526.
6. Lutheranism.
7. Erasmus.
8. The friars.
9. Erasmus believed that if there is such a thing as a just war, it is one fought in self-defense after one's country has been invaded. But he thought "just" wars seldom occurred.
10. In fact, peace was made a few months after this colloquy appeared. The Empire was victorious in Italy, and by the Treaty of Cambrai (August, 1529) France renounced its claim to Italian territory.
11. One of the judges of the dead.
12. God of the underworld.

Francis Bacon

from Novum Organum (1620)

Aphorisms Concerning the Interpretation of Nature and the Kingdom of Man

I. Man, being the servant and interpreter of Nature, can do and understand so much and so much only as he has observed in fact or in thought in the course of nature: beyond this he neither knows anything nor can do anything.

II. Neither the naked hand nor the understanding left to itself can effect much. It is by instruments and helps that the work is done, which are as much wanted for the understanding as for the hand. And as the instruments of the hand either give motion or guide it, so the instruments of the mind supply either suggestions for the understanding or cautions.

III. Human knowledge and human power meet in one; for where the cause is not known the effect cannot be produced. Nature to be commanded must be obeyed; and that which in contemplation is as the cause is in operation as the rule.

IV. Towards the effecting of works, all that man can do is to put together or put asunder natural bodies. The rest is done by nature working within.

VI. It would be an unsound fancy and self-contradictory to expect that things which have never yet been done can be done except by means which have never yet been tried.

XI. As the sciences which we now have do not help us in finding out new works, so neither does the logic which we now have help us in finding out new sciences.

XII. The logic now in use serves rather to fix and give stability to the errors which have their foundations in commonly received notions than to help the search after truth. So it does more harm than good.

XVIII. The discoveries which have hitherto been made in the sciences are such as lie close to vulgar notions, scarcely beneath the surface. In order to penetrate into the inner and further recesses of nature, it is necessary that both notions and axioms be derived from things by a more sure and guarded way; and that a method of intellectual operation be introduced altogether better and more certain.

XIX. There are and can be only two ways of searching into and discovering truth. The one flies from the senses and particulars to the most general axioms, and from these principles, the truth of which it takes for settled and immovable, proceeds to judgment and to the discovery of the middle axioms. And this way is now in fashion. The other derives axioms from the senses and particulars, rising by a gradual and unbroken ascent, so that it arrives at the most general axioms last of all. This is the true way, but as yet untried.

XXII. Both ways set out from the senses and particulars, and rest in the highest generalities; but the difference between them is infinite. For the one just glances at experiment and particulars in passing, the other dwells duly and orderly among them. The one, again, begins at once by establishing certain abstract and useless generalities, the other rises by gradual steps to that which is prior and better known in the order of nature.

XXXI. It is idle to expect any great advancement in science from the superinducing and engrafting of new things upon old. We must begin anew from the very foundations, unless we would revolve forever in a circle with mean and contemptible progress.

XXXV. It was said by Borgia of the expedition of the French into Italy, that they came with chalk in their hands to mark out their lodgings, not with arms to force their way in. I in like manner would have my doctrine enter quietly into the minds that are fit and capable of receiving it; for confutations cannot be employed, when the difference is upon first principles and very notions and even upon forms of demonstration.

XXXVI. One method of delivery alone remains to us; which is simply this: we must lead men to the particulars themselves, and their series and order; while men on their side must force themselves for awhile to lay their notions by and begin to familiarize themselves with facts.

XXXVII. The doctrine of those who have denied that certainty could be attained at all, has some agreement with my way of proceeding at the first setting out; but they end in being infinitely separated and opposed. For the holders of that doctrine assert simply that nothing can be known; I also assert that not much can be known in nature by the way which is now in use. But then they go on to destroy the authority of the senses and understanding; whereas I proceed to devise and supply helps for the same.

XXXVIII. The idols and false notions which are now in possession of the human understanding, and have taken deep root therein, not only so beset men's minds that truth can hardly find entrance, but even after entrance is obtained, they will again in the very instauration of the science meet and trouble us, unless men being forewarned of the danger fortify themselves as far as may be against their assaults.

XXXIX. There are four classes of Idols which beset men's minds. To these for distinction's sake I have assigned names, calling the first class *Idols of the Tribe*; the second, *Idols of the Cave*; the third, *Idols of the Marketplace*; the fourth, *Idols of the Theatre*.

XL. The formation of ideas and axioms by true induction is no doubt the proper remedy to be applied for the keeping off and clearing away of idols. To point them out, however, is of great use; for the doctrine of Idols is to the Interpretation of Nature what the doctrine of the refutation of Sophisms is to common Logic.

XLI. The Idols of the Tribe have their foundation in human nature itself, and in the tribe or race of men. For it is a false assertion that the sense of man is the measure of things. On the contrary, all perceptions as well of the sense as of the mind are according to the measure of the universe. And the human understanding is like a false mirror, which, receiving rays irregularly, distorts and discolours the nature of things by mingling its own nature with it.

XLII. The Idols of the Cave are the idols of the individual man. For every one (besides the errors common to human nature in general) has a cave or den of his own, which refracts and discolors the light of nature; owing either to his own proper and peculiar nature; or to his education and conversation with others; or to the reading of books, and the authority of those whom he esteems and admires; or to the differences of impressions, accordingly as they take place in a mind preoccupied and predisposed or in a mind indifferent and settled; or the like. So that the spirit of man (according as it is meted out to different individuals) is in fact a thing variable and full of perturbation, and governed as it were by chance. Whence it was observed by Heraclitus that men look for sciences in their own lesser worlds, and not in the greater or common world.

XLIII. There are also Idols formed by the intercourse and association of men with each other, which I call Idols of the Marketplace, on account of the commerce and consort of men there. For it is by discourse that men associate; and words are imposed according to the apprehension of the vulgar. And therefore the ill and unfit choice of words wonderfully obstructs the understanding. Nor do the definitions or explanations wherewith in some things learned men are wont to guard and defend themselves, by any means set the matter right. But words plainly force and overrule the understanding, and throw all into confusion, and lead men away into numberless empty controversies and idle fancies.

XLIV. Lastly, there are Idols which have immigrated into men's minds from the various dogmas of philosophies, and also from wrong laws of demonstration. These I call Idols of the Theatre; because in my judgment all the received systems are but so many stage-plays, representing worlds of their own creation after an unreal and scenic fashion. Nor is it only of the systems now in vogue, or only of the ancient sects and philosophies, that I speak; for many more plays of the same kind may yet be composed and in like artificial manner set forth; seeing that errors the most widely different have nevertheless causes for the most part alike. Neither again do I mean this only of entire systems, but also of many principles and axioms in science, which by tradition, credulity, and negligence have come to be received.

Isaac Newton

from The Mathematical Principles of Natural Philosophy (1687)

The Rules of Reasoning in Philosophy

Rule I. We are to admit no more causes of natural things, than such as are both true and sufficient to explain their appearances.

To this purpose the philosophers say, that Nature does nothing in vain, and more is in vain, when less will serve; for Nature is pleased with simplicity, and affects not the pomp of superfluous causes.

Rule II. Therefore to the same natural effects we must, as far as possible, assign the same causes.

As to respiration in a man, and in a beast; the descent of stones in Europe and in America; the light of our culinary fire and of the sun; the reflection of light in the earth, and in the planets.

Rule III. The qualities of bodies, which admit neither intension nor remission of degrees, and which are found to belong to all bodies within reach of our experiments, are to be esteemed the universal qualities of all bodies whatsoever.

For since the qualities of bodies are only known to us by experiments, we are to hold for universal, all such as universally agree with experiments; and such as are not liable to diminution, can never be quite taken away. We are certainly not to relinquish the evidence of experiments for the sake of dreams and vain fictions of our own devising; nor are we to recede from the analogy of Nature, which is wont to be simple, and always consonant to itself. We no other way know the extension of bodies, than by our senses, nor do these reach it in all bodies; but because we perceive extension in all that are sensible, therefore we ascribe it universally to all others, also. That abundance of bodies are hard we learn by experience. And because the hardness of the whole arises from the hardness of the parts, we therefore justly infer the hardness of the undivided particles not only of the bodies we feel but of all others. That all bodies are impenetrable, we gather not from reason, but from sensation. The bodies which we handle we find impenetrable, and thence conclude impenetrability to be a universal property of all bodies whatsoever. That all bodies are moveable, and endowed with certain powers (which we called the forces of inertia) or persevering in their motion or in their rest, we only infer from the like properties observed in the bodies which we have seen. The extension, hardness, impenetrability, mobility, and force of inertia of the whole, result from the extension, hardness, impenetrability, mobility, and forces of inertia of the parts: and thence we conclude that the least particles of all bodies to be also all extended, and hard, and impenetrable, and moveable, and endowed with their proper forces of inertia. And this is the foundation of all philosophy. Moreover, that the divided but contiguous particles of bodies may be separated from one another, is a matter of observation: and, in the particles that remain undivided, our minds are able to distinguish yet lesser parts, as is mathematically demonstrated. But whether the parts so distinguished, and not yet divided, may, by the powers of nature, be actually divided and separated from one another, we cannot certainly determine. Yet had we the proof of but one experiment, that any undivided particle, in breaking a hard and solid body, suffered a division, we might by virtue of this rule, conclude, that the undivided as well as the divided particles, may be divided and actually separated into infinity.

Lastly, if it universally appears, by experiments and astronomical observations, that all bodies about the earth, gravitate toward the earth; and that in proportion to the quantity of matter which they severally contain; that the moon likewise, according to the quantity of its matter, gravitates toward the earth; that on the other hand our sea gravitates toward the moon; and all the planets mutually one toward another; and the comets in like manner towards the sun; we must, in consequence of this rule, universally allow, that all bodies whatsoever are endowed with a principle of mutual gravitation. For the argument from the appearances concludes with more force for the universal gravitation of all bodies, than for the impenetrability, of which among those in the celestial regions, we have no experiments, nor any manner of observation. Not that I affirm gravity to be essential to all bodies. By their inherent force I mean nothing but their force of inertia. This is immutable. Their gravity is diminished as they recede from the earth.

Rule IV. In experimental philosophy we are to look upon propositions collected by general induction from phenomena as accurately or very nearly true, notwithstanding any contrary hypotheses that may be imagined, till such time as other phenomena occur, by which they may either be made more accurate, or liable to exceptions.

This rule we must follow that the argument of induction may not be evaded by hypotheses.

Thomas Hobbes
from Leviathan (1651)

The Introduction

Nature, the art whereby God hath made and governs the world, is by the *art* of man, as in many other things, so in this also imitated, that it can make an artificial animal. For seeing life is but a motion of limbs, the beginning whereof is in some principal part within; why may we not say that all *automata* (engines that move themselves by springs and wheels as doth a watch) have an artificial life? For what is the *heart*, but a *spring*; and the *nerves*, but so many *strings*; and the *joints*, but so many *wheels*, giving motion to the whole body, such as was intended by the artificer? *Art* goes yet further, imitating that rational and most excellent work of Nature, *man*. For by art is created that great LEVIATHAN called a COMMONWEALTH, or STATE, in Latin, CIVITAS, which is but an artificial man, though of greater stature and strength than the natural, for whose protection and defence it was intended; and in which the *sovereignty* is an artificial *soul*, as giving life and motion to the whole body; the *magistrates* and other *officers* of judicature and execution, artificial *joints*; *reward* and *punishment*, by which fastened to the seat of the sovereignty every joint and member is moved to perform his duty, are the *nerves*, that do the same in the body natural; the *wealth* and *riches* of all the particular members are the *strength*; *salus populi*, the *people's safety*, its *business*; *counsellors*, by whom all things needful for it to know are suggested unto it, are the *memory*; *equity*, and *laws*, an artificial *reason* and *will*; *concord*, *health*; *sedition*, *sickness*; and *civil war*, *death*. Lastly, the *pacts* and *covenants*, by which the parts of this body politic were at first made, set together, and united, resemble that *fiat*, or the *let us make man*, pronounced by God in creation.

Chapter XIII

Of the Natural Condition of Mankind as
Concerning Their Felicity, and Misery

Nature hath made men so equal in the faculties of the body, and mind; as that though there be found one man sometimes manifestly stronger in body, or of quicker mind than another; yet when all is reckoned together, the difference between man, and man, is not so considerable, as that one man can thereupon claim to himself any benefit, to which another may not pretend, as well as he. For as to the strength of body, the weakest has strength enough to kill the strongest, either by secret machination, or by confederacy with others, that are in the same danger with himself.

And as to the faculties of the mind, setting aside the arts grounded upon words, and especially that skill of proceeding upon general, and infallible rules, called science; which very few have, and but in few things; as being not a native faculty, born with us; nor attained, as prudence, while we look after somewhat else, I find yet a greater equality amongst men, than that of strength. For prudence, is but experience; which equal time, equally bestows on all men, in those things they equally apply themselves unto. That which may perhaps make such equality incredible, is but a vain conceit of one's own wisdom, which almost all men think they have in a greater degree, than the vulgar; that is, than all men but themselves, and a few others, whom by fame, or for concurring with themselves, they approve. For such is the nature of men, that howsoever they may acknowledge many others to be more witty, or more eloquent, or more learned; yet they will hardly believe there be many so wise as themselves; for they see their own wit at hand, and other men's at a distance. But this proveth rather that men are in that point equal, than unequal. For there is not ordinarily a greater sign of the equal distribution of any thing, than that every man is contented with his share.

From this equality of ability, ariseth equality of hope in the attaining of our ends. And therefore if any two men desire the same thing, which nevertheless they cannot both enjoy, they become enemies; and in the way to their end, which is principally their own conservation, and sometimes their delectation only, endeavour to destroy or subdue one another. And from hence it comes to pass, that where an invader hath no more to fear; than another man's single power; if one plant, sow, build, and possess a convenient seat, others may probably be expected to come prepared with forces united, to dispossess, and deprive him, not only of the fruit of his labour, but also of his life, or liberty. And the invader again is in the like danger of another.

And from this diffidence of one another, there is no way for any man to secure himself, so reasonable, as anticipation; that is, by force, or wiles, to master the persons of all men he can, so long, till he see no other power great enough to endanger him; and this is no more than his own conservation requireth, and is generally allowed. Also because there be some, that taking pleasure in contemplating their own power in the acts of conquest, which they pursue farther than their security requires; if others, that otherwise would be glad to be at ease within modest bounds, should not by invasion increase their power, they would not be able, long time, by standing only on their defence, to subsist. And by consequence, such augmentation of dominion over men being necessary to a man's conservation, it ought to be allowed him.

Again, men have no pleasure, but on the contrary a great deal of grief, in keeping company, where there is no power able to over-awe them all. For every man looketh that his companion should value him, at the same rate he sets upon himself: and upon all signs of contempt, or undervaluing, naturally endeavours, as far as he dares (which amongst them that have no common power to keep them in quiet, is far enough to make them destroy each other), to extort a greater value from his contemners, by damage; and from others, by the example.

So that in the nature of man, we find three principal causes of quarrel. First, competition; secondly, diffidence; thirdly, glory.

The first, maketh men invade for gain; the second, for safety; and the third, for reputation. The first use violence, to make themselves masters of other men's persons, wives, children, and cattle; the second, to defend them; the third, for trifles, as a word, a smile, a different opinion, and any other sign of undervalue, either direct in their persons, or by reflection in their kindred, their friends, their nation, their profession, or their name.

Hereby, it is manifest, that during the time men live without a common power to keep them all in awe, they are in that condition which is called war; and such a war, as is of every man, against every man. For WAR, consisteth not in battle only, or the act of fighting; but in a tract of time, wherein the will to contend by battle is sufficiently known; and therefore the notion of *time*, is to be considered in the nature of war; as it is in the nature of weather. For as the nature of foul weather, lieth not in a shower or two of rain; but in an inclination thereto of many days together; so the nature of war, consisteth not in actual fighting; but in the known disposition thereto, during all the time there is no assurance to the contrary. All other time is PEACE.

Whatsoever therefore is consequent to a time of war, where every man is enemy to every man; the same is consequent to the time, wherein men live without other security, than what their own strength, and their own invention shall furnish them withal. In such condition, there is no place for industry; because the fruit thereof is uncertain; and consequently no culture of the earth; no navigation, nor use of the commodities that may be imported by sea; no commodious building; no instruments of moving, and removing, such things as require much force; no knowledge of the face of the earth; no account of time; no arts; no letters; no society; and which is worst of all, continual fear, and danger of violent death; and the life of man, solitary, poor, nasty, brutish, and short.

It may seem strange to some man, that has not well weighed these things; that Nature should thus dissociate, and render men apt to invade, and destroy one another; and he may therefore, not trusting to this inference, made from the passions, desire perhaps to have the same confirmed by experience. Let him therefore consider with himself, when taking a journey, he arms himself, and seeks to go well accompanied; when going to sleep, he locks his doors; when even in his house he locks his chests; and this when he knows there will be laws, and public officers, armed, to revenge all injuries shall be done him; what opinion he has of his fellow subjects, when he rides armed; of his fellow citizens, when he locks his doors; and of his children, and servants, when he locks his chests. Does he not there as much accuse mankind by his actions, as I do by my words? But neither of us accuse man's nature in it. The desires, and other passions of man, are in themselves no sin. No more are the actions, that proceed from those passions, till they know a law that forbids them: which till laws be made they cannot know: nor can any law be made, till they have agreed upon the person that shall make it.

It may peradventure be thought, there was never such a time, nor condition of war as this, and I believe it was never generally so, over all the world: but there are many places, where they live so now. For the savage people in many places of America, except the government of small families, the concord whereof dependeth on natural lust, have no government at all; and live at this day in that brutish manner, as I said before. Howsoever, it may be perceived what manner of life there would be, where there were no common power to fear, by the manner of life, which men that have formerly lived under a peaceful government, use to degenerate, into a civil war.

But there had never been any time, wherein particular men were in a condition of war one against another; yet in all times kings and persons of sovereign authority, because of their independency, are in continual jealousies, and in the state and posture of gladiators; having their weapons pointing, and their eyes fixed on one another; that is, their forts, garrisons, and guns upon the frontiers of their kingdoms; and continual spies upon their neighbours; which is a posture of war. But because they uphold thereby, the industry of their subjects; there does not follow from it, that misery, which accompanies the liberty of particular men.

To this war of every man, against every man, this also is consequent; that nothing can be unjust. The notions of right and wrong, justice and injustice, have there no place. Where there is no common power, there is no law; where no law, no injustice. Force, and fraud, are in war the two cardinal virtues. Justice, and injustice, are none of the faculties neither of the body, or mind. If they were, they might be in a man that were alone in the world, as well as his senses, and passions. They are qualities, that relate to men in society, not in solitude. It is consequent also to the same condition that there be no propriety [property], no dominion, no *mine* and *thine* distinct; but only that to be every man's that he can get; and for so long, as he can keep it. And thus much for the ill condition, which man by mere nature is actually placed in; though with a possibility to come out of it, consisting partly in the passions, partly in his reason.

The passions that incline men to peace, are fear of death; desire of such things as are necessary to commodious living; and a hope by their industry to obtain them. And reason suggesteth convenient articles of peace, upon which men may be drawn to agreement. These articles, are they, which otherwise are called the Laws of nature, whereof I shall speak more particularly, in the two following chapters.

Chapter XIV

Of the First and Second Natural Laws, and of Contracts

The RIGHT OF NATURE, which writers commonly call *jus naturale*, is the liberty each man hath, to use his own power, as he will himself, for the preservation of his own nature; that is to say, of his own life; and consequently, of doing any thing, which in his own judgement, and reason, he shall conceive to be the aptest means thereunto.

By LIBERTY, is understood, according to the proper signification of the word, the absence of external impediments; which impediments, may oft take away part of a man's power to do what he would; but cannot hinder him from using the power left him, according as his judgement, and reason shall dictate to him.

A LAW OF NATURE, *lex naturalis*, is a precept or general rule, found out by reason, by which a man is forbidden to do that, which is destructive of his life, or taketh away the means of preserving the same, and to omit that, by which he thinketh it may be best preserved. For though they that speak of this subject, use to confound *jus*, and *lex, right* and *law;* yet they ought to be distinguished; because RIGHT, consisteth in liberty to do, or to forbear; whereas LAW determineth, and bindeth to one of them: so that law, and right, differ as much, as obligation and liberty; which in one and the same matter are inconsistent.

And because the condition of man, as hath been declared in the precedent chapter, is a condition of war of every one against every one: in which case every one is governed by his own reason; and there is nothing he can make use of, that may not be a help unto him, in preserving his life against his enemies; it followeth, that in such a condition, every man has a right to every thing; even to one another's body. And therefore, as long as this natural right of every man to every thing endureth, there can be no security to any man, how strong or wise soever he be, of living out the time, which nature ordinarily alloweth men to live. And consequently it is a precept, or general rule of reason, *that every man, ought to endeavour peace, as far as he has hope of obtaining it; and when he cannot obtain it, that he may seek, and use, all helps and advantages of war*. The first branch of which rule, containeth the first and fundamental law of nature; which is, *to seek peace and follow it*. The second, the sum of the right of nature; which is, *by all means we can, to defend ourselves*.

From this fundamental law of nature, by which men are commanded to endeavour peace, is derived this second law; *that a man be willing, when others are so too, as far forth, as for peace, and defence of himself he shall think it necessary, to lay down this right to all things; and be contented with so much liberty against other men, as he would allow other men against himself*. For as long as every man holdeth this right, of doing anything he liketh, so long are all men in the condition of war. But if other men will not lay down their right, as well as he; then there is no reason for any one, to divest himself of his: for that were to expose himself to prey, which no man is bound to, rather than to dispose himself to peace. This is that law of the Gospel: *whatsoever you require that others should do to you, that do ye to them*. And that law of all men, *quod tibi fieri non vis, alteri ne feceris*.

To *lay down* a man's right to anything, is to *divest* himself of the *liberty*, of hindering another of the benefit of his own right to the same. For he that renounceth, or passeth away his right, giveth not to any other man a right which he had not before; because there is nothing to which every man had not right by nature: but only standeth out of his way, that he may enjoy his own original right, without hindrance from him; not without hindrance from another. So that the effect which redoundeth to one man, by another man's defect of right, is but so much diminution of impediments to the use of his own right original.

Right is laid aside, either by simply renouncing it, or by transferring it to another. By *simply* RENOUNCING; when he cares not to whom the benefit thereof redoundeth. By TRANSFERRING, when he intendeth the benefit thereof to some certain person or persons. And when a man has in either manner abandoned, or granted away his right, then is he said to be OBLIGED, or BOUND, not to hinder those, to whom such right is granted, or abandoned, from the benefit of it: and that he *ought*, and it is DUTY, not to make void that voluntary act of his own: and that such hindrance is INJUSTICE, and INJURY, as being *sine jure*; the right being before renounced, or transferred. So that *injury*, or *injustice*, in the controversies of the world, is somewhat like to that, which in the disputations of scholars is called *absurdity*. For as it is there called an absurdity, to contradict what one maintained in the beginning: so in the world, it is called injustice, and injury, voluntarily to undo that, which from the beginning he had voluntarily done. The way by which a man either simply renounceth or transferreth his right, is a declaration, or signification, by some voluntary and sufficient sign, or signs, that he doth so renounce, or transfer; or hath so renounced, or transferred the same, to him that accepteth it. And these signs are either words only, or actions only; or, as it happeneth most often, both words, and actions. And the same are the BONDS, by which men are bound, and obliged: bonds, that have their strength, not from their own nature, for nothing is more easily broken than a man's word, but from fear of some evil consequence upon the rupture.

Whensoever a man transferreth his right, or renounceth it; it is either in consideration of some right reciprocally transferred to himself; or for some other good he hopeth for thereby. For it is a voluntary act: and of the voluntary acts of every man the object is some *good to himself*. And therefore there be some rights, which no man can be understood by any words, or other signs, to have abandoned, or transferred. At first a man cannot lay down the right of resisting them, that assault him by force, to take away his life; because he cannot be understood to aim thereby, at any good to himself. The same may be said of wounds, and chains, and imprisonment; both because there is no benefit consequent to such patience; as there is to the patience of suffering another to be wounded, or imprisoned: as also because a man cannot tell, when he seeth men proceed against him by violence, whether they intend his death or not. And lastly the motive, and end for which this renouncing, and transferring of right is introduced, is nothing else but the security of a man's person, in his life, and in the means of so preserving life, as not to be weary of it. And therefore if a man by words, or other signs, seem to despoil himself of the end, for which those signs were intended; he is not to be understood as if he meant it, or that it was his will; but that he was ignorant of how such words and actions were to be interpreted.

The mutual transferring of right, is that which men call CONTRACT. . . .

If a covenant be made, wherein neither of the parties perform presently, but trust one another; the condition of mere nature, which is a condition of war of every man against every man, upon any reasonable suspicion, it is void: but if there be a common power set over them both, with right and force sufficient to compel performance, it is not void. For he that performeth first, has no assurance the other will perform after; because the bonds of words are too weak to bridle men's ambition, avarice, anger, and other passions, without the fear of some coercive power; which in the condition of mere nature, where all men are equal, and judges of the justness of their own fears, cannot possibly be supposed. And therefore he which performeth first, does but betray himself to his enemy; contrary to the right, he can never abandon, of defending his life, and means of living.

But in a civil estate, where there's a power set up to constrain those that would otherwise violate their faith, that fear is no more reasonable; and for that cause, he which by the covenant is to perform first, is obliged so to do. . . .

The force of words, being, as I have formerly noted, too weak to hold men to the performance of their covenants; there are in man's nature, but two imaginable helps to strengthen it. And those are either a fear of the consequences of breaking their word; or a glory, or pride in appearing not to need to break it. This latter is a generosity too rarely found to be presumed on, especially in the pursuers of wealth, command, or sensual pleasure; which are the greatest part of mankind. The passion to be reckoned upon, is fear. . . .

Chapter XV

Of Other Laws of Nature

From that law of nature, by which we are obliged to transfer to another, such rights, as being retained, hinder the peace of mankind, there followeth a third; which is this, *that men perform their covenants made:* without which covenants are in vain, and but empty words; and the right of all men to all things remaining, we are still in the condition of war.

And in this law of nature consisteth the fountain and original of JUSTICE. For where no covenant hath preceded, there hath no right been transferred, and every man has right to every thing; and consequently, no action can be unjust. But when a covenant is made, then to break it is *unjust*; and the definition of INJUSTICE, is no other than *the not performance of covenant*. And whosoever is not unjust, is *just*.

But because covenants of mutual trust, where there is a fear of not performance on either part, as hath been said in the former chapter, are invalid; though the original of justice be the making of covenants; yet injustice actually there can be none, till the cause of such fear be taken away; which while men are in the natural condition of war, cannot be done. Therefore before the names of just, and unjust can have place, there must be some coercive power, to compel men equally to the performance of their covenants, by the terror of some punishment, greater than the benefit they expect by the breach of their covenant; and to make good that propriety, which by mutual contract men acquire, in recompense of the universal right they abandon: and such power there is none before the erection of a commonwealth. And this is also to be gathered out of the ordinary definition of justice in the Schools: for they say, that *justice is the constant will of giving to every man his own*. And therefore where there is no *own*, that is no propriety, there is no injustice; and where there is no coercive power erected, that is, where there is no commonwealth, there is no propriety; all men having right to all things: therefore where there is no commonwealth, there nothing is unjust. So that the nature of justice, consisteth in keeping of valid covenants: but the validity of covenants begins not but with the constitution of a civil power, sufficient to compel men to keep them: and then it is also that propriety begins.

Chapter XVII

Of the Causes, Generation, and Definition of a Commonwealth

The final cause, end, or design of men, who naturally love liberty, and dominion over others, in the introduction of that restraint upon themselves, in which we see them live in commonwealths, is the foresight of their own preservation, and of a more contented life thereby; that is to say, of getting themselves out from that miserable condition of war which is necessarily consequent, as hath been shown in Chapter XIII, to the natural passions of men, when there is no visible power to keep them in awe, and tie them by fear of punishment to the performance of their covenants, and observation of those laws of nature set down in the fourteenth and fifteenth chapters.

For the laws of nature, *as justice, equity, modesty, mercy*, and, in sum, *doing to others, as we would be done to*, of themselves, without the terror of some power, to cause them to be observed, are contrary to our natural passions that carry us to partiality, pride, revenge, and the like. And covenants, without the sword, are but words, and of no strength to secure a man at all. Therefore notwithstanding the laws of nature, which every one hath then kept, when he has the will to keep them, when he can do it safely, if there be no power erected, or not great enough for our security; every man will, and may lawfully rely on his own strength and art, for caution against all other men. And in all places, where men have lived by small families, to rob and spoil one another, has been a trade, and so far from being reputed against the law of nature, that the greater spoils they gained, the greater was their honour; and men observed no other laws therein, but the laws of honour; that is, to abstain from cruelty, leaving to men their lives, and instruments of husbandry. And as small families did then; so now do cities and kingdoms which are but greater families, for their own security, enlarge their dominions, upon all pretences of danger, and fear of invasion, or assistance that may be given to invaders, and endeavour as much as they can to subdue, or weaken their neighbours, by open force, and secret arts, for want of other caution, justly; and are remembered for it in after ages with honour.

Nor is it the joining together of a small number of men, that gives them this security; because in small numbers, small actions on the one side or the other, make the advantage of strength so great, as is sufficient to carry the victory; and therefore gives encouragement to an invasion. The multitude sufficient to confide in for our security, is not determined by any certain number, but by comparison with the enemy we fear; and is then sufficient, when the odds of the enemy is not of so visible and conspicuous moment, to determine the event of war, as to move him to attempt.

And be there never so great a multitude; yet if their actions be directed according to their particular judgements, and particular appetites, they can expect thereby no defence, nor protection, neither against a common enemy, nor against the injuries of one another. For being distracted in opinions concerning the best use and application of their strength, they do not help but hinder one another; and reduce their strength by mutual opposition to nothing: whereby they are easily, not only subdued by a very few that agree together; but also when there is no common enemy, they make war upon each other, for their particular interests. For if we could suppose a great multitude of men to consent in the observation of justice, and other laws of nature, without a common power to keep them all in awe; we might as well suppose all mankind to do the same; and then there neither would be, nor need to be any civil government, or commonwealth at all; because there would be peace without subjection.

Nor is it enough for the security, which men desire should last all the time of their life, that they be governed, and directed by one judgement, for a limited time; as in one battle, or one war. For though they obtain a victory by their unanimous endeavour against a foreign enemy; yet afterwards, when either they have no common enemy, or he that by one part is held for an enemy, is by another part held for a friend, they must needs by the difference of their interest dissolve, and fall again into a war amongst themselves.

It is true, that certain living creatures, as bees, and ants, live sociably one with another, which are therefore by Aristotle numbered amongst political creatures; and yet have no other direction, than their particular judgments and appetites; nor speech, whereby one of them can signify to another, what he thinks expedient for the common benefit: and therefore some man may perhaps desire to know, why mankind cannot do the same. To which I answer,

First, that men are continually in competition for honour and dignity, which these creatures are not; and consequently amongst men there ariseth on that ground, envy, and hatred, and finally war; but amongst these not so.

Secondly, that amongst these creatures, the common good differeth not from the private; and being by nature inclined to their private, they procure thereby the common benefit. But man, whose joy consisteth in comparing himself with other men, can relish nothing but what is eminent.

Thirdly, that these creatures, having not, as man, the use of their reason, do not see, nor think they see any fault, in the administration of their common business; whereas amongst men, there are very many, that think themselves wiser, and abler to govern the public, better than the rest; and these strive to perform and innovate, one this way, another that way, and thereby bring it into distraction and civil war.

Fourthly, that these creatures, though they have some use of voice, in making known to one another their desires, and other affections; yet they want that art of words, by which some men can represent to others, that which is good, in the likeness of evil; and evil, in the likeness of good; and augment, or diminish the apparent greatness of good and evil; discontenting men and, troubling their peace at their pleasure.

Fifthly, irrational creatures cannot distinguish between *injury,* and *damage*; and therefore as long as they be at ease, they are not offended with their fellows; whereas man is then most troublesome, when he is most at ease: for then it is that he loves to shew his wisdom, and control the actions of them that govern the commonwealth.

Lastly, the agreement of these creatures is natural; that of men, is by covenant only, which is artificial: and therefore it is no wonder if there be somewhat else required, besides covenant, to make their agreement constant and lasting; which is a common power, to keep them in awe, and to direct their actions to the common benefit.

The only way to erect such a common power, as may be able to defend them from the invasion of foreigners, and the injuries of one another, and thereby to secure them in such sort, as that by their own industry, and by the fruits of the earth, they may nourish themselves and live contentedly; is to confer all their power and strength upon one man, or upon one assembly of men, that may reduce all their wills, by plurality of voices, unto one will: which is as much as to say, to appoint one man, or assembly of men, to bear their person; and every one to own, and acknowledge himself to be author of whatsoever he that so beareth their person, shall act, or cause to be acted, in those things which concern the common peace and safety; and therein to submit their wills, every one to his will, and their judgements, to his judgement. This is more than consent, or concord; it is a real unity of them all, in one and the same person, made by covenant of every man with every man, in such manner, as if every man should say to every man: *I authorise and give up my right of governing myself, to this man, or to this assembly of men, on this condition, that thou give up thy right to him, and authorise all his actions in like manner.* This done, the multitude so united in one person is called a COMMONWEALTH, in Latin, CIVITAS. This is the generation of that great LEVIATHAN, or rather, to speak more reverently, of that *mortal god,* to which we owe, under the *immortal God,* our peace and defence. For by this authority, given him by every particular man in the commonwealth, he hath the use of so much power and strength conferred on him, that by terror thereof, he is enabled to perform the wills of them all, to peace at home, and mutual aid against their enemies abroad. And in him consisteth the essence of the commonwealth; which, to define it, is *one person of whose acts a great multitude, by mutual covenants one with another, have made themselves every one the author, to the end he may use the strength and means of them all, as he shall think expedient, for their peace and common defence.*

And he that carrieth this person, is called SOVEREIGN, and said to have *sovereign power*; and every one besides, his SUBJECT.

II. Europeans and Others: Travel, Colonialism, and Philosophy

Encounters with other cultures, both within Europe and around the globe, played a significant role in the shaping of European ideas, social practices, and political and economic systems. The outline of these encounters, at least politically and economically, is familiar. In 1500, east and south of Europe lay Russia and the Ottoman Empire, which had conquered the remains of the Byzantine empire and taken its capital, Constantinople, in 1453. Beyond were India, China, Africa, all known to Europeans only in sketchy, often fantastic terms. By late in the next century, the Ottoman empire stretched from Morocco to the Persian gulf and from the Crimea almost to Vienna. European powers were concerned, first about the threat of invasion (Ottoman armies besieged Vienna in 1683), and later (especially in the nineteenth and early twentieth centuries) about the political effects of both the gradual dissolution of the Ottoman empire and the increasing power of imperial Russia in Europe and the East.

What lay west of Europe was also poorly known in 1500, though that changed dramatically in the centuries that followed as Europeans explored the area they called the 'New World,' conquered the local inhabitants with the aid of technological advantages and disease, and established their own settlements. By the eighteenth century several European states—especially Spain, Britain, France, and the Netherlands—had substantial empires in the New World, with territory in Africa and India as well. As independence movements in the Americas contested European rule in the late eighteenth and nineteenth centuries, European states expanded their empires to the east and south, claiming political and economic dominance over much of Africa, India, and Asia.

Encounters such as these were affected by European assumptions about other cultures, and provided images, practices, experiences, and ideas that affected European cultures in return. Speculation about other peoples was hardly new, of course, but became increasingly common and important as trade networks expanded, imperial rivalries intensified, and travel to other countries within Europe and around the globe became easier. At home and abroad, in philosophical essays, letters, novels, and histories, Europeans wrote about other cultures, often as a means of defining—or celebrating—their own national and cultural identities or of explaining their political dominance. Ancient Greeks had defined themselves in contrast to nonGreeks, commonly referring to them as 'barbarians'; Christians in Europe had characterized others, especially Moslems, as 'infidels.' In early modern France, to take one example, the social mores, art forms, and ideas of other cultures—English, Russian, and Greek as well as African, Chinese, or Indian—continued to appear at once fascinating and disturbing.

Directly and indirectly, then, Europeans asked questions such as these: what accounts for differences between cultures? what does it mean to be 'civilized'? are some cultures better than others? is slavery acceptable, or wrong? is technological superiority proof of cultural superiority? is it just for one people to govern another? what are, and what should be, the relations between different peoples, cultures, and nationalities?

As the texts in this and later sections demonstrate, the situations in which these questions have been addressed in the last 500 years have varied enormously. Michel de Montaigne (1533-1592), a French aristocrat from Bordeaux, created the literary essay as a form for introspection. Drawing on both life experience and reading, he wrote three volumes of essays in which he endeavored to strip away surface opinions and get at the core of human nature and society. For Montaigne, late in the sixteenth century, writing "On Cannibals" enabled him to turn a critical eye toward Europeans, to ask why and how they distinguished between 'civilized' and 'barbarian' peoples.

Over a century later, in 1716, Mary Wortley Montagu (1689–1762) accompanied her husband to Constantinople, where he had been sent as ambassador from England. The journey took them through central Europe, across the Balkans, scarred by battles between armies of the Holy Roman and Ottoman empires, to Constantinople; two years later she returned to England by way of Tunis and France. During the course of her travels she wrote long descriptive letters (to her sister the Countess of Mar, the poet Alexander Pope, and other friends) in which she measured English ideas about everything from Turks to the Austrian court against her experiences. Years later Mary Wortley Montagu prepared the letters, well-known in her lifetime, for publication; despite objections from her daughter, who shared the assumption of her class that women should not be known as authors, the book appeared within a year of her death.

While Mary Wortley Montagu wrote about her own real-life travels, other eighteenth-century European writers used travel as a fictional device in order to comment satirically on the excesses of their own society and political order by contrasting them with those of other people, real or imagined. Perhaps the best-known examples of this are *Gulliver's Travels* (1726), by Jonathan Swift, and *Persian Letters* (1721), by Charles de Secondat, Baron de Montesquieu (1689–1755). Swift's novel is about an Englishman who travels to imaginary countries; Montesquieu's about two Persians traveling in Europe. Montesquieu revisited the topic of cultural and political differences in a very different way a few decades later in *The Spirit of Laws*, a philosophical treatise on government influenced by the Enlightenment emphasis on reason and science. One of Montesquieu's arguments was that different political systems seem to be appropriate in different times and places, depending on variables such as social customs, religion and tradition, and climate. In the section included here, he speculates about the relationship between climate, national character, and laws.

It is ironically appropriate, perhaps, that independence movements around the globe in the nineteenth and twentieth centuries have found some of their most powerful arguments against European domination in Enlightenment philosophy. With the growth of empires abroad came the spread of European cultural institutions, which served to disseminate and claim the cultural superiority of European modes of thought. In the decades following the American and French revolutions, as opposition to European rule in Latin America grew, members of the social elite invoked Enlightenment ideals about liberty and equality that had helped to inspire those earlier revolutions. Schooled in European history and philosophy, they made use of it in impassioned arguments against European domination. In a letter written while he was temporarily in exile in Jamaica during the fight for Latin American independence, Símon Bolívar (1783–1830), born into the creole elite in Caracas, offers "a candid statement" of the situation, responding to European colonialism with arguments that would be echoed in the next century during anti-colonial struggles in India, Asia, and Africa.

MICHEL DE MONTAIGNE

from Essays (1572)

On Cannibals

When King Pyrrhus entered Italy, and saw the order of the Roman army that was sent to meet him, "I know not," said he, "what kind of barbarians" (for so the Greeks call other nations) "these may be, but the disposition of the army which I now see has nothing of the barbarian in it." The same was said by the Greeks concerning the army which Flaminius sent into their country; and by Philip, when he discovered from an eminence the order and distribution of the Roman camp in his kingdom, under Publius Sulpicius Galba. By this it appears how cautious men ought to be of taking things upon trust from vulgar opinion, and that we are to judge by the eye of reason, and not from common report.

I had a man with me a long time who had lived ten or twelve years in that other world lately discovered, in that part of it which Villegaignon went after, which he surnamed Antarctic France. This discovery of so vast a country seems to be of very great importance; and we are not sure that there may not be another discovered hereafter, so many greater men than we having been deceived in this. I am afraid that our eyes are bigger than our bellies, and that our curiosity is greater than our capacity. We grasp at everything, and catch nothing but air. . . .

This manservant of mine is a plain honest fellow, and therefore the more likely to tell truth. Your men of fine parts, indeed, are much more curious in their observations, and discover more particulars; but then they make comments upon them, and to give the better air to their glosses, and to gain them a credit, they cannot help making a little alteration in the story. The never represent things to you simply as they are, but turn and wind them according to the light they appeared in to themselves; and, in order to gain a reputation to their judgment, and to draw you in to trust it, they are apt to lengthen and amplify the subject with something of their own invention. Either a man must be of undoubted veracity, or so simple that he has not wherewithal to contrive to give an air of truth to fiction; and he must be wedded to no opinion. Such a one was my man, and, besides, he has divers times showed me several sailors and merchants who went the same voyage with him. Therefore I content myself with his information, without inquiring what the cosmographers say of it. We would have topographers to give us a particular account of the places where they were. But, because they have had this advantage over us of seeing the Holy Land, they would have the privilege, forsooth, of telling us stories of all the other parts of the world. I would have every one write what he knows, and as much as he knows of it, not only on this, but on all other subjects. For a man may have some particular knowledge or experience of the nature of such a river, or such a spring, who, as to other things, knows no more than what everybody does, and nevertheless, for the sake of propagating this smattering knowledge of his, he will undertake to write a whole history of natural philosophy: a vice which is the source of several great inconveniences.

Moreover, I find, to return to my subject, by what I am told of it, that there is nothing wild and barbarous in this nation, excepting that every one gives the denomination of barbarism to what is not the custom of his country. As, indeed, we have no other level for aiming at truth and reason but the example and idea of the opinions and customs of the country wherein we live. There is always the true religion, there is perfect government, and there the use of all things is complete and perfect. There the people are wild, just as we call fruits wild which nature produces of itself, and in its ordinary progress; whereas in truth we ought rather to call those wild whose natures we have changed by our artifice and diverted from the common order. In the former, their genuine and most useful and natural virtues and properties are vigorous and sprightly; but the latter are degenerated, by our accommodating them to the pleasure of our corrupted taste. And yet our palates ever find a flavour and delicacy, excellent even to emulation of the best of ours, in several fruits of those countries that grow without cultivation. It is not reasonable that art should gain the pre-eminence of our great and powerful mother, Nature. We have so surcharged the beauty and richness of her works by our own inventions that we have almost smothered her. Yet, wherever she shines in her own pure lustre, she wonderfully disgraces our vain and frivolous attempts.

> "Et veniunt hederae sponte suâ melius;
> Surgit et in solis formosior arbutus antris; . . .
> Et volucres nullâ dulcius arte canunt." (Propertius)

"The ivy thrives best when left to itself; the wild strawberry in rocky shades; and wild birds sing better than art can teach them." With all our skill, we are not able to frame such a nest as that of the least of the small birds, neither for its contexture, beauty, nor convenience; nor can we weave such a web as the poor spider does. All things, says Plato, are produced either by nature, or by chance, or by art. The largest and The most beautiful by one or other of the two first, the least and imperfect ones by the last.

These nations, then, seem to me to be so far barbarous as very little care has been taken to form their minds, and as their native simplicity is still unimproved. They are still governed by the laws of nature, as yet very little adulterated by ours, but remaining in such purity that I am sometimes sorry that we were not acquainted with the people sooner, when there were men better able to judge of them than we are. I am vexed that Lycurgus and Plato had no knowledge of them; for, in my opinion, what we see in those nations by experience does not only surpass all the paintings with which the poets have embellished the golden age, and all their inventions in representing the then happy state of mankind, but also the conception and desire of philosophy itself. Such a native and pure simplicity, as we see in them by experience, could never enter into their imagination, nor could they ever believe that society could be maintained with so little human artifice and cement.

Should I say to Plato, it is a nation wherein there is no sort of traffic, no knowledge of letters, no science of numbers, no title of magistracy or of political superiority; no use of service, riches or poverty; no contract, no successions, no dividends, no occupations but idle ones; no respect of kindred, but all common; no clothes, no agriculture, no metal, no use of wine or corn, and that they never heard the mention of such words as signify lying, treason, dissimulation, avarice, envy, detraction, and pardon, how far would he find his imaginary republic short of this perfection! *Viri a diis recentes*, "Fresh from God's hands." *Hos natura modos primum dedit*, "Nature first showed us the way." (Virgil) For the rest, they live in a very pleasant country and temperate climate; so that, as my authors tell me, it is rare to see a man sick there; and they assured me they never saw any of the natives either paralytic, blear-eyed, toothless, or decrepit with age. The situation of their country is all along by the sea-shore, being shut up on the land side by great high mountains, from which it is one hundred leagues or thereabouts to the sea. Here are fish and flesh in abundance that have no resemblance with what comes to our tables; and they use no cookery, but plain boiling, broiling, roasting, or baking on the coals. The first man that ever came to them on horseback, though he had made an acquaintance with them by several voyages, so frightened them by his appearance of half man and half horse, that they killed him with their arrows before they discovered their mistake. Their buildings, which are very long, and capable of entertaining 200 or 300 people, are made of the bark of tall trees, fixed with one end to the ground, and leaning to and supporting one another at the top, like some of our barns, the roof of which descends almost to the ground, and serves instead of the side walls. They have wood so hard that they cleave it and make swords of it, and grills to broil their meat on. Their beds, which are of cotton, are hung up to the roof, like our seamen's hammocks, and hold but one person; for the wives lie apart from their husbands. They rise with the sun, and immediately fall to eating, when they make one meal, which serves them for the whole day. They do not then drink (as Suidas reports of some people of the East, who never drank at their meals), but they drink several times in a day, and to a hearty pitch. Their liquor is made of a certain root, and is of the colour of claret; and they always drink it lukewarm. It will not keep above two or three days, has a brisk savour, is not at all heady, is very good for the stomach, but proves laxative to those who are not used to it, though to those who are it is a very pleasant beverage. Instead of bread, they make use of a certain white compound, like coriander comfits, which I have tasted, and found to be sweet, but a little flat. They spend the whole day in dancing. The young men go out to hunt the wild beast with bows and arrows. Part of their women, in the meantime, are employed in warming their drink, which is their chief employment. One of their old men, in the morning before they fall to eating, preaches to the whole household in common, walking from one end of the house to the other, several times repeating the same sentences, till he has gone all round the family (for their buildings are at least 100 yards long), to whom he only recommends two things—valour against their enemies, and love to their wives. And they never fail to put them in mind how much they are the more obliged to the latter, because it is the women who provide them their drink warm, and well relished. In several places, and at my house amongst others, may be seen the form of their beds, swords, and wooden gauntlets, with which they guard their wrists in battle, and their canes hollow at one end, by the sound of which they keep time in their dancing. They shave all their hairy parts, and much more nicely than we, without any razor but what is of wood or stone. They believe the soul to be eternal, and that those who have deserved well of the gods are lodged in that part of the heaven where the sun rises, and the damned on the western side.

They have I know not what kind of priests and prophets, who live in the mountains, and are seldom seen by the people. Whenever they come down to them there is a great festival, and a solemn assembly of the people from many villages (or barns, as I have described them), which are about a French league from one another. The prophet then speaks to them in public, exhorting them to their virtue and their duty; but their whole system of morality consists in these two articles—resolution in war, and affection to their wives. He also foretells to them things to come, and what they must expect will be the event of their enterprises, and he either persuades them to or dissuades them from war; but woe be to him if he does not guess right! for it if happens to them otherwise than he foretold, they condemn him for a false prophet, and, if they can catch him, cut him in a thousand pieces. For this reason, if any one finds himself mistaken, he keeps out of sight. Divination is a gift of God; therefore to abuse it is an imposture that ought to be punished.

Among the Scythians, when their diviners failed in their predictions, they were bound hand and foot, and laid on a cart laden with furze, and drawn by oxen, on which they were burnt to death. They who only meddle with things within the sphere of human capacity are excusable in doing the best they can; but as for those other people that come and delude us with assurances of an extraordinary faculty beyond our understanding, ought they not to be punished for not making good their promise, and for the temerity of their imposture?

They have wars with the nations that are beyond their mountains, farther within the mainland, to which they go stark naked, without any weapons but bows or wooden swords, pointed at the end like the heads of our javelins. Their obstinacy in battles is wonderful, as they never end without great effusion of blood; for they know not what it is to be frightened and to run away. Every one brings home for a trophy the head of some enemy that he has killed, which he sets up over the door of his house. After having treated their prisoners a good while in the handsomest manner they can think of, the person who has the property of them invites a great number of his acquaintance, and when they are come ties a cord to one of the prisoner's arms, by one end of which he holds him some paces at a distance, that he may not hurt him, and gives to the friend he loves best the other arm to hold in the same manner, and then they two, in presence of the whole assembly, run him through the body with their swords. This done, they roast him and eat him in common, and send some slices of him to their absent friends. They do not do this, as it is imagined, for the sake of nourishment, as the Scythians did of old, but to denote the last degree of revenge; as will appear by this. For, perceiving that, when the Portuguese had taken any prisoners, they inflicted another sort of death upon them, which was to set them in the earth up to the waist, to let fly their arrows at the upper part, and then to hang them, they were of opinion that these people of the other world (as they had made their neighbours acquainted with a great many vices, and far outstripped them in all sorts of mischief) had a reason for taking this sort of revenge, and that it must be more severe than theirs, and so began to leave their old way and to follow this. I am not sorry that we should here take notice of the barbarous cruelty of such an action, but rather that, while we judge so nicely of their faults, we are so blind to our own. I think there is more barbarity in eating a man alive than when he is dead; in tearing a body limb from limb, by racks and torments, while it has the sense of feeling; in roasting it by degrees, in causing it to be bit and worried by dogs and swine (as we have not only read but lately seen, not between veteran enemies, but between neighbours and fellow-citizens, and what is worse, under pretence of piety and religion), than in roasting and eating it after it is dead. Chrysippus and Zeno, the two heads of the Stoical sect, were of opinion that there was no hurt in making use of our dead bodies to any purpose whatsoever, to serve our occasions and even for our nourishment, as our ancestors, when besieged by Caesar in the city Alexia, resolved to keep themselves from being starved to death by the bodies of their old men, women, and other persons incapable of bearing arms.

> "Vascones, ut fama est, alimentis talibus usi
> Produxere animas." (Juvenal)

"'Tis said the Gascons prolonged their lives with such nourishment." And the physicians scruple not to make use of human flesh every way, either inwardly or outwardly, for our health. But the savages here treated of never maintained any opinion so enormous as to excuse treason, disloyalty, tyranny, and cruelty, which are our familiar vices. We may, therefore, style them barbarous, with an eye to the laws of reason, but not in respect to ourselves, who exceed them in all kinds of barbarity.

Their warfare is quite noble and generous, and is as excusable and commendable as that human malady is capable of, it having no foundation with them but the sole jealousy of virtue. They do not contend for the conquest of new lands; for those they possess still enjoy their natural fertility, which furnishes them, without labour and toil, with such an abundance of all necessaries that they have no need to enlarge their borders. They are also happy in this circumstance, that they desire no more than what the necessities of nature demand, everything beyond that being to them superfluous. Men of the same age generally call one another brothers, those who are younger children, and the old men are fathers to all. These leave to their heirs in common the full possession of their goods and chattels, without any division or any other title than what Nature bestows upon her creatures at bringing them into the world. If their neighbours come over the mountains to attack them, and obtain a victory over them, all that the conquerors gain by it is glory, and the advantage of proving their superiority in valour and prowess; for they take no spoils from the vanquished, but return home to their own country, where they have no want of any necessaries, nor of that happy knowledge how to live contentedly in their condition. And these in their turn do the same. They demand no other ransom of the prisoners they take than the confession and acknowledgment of being vanquished. But there is not a man of them to be found in a whole century who had not rather perish than abate an ace of the grandeur of his invincible courage, either by look or word. There is not one who had not rather be killed and eaten than so much as open his mouth to desire he may not be so treated. They indulge them with full liberty, that their lives may be so much the dearer to them, yet commonly accost them with menaces of their approaching death, of the torments which they are to suffer, of the preparations making for that purpose, of the mutilation of their members, and of the feast that is to be made on their carcases. And all this they do for no other purpose but to extort some gentle or submissive word from them, or to put it into their heads to make their escape, for the sake of gaining the advantage of having terrified them, and shaken their constancy. And, indeed, if the thing be rightly considered, it is in this point only that true victory consists.

————"Victoria nulla est,
Quam quae confessos animo quoque subjugat hostes."(Claudian)

"There is no victory so complete as when the vanquished own its justice." . . .

To return to my story. These prisoners are so far from being humbled by anything done to them, that, on the contrary, during the two or three months that they are kept under guard, they appear with a brisk countenance, urge their keepers to make haste to bring them to the test, defy, rail at them, reproach them with cowardice, and with the number of battles they have lost. I have a song made by one of these prisoners, wherein he says, "They shall be welcome to meet, one and all, to dine upon him, and thereby eat their fathers and grandfathers, whose flesh had served to feed and nourish him. These muscles," says he, "this flesh, and these veins, they are your own. Poor souls as you are! you little think that the substance of the limbs of your ancestors is here still. Do but mind the taste, and you will perceive the relish of your own flesh." This is a composition that has nothing of the taste of barbarism. They who paint him dying after being stabbed, paint the prisoner spitting in the faces of his executioners, and making mouths at them; and, in truth, they never cease to brave and defy them, both by looks and language, to the very last gasp. Now, without any lying, these men, compared to us, are very savage; for, in good faith, either they must needs be such, or else we must, there being a wonderful difference betwixt their manners and ours.

The men here have a plurality of wives, and the more eminent they are for their valour, the more wives they have. There is one very extraordinary thing to be observed in their married state—viz., that, as the jealousy of our wives excites them to hinder us from the friendship and favour of other women, their wives have the same emulation to procure that happiness for their husbands; for, being more careful to promote the honour of their husbands than of any one thing besides, they seek out very eagerly for as many companions as they can find for the husband, it being a testimony of his valour. Our wives will say this is monstrous; but it is not so. It is a virtue truly matrimonial, though of the highest form. We find in the Bible that Sarah the wife of Abraham, and Jacob's wives, Leah and Rachel, furnished their husbands with their beautiful maids; and Livia favoured Augustus to her own prejudice; while Stratonice, the wife of King Dejotarus, not only did so, but carefully brought up all the children he thus had, and helped them to succeed to their father's dominions. And, lest it should be thought that all this is done merely from a servile obligation to their customs, and by the impression of the authority of their ancient practice, without reason and without judgment, and for want of sense to take another course, it is necessary in this place to give some touches of their capacity. Besides what I just now repeated from one of their military songs, I have another, a love-song of theirs, which begins in this manner—viz., "Stay, adder, stay, that by thy likeness my sister may draw the fashion and work of a rich belt for me to make a present of to my sweetheart, by which means thy beauty and thy disposition may at all times give thee the preference before all other serpents." The first couplet, "Stay, adder," etc., makes the burden of the song. Now I converse enough with poetry to judge thus much, that not only there is nothing barbarous in this thought, but that it is perfectly Anacreontic. Their language, moreover, is soft, and of a pleasing accent, resembling the termination of the Greek. Three of these people, foreseeing how dear the knowledge of the corruption of this part of the world would one day cost their happiness and repose, and that this correspondence would in the end prove their ruin, as I suppose it to be already in a fair way of doing so (wretched men! to suffer themselves to be deluded with desire of novelty, and to leave their own serene sky to come and gaze at ours), were at Roan when the late King Charles IX was there. The monarch himself talked to them a good while, and they were made to see our fashions, our pomp, and the form of a fine city; after which somebody asked their opinion, and wanted to know of them what things they most admired of all they had seen. To which they made answer, three things, of which I am sorry I have forgot the third, but two I yet remember. They said, in the first place, they thought it very strange that so many tall men, wearing great beards, strong and well armed about the king's person (by whom it is likely they meant his Swiss guards), should submit to obey a child, and did not rather choose out one among themselves to command; secondly, that they had taken notice of men amongst us who were fat and crammed with all manner of good things, whilst their halves were begging at the gates, lean and half starved with hunger and poverty; and they wondered how these necessitous halves could put up with such unjust fare, and not take the others by the throat or set fire to their houses.

I talked with one of them a good while, but I had so sorry an interpreter, who was so perplexed by his stupidity to apprehend my meaning, that I could get nothing of any moment out of him. Asking of what advantage his superiority over the people was to him (for he was a captain, and our mariners styled him king), he told me, "To march at the head of them to war." And demanding further of him how many men he had to follow him, he showed me a space of ground, to signify as many as could stand in such a compass, which might be four or five thousand men. Then putting the question to him whether or no his authority expired with the war, he told me, "This part of it remained, that when he went to visit the villages of his dependence, they made paths for him through their thickest woods, so that he could pass from one place to another with ease." And, upon the whole, this was not a bad thing. If you ask why, I answer, because they wear no breeches.

MARY WORTLEY MONTAGU
from Letters (1763)

To the Countess of B. [Bristol].

Nuremberg, Aug. 22, O.S. [1716].

After five days travelling post, I am sure I could sit down to write on no other occasion, but to tell my dear Lady _____, that I have not forgot her obliging command, of sending her some account of my travels.

I have already passed a large part of Germany, have seen all that is remarkable in Cologne, Frankfort, Wurtsburg, and this place; and 'tis impossible not to observe the difference between the free towns and those under the government of absolute princes, as all the little sovereigns of Germany are. In the first, there appears an air of commerce and plenty. The streets are well built, and full of people, neatly and plainly dressed. The shops loaded with merchandise, and the commonalty clean and cheerful. In the other, a sort of shabby finery, a number of dirty people of quality tawdered out; narrow nasty streets out of repair, wretchedly thin of inhabitants, and above half of the common sort asking alms. I cannot help fancying one under the figure of a handsome clean Dutch citizen's wife, and the other like a poor town lady of pleasure, painted and ribboned out in her head-dress, with tarnished silver-laced shoes and a ragged under-petticoat, a miserable mixture of vice and poverty.

They have sumptuary laws in this town, which distinguish their rank by their dress, and prevent the excess which ruins so many other cities, and has a more agreeable effect to the eye of a stranger than our fashions. I think, after the Archbishop of Cambray having declared for them, I need not be ashamed to own, that I wish these laws were in force in other parts of the world. When one considers impartially the merits of a rich suit of clothes in most places, the respect and the smiles of favour that it procures, not to speak of the envy and the sighs it occasions (which is very often the principal charm to the wearer), one is forced to confess, that there is need of an uncommon understanding to resist the temptation of pleasing friends and mortifying rivals; and that it is natural to young people to fall into a folly, which betrays them to that want of money which is the source of a thousand basenesses. What numbers of men have begun the world with generous inclinations, that have afterwards been the instruments of bringing misery on a whole people, being led by a vain expence into debts, that they could clear no other way but by the forfeit of their honour, and which they would never have contracted, if the respect the many pay to habits was fixed by law only to a particular colour or cut of plain cloth! These reflections draw

41

after them others that are too melancholy. I will make haste to put them out of your head by the farce of relics, with which I have been entertained in all the Romish churches.

The Lutherans are not quite free from these follies. I have seen here, in the principal church, a large piece of the cross set in jewels, and the point of the spear, which they told me, very gravely, was the same that pierced the side of our Saviour. But I was particularly diverted in a little Roman Catholic church which is permitted here, where the professors of that religion are not very rich, and consequently cannot adorn their images in so rich a manner as their neighbours. For, not to be quite destitute of all finery, they have dressed up an image of our Saviour over the altar in a fair full-bottomed wig very well powdered. I imagine I see your ladyship stare at this article, of which you very much doubt the veracity; but, upon my word, I have not yet made use of the privilege of a traveller; and my whole account is writ with the same plain sincerity of heart, with which I assure you that I am, dear madam, your ladyship's, &c.

To the Countess of _____ [Mar].

Vienna, Sept. 14, O.S. [1716].

Though I have so lately troubled you, my dear sister, with a long letter, yet I will keep my promise in giving you an account of my first going to court.

In order to that ceremony, I was squeezed up in a gown, and adorned with a gorget and the other implements thereunto belonging: a dress very inconvenient, but which certainly shews the neck and shape to great advantage. I cannot forbear in this place giving you some description of the fashions here, which are more monstrous and contrary to all common sense and reason, than 'tis possible for you to imagine. They build certain fabrics of gauze on their heads about a yard high, consisting of three or four stories, fortified with numberless yards of heavy ribbon. The foundation of this structure is a thing they call a *Bourle* which is exactly of the same shape and kind, but about four times as big, as those rolls our prudent milk-maids make use of to fix their pails upon. This machine they cover with their own hair, which they mix with a great deal of false, it being a particular beauty to have their heads too large to go into a moderate tub. Their hair is prodigiously powdered, to conceal the mixture, and set out with three or four rows of bodkins (wonderfully large, that stick [out] two or three inches from their hair), made of diamonds, pearls, red, green, and yellow stones, that it certainly requires as much art and experience to carry the load upright, as to dance upon May-day with the garland. Their whalebone petticoats outdo ours by several yards circumference, and cover some acres of ground.

You may easily suppose how much this extraordinary dress sets off and improves the natural ugliness with which God Almighty has been pleased to endow them all generally. Even the lovely empress herself is obliged to comply, in some degree, with these absurd fashions, which they would not quit for all the world. I had a private audience (according to ceremony) of half an hour, and then all the other ladies were permitted to come [and] make their court. I was perfectly charmed with the empress: I cannot, however, tell you that her features are regular; her eyes are not large, but have a lively look, full of sweetness; her complexion the finest I ever saw; her nose and forehead well made, but her mouth has ten thousand charms that touch the soul. When she smiles, 'tis with a beauty and sweetness that forces adoration. She has a vast quantity of fine fair hair; but then her person!—

one must speak of it poetically to do it rigid justice; all that the poets have said of the mien of Juno, the air of Venus, come not up to the truth. The Graces move with her; the famous statues of Medecis was not formed with more delicate proportions; nothing can be added to the beauty of her neck and hands. Till I saw them, I did not believe there were any in nature so perfect, and I was almost sorry that my rank here did not permit me to kiss them; but they are kissed sufficiently; for every body that waits on her pays that homage at their entrance, and when they take leave.

When the ladies were come in, she sat down to Quinze. I could not play at a game I had never seen before, and she ordered me a seat at her right hand, and had the goodness to talk to me very much, with that grace so natural to her. I expected every moment, when the men were to come in to pay their court; but this drawing-room is very different from that of England; no man enters it but the old grand-master, who comes in to advertize the empress of the approach of the emperor. His imperial majesty did me the honour of speaking to me in a very obliging manner; but he never speaks to any of the other ladies; and the whole passes with a gravity and air of ceremony that has something very formal in it.

To the Countess of _____ [Mar].

Blankenburg, Dec. 17, O.S. [1716].

You will not forgive me, if I do not say something of Hanover; I cannot tell you that the town is either large or magnificent. The opera-house, which was built by the late Elector, is much finer than that of Vienna. I was very sorry that the ill weather did not permit me to see Hernhausen in all its beauty; but, in spite of the snow, I thought the gardens very fine. I was particularly surprised at the vast number of orange trees, much larger than I have ever seen in England, though this climate is certainly colder. But I had more reason to wonder that night at the king's table. There was brought to him from a gentleman of this country, two large baskets full of ripe oranges and lemons of different sorts, many of which were quite new to me; and, what I thought worth all the rest, two ripe ananas, which, to my taste, are a fruit perfectly delicious. You know they are naturally the growth of Brazil, and I could not imagine how they could come there but by enchantment. Upon enquiry, I learnt that they have brought their stoves to such perfection, they lengthen the summer as long as they please, giving to every plant the degree of heat it would receive from the sun in its native soil. The effect is very near the same; I am surprised we do not practise in England so useful an invention.

This reflection naturally leads me to consider our obstinacy in shaking with cold six months in the year, rather than make use of stoves, which are certainly one of the greatest conveniences of life; and so far from spoiling the form of a room, they add very much to the magnificence of it, when they are painted and gilt, as at Vienna, or at Dresden, where they are often the shape of china jars, statues, or fine cabinets, so naturally represented, they are not to be distinguished. If ever I return, in defiance to the fashion, you shall certainly see one in the chamber of,

Dear sister, &c.

To the Countess of _____ [Mar].

Peterwaradin, Jan. 30, O.S. [1717].

. . . Leaving Comora on the other side [of] the river, we went the eighteenth to Nosmuhl, a small village, where, however, we made shift to find tolerable accommodation. We continued two days travelling between this place and Buda, through the finest plains in the world, as even as if they were paved, and extremely fruitful; but for the most part desert and uncultivated, laid waste by the long war between the Turk and emperor, and the more cruel civil war occasioned by the barbarous persecution of the Protestant religion by the Emperor Leopold. That prince has left behind him the character of an extraordinary piety, and was naturally of a mild merciful temper; but, putting his conscience into the hands of a Jesuit, he was more cruel and treacherous to his poor Hungarian subjects, than ever the Turk has been to the Christians; breaking, without scruple, his coronation oath, and his faith, solemnly given in many public treaties. Indeed, nothing can be more melancholy than, travelling through Hungary, reflecting on the former flourishing state of that kingdom, and seeing such a noble spot of earth almost uninhabited. This is also the present circumstances of Buda (where we arrived very early the twenty-second), once the royal seat of the Hungarian kings, where their palace was reckoned one of the most beautiful buildings of the age, now wholly destroyed, no part of the town having been repaired since the last siege, but the fortifications and the castle, which is the present residence of the governor-general Ragule, an officer of great merit. He came immediately to see us, and carried us in his coach to his house, where I was received by his lady with all possible civility, and magnificently entertained.

To Mr. P. [Pope].

Belgrade, Feb. 12, O.S. [1717].

. . . This little digression has interrupted my telling you we passed over the fields of Carlowitz, where the last great victory was obtained by Prince Eugene over the Turks. The marks of that glorious bloody day are yet recent, the field being strewed with the skulls and carcases of unburied men, horses, and camels. I could not look without horror, on such numbers of mangled human bodies, and reflect on the injustice of war, that makes murder not only necessary but meritorious. Nothing seems to be a plainer proof of the irrationality of mankind (whatever fine claims we pretend to reason) than the rage with which they contest for a small spot of ground, when such large parts of fruitful earth lie quite uninhabited. It is true, custom has now made it unavoidable; but can there be a greater demonstration of want of reason, than a custom being firmly established, so plainly contrary to the interest of man in general? I am a good deal inclined to believe Mr. Hobbes, that the state of nature is a state of war; but thence I conclude human nature not rational, if the word reason means common sense, as I suppose it does. I have a great many admirable arguments to support this reflection; but I won't trouble you with them, but return, in a plain style, to the history of my travels.

To the Lady _____.
Adrianople, April 1, O.S. [1717].

I am now got into a new world, where everything I see appears to me a change of scene; and I write to your ladyship with some content of mind, hoping at least that you will find the charm of novelty in my letters, and no longer reproach me, that I tell you nothing extraordinary.

I won't trouble you with a relation of our tedious journey; but I must not omit what I saw remarkable at Sophia, one of the most beautiful towns in the Turkish empire, and famous for its hot baths, that are resorted to both for diversion and health. I stopped here one day on purpose to see them. Designing to go *incognita*, I hired a Turkish coach. These voitures are not at all like ours, but much more convenient for the country, the heat being so great that glasses would be very troublesome. . . .

. . . I went to the bagnio about ten o'clock. It was already full of women. It is built of stone, in the shape of a dome, with no windows but in the roof, which gives light enough. There were five of these domes joined together, the outmost being less than the rest, and serving only as a hall, where the portress stood at the door. Ladies of quality generally give this woman the value of a crown or ten shillings; and I did not forget that ceremony. The next room is a very large one paved with marble, and all round it, raised, two sofas of marble, one above another. There were four fountains of cold water in this room, falling first into marble basins, and then running on the floor in little channels made for that purpose, which carried the streams into the next room, something less than this, with the same sort of marble sofas, but so hot with steams of sulphur proceeding from the baths joining to it, it was impossible to stay there with one's clothes on. The two other domes were the hot baths, one of which had cocks of cold water turning into it, to temper it to what degree of warmth the bathers have a mind to.

I was in my travelling habit, which is a riding dress, and certainly appeared very extraordinary to them. Yet there was not one of them that shewed the least surprise or impertinent curiosity, but received me with all the obliging civility possible. I know no European court where the ladies would have behaved themselves in so polite a manner to a stranger. I believe in the whole, there were two hundred women, and yet none of those disdainful smiles, or satiric whispers, that never fail in our assemblies when any body appears that is not dressed exactly in the fashion. They repeated over and over to me, "Uzelle, pék uzelle," which is nothing but Charming, very charming.—The first sofas were covered with cushions and rich carpets, on which sat the ladies; and on the second, their slaves behind them, but without any distinction of rank by their dress, all being in the state of nature, that is, in plain English, stark naked, without any beauty or defect concealed. Yet there was not the least wanton smile or immodest gesture amongst them. They walked and moved with the same majestic grace which Milton describes of our general mother. There were many amongst them as exactly proportioned as ever any goddess was drawn by the pencil of Guido or Titian,—and most of their skins shiningly white, only adorned by their beautiful hair divided into many tresses, hanging on their shoulders, braided either with pearl or ribbon, perfectly representing the figures of the Graces.

I was here convinced of the truth of a reflection I had often made, that if it was the fashion to go naked, the face would be hardly observed. I perceived that the ladies with the finest skins and most delicate shapes had the greatest share of my admiration, though their faces were sometimes less beautiful than those of their companions. To tell you the truth, I had wickedness enough to wish secretly that Mr. Jervas could have been there invisible. I fancy it would have very much improved his art, to see so many fine women naked, in different postures, some in conversation, some working, others drinking coffee or sherbet, and many negligently lying on their cushions, while their slaves (generally pretty girls of seventeen or eighteen) were employed in braiding their hair in several pretty fancies. In short, it is the women's coffee-house, where all the news of the town is told, scandal invented, &c.—They generally take this diversion once a-week, and stay there at least four or five hours, without getting cold by immediate coming out of the hot bath into the cold room, which was very surprising to me. The lady that seemed the most consider-able among them, entreated me to sit by her, and would fain have undressed me for the bath. I excused myself with some difficulty. They being all so earnest in persuading me, I was at last forced to open my shirt, and shew them my stays; which satisfied them very well, for, I saw, they believed I was so locked up in that machine, that it was not in my own power to open it, which contrivance they attributed to my husband.—I was charmed with their civility and beauty, and should have been very glad to pass more time with them; but Mr. W_____[Wortley] resolving to pursue his journey the next morning early, I was in haste to see the ruins of Justinian's church, which did not afford me so agreeable a prospect as I had left, being little more than a heap of stones.

Adieu, madam: I am sure I have now entertained you with an account of such a sight as you never saw in your life, and what no book of travels could inform you of. 'Tis no less than death for a man to be found in one of these places.

To Mrs. S. C_____ [Miss Sarah Chiswell].
Adrianople, April 1, O.S. [1717].

A propos of distempers, I am going to tell you a thing that I am sure will make you wish yourself here. The small-pox, so fatal, and so general amongst us, is here entirely harmless by the invention of *ingrafting*, which is the term they give it. There is a set of old women who make it their business to perform the operation every autumn, in the month of Sep-tember, when the great heat is abated. People send to one another to know if any of their family has a mind to have the small-pox: they make parties for this purpose, and when they are met (commonly fifteen or sixteen together), the old woman comes with a nut-shell full of the matter of the best sort of small-pox, and asks what veins you please to have opened. She immediately rips open that you offer to her with a large needle (which gives you no more pain than a common scratch), and puts into the vein as much venom as can lie upon the head of her needle, and after binds up the little wound with a hollow bit of shell; and in this manner opens four or five veins. The Grecians have commonly the superstition of opening one in the middle of the forehead, in each arm, and on the breast, to mark the sign of the cross; but this has a very ill effect, all these wounds leaving little scars, and is not done by those that are not superstitious, who choose to have them in the legs, or that part of the arm that is concealed. The children or young patients play together all the rest of the day, and are in perfect health to the eighth. Then the fever begins to seize them, and they keep their beds two days, very seldom three. They have very rarely above twenty or thirty in their faces, which never mark; and in eight days' time they are as well as before their illness. Where they are wounded, there remain running sores during the distemper, which I don't doubt is a great relief to it. Every year thousands undergo this operation; and the French embassador says pleasantly, that they take the small-pox here by way of diversion, as they take the waters in other countries. There is no example of any one that has died in it; and you may believe I am very well satisfied of the safety of this experiment, since I intend to try it on my dear little son.

I am patriot enough to take pains to bring this useful invention into fashion in England; and I should not fail to write to some of our doctors very particularly about it, if I knew any one of them that I thought had virtue enough to destroy such a considerable branch of their revenue for the good of mankind. But that distemper is too beneficial to them not to expose to all their resentment the hardy wight that should undertake to put an end to it. Perhaps, if I live to return, I may, however, have courage to war with them. Upon this occasion admire the heroism in the heart of your friend, &c.

To the Lady _____.

Belgrade Village, June 17, O.S. [1717].

I heartily beg your ladyship's pardon; but I really could not forbear laughing heartily at your letter, and the commissions you are pleased to honour me with.

You desire me to buy you a Greek slave, who is to be mistress of a thousand good qualities. The Greeks are subjects, and not slaves. Those who are to be bought in that manner, are either such as are taken to war, or stolen by the Tartars from Russia, Circassia, or Georgia, and are such miserable, awkward, poor wretches, you would not think any of them worthy to be your housemaids. 'Tis true that many thousands were taken in the Morea; but they have been, most of them, redeemed by the charitable contributions of the Christians, or ransomed by their own relations at Venice. The fine slaves that wait upon the great ladies, or serve the pleasures of the great men, are all bought at the age of eight or nine years old, and educated with great care, to accomplish them in singing, dancing, embroidery, &c. They are commonly Circassians, and their patron never sells them, except it is as a punishment for some very great fault. If ever they grow weary of them, they either present them to a friend, or give them their freedom. Those that are exposed to sale at the markets are always either guilty of some crime, or so entirely worthless that they are of no use at all. I am afraid you will doubt the truth of this account, which I own is very different from our common notions in England; but it is no less truth for all that.

Your whole letter is full of mistakes from one end to the other. I see you have taken your ideas of Turkey from that worthy author Dumont, who has written with equal ignorance and confidence. 'Tis a particular pleasure to me here, to read the voyages to the Levant, which are generally so far removed from truth, and so full of absurdities, I am very well diverted with them. They never fail giving you an account of the women, whom 'tis certain they never saw, and talking very wisely of the genius of the men, into whose company they are never admitted; and very often describe mosques, which they dare not peep into. The Turks are very proud, and will not converse with a stranger they are not assured is considerable in his own country. I speak of the men of distinction; for, as to the ordinary fellows, you may imagine what ideas their conversation can give of the general genius of the people. . . .

To Mrs. T. [Thistlethwayte].

Pera of Constantinople, Jan. 4, O.S. [1718].

. . . To say the truth, I am, at this present writing, not very much turned for the recollection of what is diverting, my head being wholly filled with the preparations necessary for the increase of my family, which I expect every day. You may easily guess at my uneasy situation. But I am, however, in some degree comforted, by the glory that accrues to me from it, and a reflection on the contempt I should otherwise fall under. You won't know what to make of this speech: but, in this country, it is more despicable to be married and not fruitful, than it is with us to be fruitful before marriage. They have a notion, that, whenever a woman leaves off bringing children, it is because she is too old for that business, whatever her face says to the contrary, and this opinion makes the ladies here so ready to make proofs of their youth, (which is as necessary, in order to be a received beauty, as it is to shew the proofs of nobility, to be admitted knight of Malta,) that they do not content themselves with using the natural means, but fly to all sorts of quackeries, to avoid the scandal of being past child-bearing, and often kill themselves by them. Without any exaggeration, all the women of my acquaintance that have been married ten years, have twelve or thirteen children; and the old ones boast of having had five-and-twenty or thirty a-piece, and are respected according to the number they have produced. Whey they are with child, it is their common expression to say, They hope God will be so merciful to them to send two this time; and when I have asked them sometimes, How they expected to provide for such a flock as they desire? they answered, That the plague will certainly kill half of them; which, indeed, generally happens, without much concern to the parents, who are satisfied with the vanity of having brought forth so plentifully.

The French embassadress is forced to comply with this fashion as well as myself. She has not been here much above a year, and has lain in once, and is big again. What is most wonderful is, the exemption they seem to enjoy from the curse entailed on the sex. They see all company the day of their delivery, and, at the fortnight's end, return visits, set out in their jewels and new clothes. I wish I may find the influence of the climate in this particular. But I fear I shall continue an Englishwoman in that affair. . . .

But, having entertained you with things I don't like, it is but just I should tell you something that pleases me. The climate is delightful in the extremest degree. I am now sitting, this present fourth of January, with the windows open, enjoying the warm shine of the sun, while you are freezing over a sad sea-coal fire; and my chamber set out with carnations, roses, and jonquils, fresh from my garden. I am also charmed with many points of the Turkish law, to our shame be it spoken, better designed and better executed than ours; particularly, the punishment of convicted liars (triumphant criminals in our country, God knows): They are burnt in the forehead with a hot iron, being proved the authors of any notorious falsehood. How many white foreheads should we see disfigured, how many fine gentlemen would be forced to wear their wigs as low as their eyebrows, were this law in practice with us! I should go on to tell you many other parts of justice, but I must send for my midwife.

To Mr. P_____.

I have been running about Paris at a strange rate with my sister, and strange sights have we seen. They are, at least, strange sights to me, for after having been accustomed to the gravity of the Turks, I can scarcely look with an easy and familiar aspect at the levity and agility of the airy phantoms that are dancing about me here, and I often think that I am at a puppet-shew amidst the representations of real life. I stare prodigiously, but nobody remarks it, for every body stares here; staring is à la mode—there is a stare of attention and *intérêt*, a stare of curiosity, a stare of expectation, a stare of surprise, and it would greatly amuse you to see what trifling objects excite all this staring. This staring would have rather a solemn kind of air, were it not alleviated by grinning, for at the end of a stare there comes always a grin, and very commonly the entrance of a gentleman or a lady into a room is accompanied with a grin, which is designed to express complacence and social pleasure, but really shews nothing more than a certain contortion of muscles that must make a stranger laugh really, as they laugh artificially. The French grin is equally remote from the cheerful serenity of a smile, and the cordial mirth of an honest English horse-laugh. I shall not perhaps stay here long enough to form a just idea of French manners and characters, though this, I believe, would require but little study, as there is no great depth in either. It appears, on a superficial view, to be a frivolous, restless, and agreeable people. . . .

CHARLES DE SECONDAT, BARON DE MONTESQUIEU

from The Spirit of Laws (1748)

Book XIV
Of Laws in Relation to the Nature of the Climate

1. —General Idea

If it be true that the temper of the mind and the passions of the heart are extremely different in different climates, the laws ought to be in relation both to the variety of those passions and to the variety of those tempers.

2. —Of the Difference of Men in Different Climates

Cold air constringes the extremities of the external fibres of the body;[1] this increases their elasticity, and favours the return of the blood from the extreme parts to the heart. It contracts[2] those very fibres; consequently it increases also their force. On the contrary, warm air relaxes and lengthens the extremes of the fibres; of course it diminishes their force and elasticity.

People are therefore more vigorous in cold climates. Here the action of the heart and the reaction of the extremities of the fibres are better performed, the temperature of the humours is greater, the blood moves more freely towards the heart, and reciprocally the heart has more power. This superiority of strength must produce various effects; for instance, a greater boldness, that is, more courage; a greater sense of superiority, that is, less desire of revenge; a greater opinion of security, that is, more frankness, less suspicion, policy, and cunning. In short, this must be productive of very different tempers. Put a man into a close, warm place, and for the reasons above given he will feel a great faintness. If under this circumstance you propose a bold enterprise to him, I believe you will find him very little disposed towards it; his present weakness will throw him into despondency; he will be afraid of everything, being in a state of total incapacity. The inhabitants of warm countries are, like old men, timorous; the people in cold countries are, like young men, brave. If we reflect on the late wars,[3] which are more recent in our memory, and in which we can better distinguish some particular effects that escape us at a greater distance of time, we shall find that the northern people, transplanted into southern regions,[4] did not perform such exploits as their countrymen, who, fighting in their own climate, possessed their full vigour and courage.

This strength of the fibres in northern nations is the cause that the coarser juices are extracted from their aliments. Hence two things result: one, that the parts of the chyle or lymph are more proper, by reason of their large surface, to be applied to and to nourish the fibres; the other, that they are less proper, from their coarseness, to give a certain subtilty to the nervous juice. Those people have therefore large bodies and but little vivacity.

The nerves that terminate from all parts in the cutis form each a nervous bundle; generally speaking, the whole nerve is not moved, but a very minute part. In warm climates, where the cutis is relaxed, the ends of the nerves are expanded and laid open to the weakest action of the smallest objects. In cold countries the cutis is constringed and the papillae compressed: the miliary glands are in some measure paralytic; and the sensation does not reach the brain, except when it is very strong and proceeds from the whole nerve at once. Now, imagination, taste, sensibility, and vivacity depend on an infinite number of small sensations.

I have observed the outermost part of a sheep's tongue, where, to the naked eye, it seems covered with papillae. On these papillae I have discerned through a microscope small hairs, or a kind of down; between the papillae were pyramids shaped towards the ends like pincers. Very likely these pyramids are the principal organ of taste.

I caused the half of this tongue to be frozen, and observing it with the naked eye I found the papillae considerably diminished: even some rows of them were sunk into their sheath. The outermost part I examined with the microscope, and perceived no pyramids. In proportion as the frost went off, the papillae seemed to the naked eye to rise, and with the microscope the miliary glands began to appear.

This observation confirms what I have been saying, that in cold countries the nervous glands are less expanded: they sink deeper into their sheaths, or they are sheltered from the action of external objects; consequently they have not such lively sensations.

In cold countries they have very little sensibility for pleasure; in temperate countries, they have more; in warm countries, their sensibility is exquisite. As climates are distinguished by degrees of latitude, we might distinguish them also in some measure by those of sensibility. I have been at the opera in England and in Italy, where I have seen the same pieces and the same performers; and yet the same music produces such different effects on the two nations: one is so cold and phlegmatic, and the other so lively and enraptured, that it seems almost inconceivable.

It is the same with regard to pain, which is excited by the laceration of some fibre of the body. The Author of nature has made it an established rule that this pain should be more acute in proportion as the laceration is greater: now it is evident that the large bodies and coarse fibres of the people of the north are less capable of laceration than the delicate fibres of the inhabitants of warm countries; consequently the soul is there less sensible of pain. You must flay a Muscovite alive to make him feel.

From this delicacy of organs peculiar to warm climates it follows that the soul is most sensibly moved by whatever relates to the union of the two sexes: here everything leads to this object.

In northern climates scarcely has the animal part of love a power of making itself felt. In temperate climates, love, attended by a thousand appendages, endeavours to please by things that have at first the appearance, though not the reality, of this passion. In warmer climates it is liked for its own sake, it is the only cause of happiness, it is life itself.

In southern countries a machine of a delicate frame but strong sensibility resigns itself either to a love which rises and is incessantly laid in a seraglio, or to a passion which leaves women in a greater independence, and is consequently exposed to a thousand inquietudes. In northern regions a machine robust and heavy finds pleasure in whatever is apt to throw the spirits into motion, such as hunting, travelling, war, and wine. If we travel towards the north, we meet with people who have few vices, many virtues, and a great share of frankness and sincerity. If we draw near the south, we fancy ourselves entirely removed from the verge of morality; here the strongest passions are productive of all manner of crimes, each man endeavouring, let the means be what they will, to indulge his inordinate desires. In temperate climates we find the inhabitants inconstant in their manners, as well as in their vices and virtues: the climate has not a quality determinate enough to fix them.

The heat of the climate may be so excessive as to deprive the body of all vigour and strength. Then the faintness is communicated to the mind; there is no curiosity, no enterprise, no generosity of sentiment; the inclinations are all passive; indolence constitutes the utmost happiness; scarcely any punishment is so severe as mental employment; and slavery is more supportable than the force and vigour of mind necessary for human conduct.

3. —Contradiction in the Tempers of Some Southern Nations

The Indians[5] are naturally a pusillanimous people; even the children[6] of Europeans born in India lose the courage peculiar to their own climate. But how shall we reconcile this with their customs and penances so full of barbarity? The men voluntarily undergo the greatest hardships, and the women burn themselves: here we find a very odd compound of fortitude and weakness.

Nature, having framed those people of a texture so weak as to fill them with timidity, has formed them at the same time of an imagination so lively that every object makes the strongest impression upon them. That delicacy of organs which renders them apprehensive of death contributes likewise to make them dread a thousand things more than death: the very same sensibility induces them to fly and dare all dangers.

As a good education is more necessary to children than to such as have arrived at maturity of understanding, so the inhabitants of those countries have much greater need than the European nations of a wiser legislator. The greater their sensibility, the more it behoves them to receive proper impressions, to imbibe no prejudices, and to let themselves be directed by reason.

At the time of the Romans the inhabitants of the north of Europe were destitute of arts, education, and almost of laws; and yet the good sense annexed to the gross fibres of those climates enabled them to make an admirable stand against the power of Rome, till the memorable period in which they quitted their woods to subvert that great empire.

4. —Cause of the Immutability of Religion, Manners, Customs, and Laws in the Eastern Countries

If to that delicacy of organs which renders the eastern nations so susceptible of every impression you add likewise a sort of indolence of mind, naturally connected with that of the body, by means of which they grow incapable of any exertion or effort, it is easy to comprehend that when once the soul has received an impression it cannot change it. This is the reason that the laws, manners, and customs,[7] even those which seem quite indifferent, such as their mode of dress, are the same to this very day in eastern countries as they were a thousand years ago.

5. —That Those are Bad Legislators Who Favour the Vices of the Climate, and Good Legislators Who Oppose Those Vices

The Indians believe that repose and non-existence are the foundation of all things, and the end in which they terminate. Hence they consider entire inaction as the most perfect of all states, and the object of their desires. To the Supreme Being they give the title of immovable.[8] The inhabitants of Siam believe that their utmost happiness[9] consists in not being obliged to animate a machine, or to give motion to a body.

In those countries where the excess of heat enervates and exhausts the body, rest is so delicious, and motion so painful, that this system of metaphysics seems natural; and Foe,[10] the legislator of the Indies, was directed by his own sensations when he placed mankind in a state extremely passive; but his doctrine arising from the laziness of the climate favoured it also in its turn; which has been the source of an infinite deal of mischief.

The legislators of China were more rational when, considering men not in the peaceful state which they are to enjoy hereafter, but in the situation proper for discharging the several duties of life, they made their religion, philosophy, and laws all practical. The more the physical causes incline mankind to inaction, the more the moral causes should estrange them from it.

10. —Of the Laws in Relation to the Sobriety of the People

In warm countries the aqueous part of the blood loses itself greatly by perspiration;[11] it must therefore be supplied by a like liquid. Water is there of admirable use; strong liquors would congeal the globules[12] of blood that remain after the transuding of the aqueous humour.

In cold countries the aqueous part of the blood is very little evacuated by perspiration. They may therefore make use of spirituous liquors, without which the blood would congeal. They are full of humours; consequently strong liquors, which give a motion to the blood, are proper for those countries.

The law of Mahomet, which prohibits the drinking of wine, is therefore fitted to the climate of Arabia: and indeed, before Mahomet's time, water was the common drink of the Arabs. The law[13] which forbade the Carthaginians to drink wine was a law of the climate; and, indeed, the climate of those two countries is pretty nearly the same.

Such a law would be improper for cold countries, where the climate seems to force them to a kind of national intemperance, very different from personal ebriety. Drunkenness predominates throughout the world, in proportion to the coldness and humidity of the climate. Go from the equator to the north pole, and you will find this vice increasing together with the degree of latitude. Go from the equator again to the south pole, and you will find the same vice travelling south,[14] exactly in the same proportion.

It is very natural that where wine is contrary to the climate, and consequently to health, the excess of it should be more severely punished than in countries where intoxication produces very few bad effects to the person, fewer to the society, and where it does not make people frantic and wild, but only stupid and heavy. Hence those laws[15] which inflicted a double punishment for crimes committed in drunkenness were applicable only to a personal, and not to a national, ebriety. A German drinks through custom, and a Spaniard by choice.

In warm countries the relaxing of the fibres produces a great evacuation of the liquids, but the solid parts are less transpired. The fibres, which act but faintly, and have very little elasticity, are not much impaired; and a small quantity of nutritious juice is sufficient to repair them; for which reason they eat very little.

It is the variety of wants in different climates that first occasioned a difference in the manner of living, and this gave rise to a variety of laws. Where people are very communicative there must be particular laws, and others where there is but little communication.

13. —Effects Arising from the Climate of England

In a nation so distempered by the climate as to have a disrelish of everything, nay, even of life, it is plain that the government most suitable to the inhabitants is that in which they cannot lay their uneasiness to any single person's charge, and in which, being under the direction rather of the laws than of the prince, it is impossible for them to change the government without subverting the laws themselves.

And if this nation has likewise derived from the climate a certain impatience of temper, which renders them incapable of bearing the same train of things for any long continuance, it is obvious that the government above mentioned is the fittest for them.

This impatience of temper is not very considerable of itself; but it may become so when joined with courage.

It is quite a different thing from levity, which makes people undertake or drop a project without cause; it borders more upon obstinacy, because it proceeds from so lively a sense of misery that it is not weakened even by the habit of suffering.

This temper in a free nation is extremely proper for disconcerting the projects of tyranny,[16] which is always slow and feeble in its commencement, as in the end it is active and lively: which at first only stretches out a hand to assist, and exerts afterwards a multitude of arms to oppress.

Slavery is ever preceded by sleep. But a people who find no rest in any situation, who continually explore every part, and feel nothing but pain, can hardly be lulled to sleep.

Politics are a smooth file, which cuts gradually, and attains its end by a slow progression. Now the people of whom we have been speaking are incapable of bearing the delays, the details, and the coolness of negotiations: in these they are more unlikely to succeed than any other nation; hence they are apt to lose by treaties what they obtain by their arms.

14. —Other Effects of the Climate

Our ancestors, the ancient Germans, lived in a climate where the passions were extremely calm. Their laws decided only in such cases where the injury was visible to the eye, and went no farther. And as they judged of the outrages done to men from the greatness of the wound, they acted with no other delicacy in respect to the injuries done to women. The law of the Alemans[17] on this subject is very extraordinary. If a person uncovers a woman's head, he pays a fine of fifty sous; if he uncovers her leg up to the knee, he pays the same; and double from the knee upwards. One would think that the law measured the insults offered to women as we measure a figure in geometry; it did not punish the crime of the imagination, but that of the eye. But upon the migration of a German nation into Spain, the climate soon found a necessity for different laws. The law of the Visigoths inhibited the surgeons to bleed a free woman, except either her father, mother, brother, son, or uncle was present. As the imagination of the people grew warm, so did that of the legislators; the law suspected everything when the people had become suspicious.

These laws had, therefore, a particular regard for the two sexes. But in their punishments they seem rather to humour the revengeful temper of private persons than to administer public justice. Thus, in most cases, they reduced both the criminals to be slaves to the offended relatives or to the injured husband; a free-born woman[18] who had yielded to the embraces of a married man was delivered up to his wife to dispose of her as she pleased. They obliged the slaves,[19] if they found their master's wife in adultery, to bind her and carry her to her husband; they even permitted her children to be her accusers, and her slaves to be tortured in order to convict her. Thus their laws were far better adapted to refine, even to excess, a certain point of honour than to form a good civil administration. We must not, therefore, be surprised if Count Julian was of opinion that an affront of that kind ought to be expiated by the ruin of his king and country: we must not be surprised if the Moors, with such a conformity of manners, found it so easy to settle and to maintain themselves in Spain, and to retard the fall of their empire.

15. —Of the Different Confidence Which the Laws Have in the People, According to the Difference of Climates

The people of Japan are of so stubborn and perverse a temper that neither their legislators nor magistrates can put any confidence in them: they set nothing before their eyes but judgments, menaces, and chastisements; every step they take is subject to the inquisition of the civil magistrate. Those laws which out of five heads of families establish one as a magistrate over the other four; those laws which punish a family or a whole ward for a single crime; those laws, in fine, which find nobody innocent where one may happen to be guilty, are made with a design to implant in the people a mutual distrust, and to make every man the inspector, witness, and judge of his neighbour's conduct.

On the contrary, the people of India are mild,[20] tender, and compassionate. Hence their legislators repose great confidence in them. They have established[21] very few punishments; these are not severe, nor are the rigorously executed. They have subjected nephews to their uncles, and orphans to their guardians, as in other countries they are subjected to their fathers; they have regulated the succession by the acknowledged merit of the successor. They seem to think that every individual ought to place entire confidence in the good nature of his fellow-subjects.[22]

They enfranchise their slaves without difficulty, they marry them, they treat them as their children.[23] Happy climate which gives birth to innocence, and produces a lenity in the laws!

Notes

1. This appears even in the countenance: in cold weather people look thinner.
2. We know that it shortens iron.
3. Those for the succession to the Spanish monarchy.
4. For instance, in Spain.
5. "One hundred European soldiers," says Tavernier, "would without any great difficulty beat a thousand Indian soldiers."
6. Even the Persians who settle in the Indies contract in the third generation the indolence and cowardice of the Indians. See Bernier on the Mogul, tom. i. p. 182.
7. We find by a fragment of Nicolaus Damascenus, collected by Constantine Porphyrogenitus, that it was an ancient custom in the East to strangle a governor who had given any displeasure; it was in the time of the Medes.
8. Panamanack: See Kircher.
9. La Loubiere, Relation of Siam, p. 446.
10. Foe endeavoured to reduce the heart to a mere vacuum: "We have eyes and ears, but perfection consists in neither seeing nor hearing; a mouth, hands, &c., but perfection requires that these members should be inactive." This is taken from the dialogue of a Chinese philosopher, quoted by Father Du Halde, tom. iii.
11. "My body is a sieve; scarcely have I swallowed a pint of water, but I see it transude like dew out of all my limbs, even to my fingers' ends. I drink ten pints a day, and it does me no manner of harm."—Berniers Travels, tom. ii. p. 261.
12. In the blood there are red globules, fibrous parts, white globules and water, in which the whole swims.
13. Plato, book II. of Laws; Aristotle, of the care of domestic affairs; Eusebius's Evangelical Preparation, book XII. chap. xvii.
14. This is seen in the Hottentots, and the inhabitants of the most southern part of Chili.
15. As Pittacus did, according to Aristotle, *Polit.* lib. I. cap. iii. He lived in a climate where drunkenness is not a national vice.
16. Here I take this word for the design of subverting the established power, and espeically that of democracy; this is the signification in which it was understood by the Greeks and Romans.
17. Chap. lviii. 1 and 2.
18. Law of the Visigoths, book III. tit. 4, 9.
19. Ibid. book III. tit. 4, 6.
20, See Bernier, tom. ii. p. 140.
21. See in the 14th Collection of the Edifying Letters, p. 403, the principal laws or customs of the inhabitants of the peninsula on this side the Ganges.
22. See Edifying Letters, IX. 378.
23. I had once thought that the lenity of slavery in India had made Diodorus say that there was neither master nor slave in that country; but Diodorus has attributed to the whole continent of India what, according to Strabo, lib. XV., belonged only a particular nation.

Simón Bolívar

from The Jamaica Letter (1815)

Kingston, Jamaica,
September 6, 1815

My dear Sir:

I hasten to reply to the letter of the 29th ultimo which you had the honor of sending me and which I received with the greatest satisfaction.

Sensible though I am of the interest you desire to take in the fate of my country, and of your commiseration with her for the tortures she has suffered from the time of her discovery until the present at the hands of her destroyers, the Spaniards, I am no less sensible of the obligation which your solicitous inquiries about the principal objects of American policy place upon me. Thus, I find myself in conflict between the desire to reciprocate your confidence, which honors me, and the difficulty of rewarding it, for lack of documents and books and because of my own limited knowledge of a land so vast, so varied, and so little known as the New World.

In my opinion it is impossible to answer the questions that you have so kindly posed. Baron von Humboldt himself, with his encyclopedic theoretical and practical knowledge, could hardly do so properly, because, although some of the facts about America and her development are known, I dare say the better part are shrouded in mystery. Accordingly, only conjectures that are more or less approximate can be made, especially with regard to her future and the true plans of the Americans, inasmuch as our continent has within it potentialities for every facet of development revealed in the history of nations, by reason of its physical characteristics and because of the hazards of war and the uncertainties of politics.

As I feel obligated to give due consideration to your esteemed letter and to the philanthropic intentions prompting it, I am impelled to write you these words, wherein you will certainly not find the brilliant thoughts you seek but rather a candid statement of my ideas.

"Three centuries ago," you say, "began the atrocities committed by the Spaniards on this great hemisphere of Columbus." Our age has rejected these atrocities as mythical, because they appear to be beyond the human capacity for evil. Modern critics would never credit them were it not for the many and frequent documents testifying to these horrible truths. The humane Bishop of Chiapas, that apostle of America, Las Casas [1474–1564], has left to posterity a brief description of these horrors, extracted from the trial records in Sevilla relating to the cases brought against the *conquistadores*, and containing the testimony of every respectable person then in the New World, together with the charges [*procesos*], which the tyrants made against each other. All this is attested by the foremost historians of that time. Every impartial person has admitted the zeal, sincerity and high character of that friend of humanity, who so fervently and so steadfastly denounced to his government and to his contemporaries the most horrible acts of sanguinary frenzy.

With what a feeling of gratitude I read that passage in your letter in which you say to me: "I hope that the success which then followed Spanish arms may now turn in favor of their adversaries, the badly oppressed people of South America." I take this hope as a prediction, if it is justice that determines man's contests. Success will crown our efforts, because the destiny of America has been irrevocably decided; the tie that bound her to Spain has been severed. Only a concept maintained that tie and kept the parts of that immense monarchy together. That which formerly bound them now divides them. The hatred that the Peninsula [Spain] has inspired in us is greater than the ocean between us. It would be easier to have the two continents meet than to reconcile the spirits of the two countries. The habit of obedience; a community of interest, of understanding, of religion; mutual goodwill; a tender regard for the birthplace and good name of our forefathers; in short, all that gave rise to our hopes, came to us from Spain. As a result there was born a principle of affinity that seemed eternal, notwithstanding the misbehavior of our rulers which weakened that sympathy, or, rather, that bond enforced by the domination of their rule. At present the contrary attitude persists: we are threatened with the fear of death, dishonor, and every harm; there is nothing we have not suffered at the hands of that unnatural stepmother—Spain. The veil has been torn asunder. We have already seen the light, and it is not our desire to be thrust back into darkness. The chains have been broken; we have been freed, and now our enemies seek to enslave us anew. For this reason America fights desperately, and seldom has desperation failed to achieve victory.

Because successes have been partial and spasmodic, we must not lose faith. In some regions the Independents triumph, while in others the tyrants have the advantage. What is the end result? Is not the entire New World in motion, armed for defense? We have but to look around us on this hemisphere to witness a simultaneous struggle at every point.

The war-like state of the La Plata River provinces [Argentina] has purged that territory and led their victorious armies to Upper Perú arousing Arequipa and worrying the royalists in Lima. Nearly one million inhabitants there now enjoy liberty.

The territory of Chile, populated by 800,000 souls, is fighting the enemy who is seeking her subjugation; but to no avail, because those who long ago put an end to the conquests of this enemy, the free and indomitable Araucanians, are their neighbors and compatriots. Their sublime example is proof to those fighting in Chile that a people who love independence will eventually achieve it.

The viceroyalty of Perú, whose population approaches a million and a half inhabitants, without doubt suffers the greatest subjection and is obliged to make the most sacrifices for the royal cause; and, although the thought of cooperating with that part of America may be vain, the fact remains that it is not tranquil, nor is it capable of restraining the torrent that threatens most of its provinces.

New Granada [Colombia], which is, so to speak, the heart of America, obeys a general government, save for the territory of Quito which is held only with the greatest difficulty, by its enemies, as it is strongly devoted to the country's cause; and the provinces of Panamá and Santa Marta endure, not without suffering, the tyranny of their masters. Two and a half million people inhabit New Granada and are actually defending that territory against the Spanish army under General Morillo, who will probably suffer defeat at the impregnable fortress of Cartagena. But should he take that city, it will be at the price of heavy casualties, and he will then lack sufficient forces to subdue the unrestrained and brave inhabitants of the interior.

With respect to heroic and hapless Venezuela, events there have moved so rapidly and the devastation has been such that it is reduced to frightful desolation and almost absolute indigence, although it was once among the fairest regions that are the pride of America. Its tyrants govern a desert, and they oppress only those unfortunate survivors who, having escaped death, lead a precarious existence. A few women, children, and old men are all that remain. Most of the men have perished rather than be slaves; those who survive continue to fight furiously on the fields and in the inland towns, until they expire or hurl into the sea those who, insatiable in their thirst for blood and crimes, rival those first monsters who wiped out America's primitive race. Nearly a million persons formerly dwelt in Venezuela, and it is no exaggeration to say that one out of four has succumbed either to the land, sword, hunger, plague, flight, or privation, all consequences of the war, save the earthquake.

According to Baron von Humboldt, New Spain, including Guatemala, had 7,800,000 inhabitants in 1808. Since that time, the insurrection, which has shaken virtually all of her provinces, has appreciably reduced that apparently correct figure, for over a million men have perished, as you can see in the report of Mr. Walton, who describes faithfully the bloody crimes committed in that abundant kingdom. There the struggle continues by dint of human and every other type of sacrifice, for the Spaniards spare nothing that might enable them to subdue those who have had the misfortune of being born on this soil, which appears to be destined to flow with the blood of its offspring. In spite of everything, the Mexicans will be free. They have embraced the country's cause, resolved to avenge their forefathers or follow them to the grave. Already they say with Raynal [French philosopher]: The time has come at last to repay the Spaniards torture for torture and to drown that race of annihilators in its own blood or in the sea.

The islands of Puerto Rico and Cuba, with a combined population of perhaps 700,000 to 800,000 souls, are the most tranquil possessions of the Spaniards, because they are not within range of contact with the Independents. But are not the people of those islands Americans? Are they not maltreated? Do they not desire a better life?

This picture represents, on a military map, an area of 2,000 longitudinal and 900 latitudinal leagues at its greatest point, wherein 16,000,000 Americans either defend their rights or suffer repression at the hands of Spain, which, although once the world's greatest empire, is now too weak, with what little is left her, to rule the new hemisphere or even to maintain herself in the old. And shall Europe, the civilized, the merchant, the lover of liberty allow an aged serpent, bent only on satisfying its venomous rage, devour the fairest part of our globe? What! Is Europe deaf to the clamor of her own interests? Has she no eyes to see justice? Has she grown so hardened as to become insensible? The more I ponder these questions, the more I am confused. I am led to think that America's disappearance is desired; but this is impossible because all Europe is not Spain. What madness for our enemy to hope to reconquer America when she has no navy, no funds, and almost no soldiers! Those troops which she has are scarcely adequate to keep her own people in a state of forced obedience and to defend herself from her neighbors. On the other hand, can that nation carry on the exclusive commerce of one-half the world when it lacks manufactures, agricultural products, crafts and sciences, and even a policy? Assume that this mad venture were successful, and further assume that pacification ensued, would not the sons of the Americans of today, together with the sons of the European *reconquistadores* twenty years hence, conceive the same patriotic designs that are now being fought for?

Europe could do Spain a service by dissuading her from her rash obstinacy, thereby at least sparing her the costs she is incurring and the blood she is expending. And if she will fix her attention on her own precincts she can build her prosperity and power upon more solid foundations than doubtful conquests, precarious commerce, and forceful exactions from remote and powerful peoples. Europe herself, as a matter of common sense policy, should have prepared and executed the project of American independence, not alone because the world balance of power so necessitated, but also because this is the legitimate and certain means through which Europe can acquire overseas commercial establishments. A Europe which is not moved by the violent passions of vengeance, ambition, and greed, as is Spain, would seem to be entitled, by all the rules of equity, to make clear to Spain where her best interests lie.

All of the writers who have treated this matter agree on this point. Consequently, we have had reason to hope that the civilized nations would hasten to our aid in order that we might achieve that which must prove to be advantageous to both hemispheres. How vain has been this hope! Not only the Europeans but even our brothers of the North [United States] have been apathetic bystanders in this struggle which, by its very essence, is the most just, and in its consequences the most noble and vital of any which have been raised in ancient or in modern times. Indeed, can the far-reaching effects of freedom for the hemisphere which Columbus discovered ever be calculated?

"The criminal action of Bonaparte," you say, "in seizing Charles IV and Ferdinand VII, the monarchs of that nation which three centuries ago treacherously imprisoned two rulers of South America, is a most evident sign of divine retribution, and, at the same time, positive proof that God espouses the just cause of the Americans and will grant them independence."

"These several months," you add, "I have given much thought to the situation in America and to her hopes for the future. I have a great interest in her development, but I lack adequate information respecting her present state and the aspirations of her people. I greatly desire to know about the politics of each province, also its peoples, and whether they desire a republic or a monarchy; or whether they seek to form one unified republic or a single monarchy? If you could supply me with this information or suggest the sources I might consult, I should deem it a very special favor."

Generous souls always interest themselves in the fate of a people who strive to recover the rights to which the Creator and Nature have entitled them, and one must indeed be wedded to error and passion not to harbor this noble sentiment. You have given thought to my country and are concerned in its behalf, and for your kindness I am warmly grateful.

I have listed the population, which is based on more or less exact data, but which a thousand circumstances render deceiving. This inaccuracy cannot easily be remedied, because most of the inhabitants live in rural areas and are often nomadic; they are farmers, herders, and migrants, lost amidst thick giant forests, solitary plains, and isolated by lakes and mighty streams. Who is capable of compiling complete statistics of a land like this? Moreover, the tribute paid by the Indians, the punishments of the slaves, the first fruits of the harvest [*primicias*], tithes [*diezmas*], and taxes levied on farmers, and other impositions have driven the poor Americans from their homes. This is not to mention the war of extermination that has already taken a toll of nearly an eighth part of the population and frightened another large part away. All in all, the difficulties are insuperable, and the tally is likely to show only half the true count.

It is even more difficult to foresee the future fate of the New World, to set down its political principles, or to prophesy what manner of government it will adopt. Every conjecture relative to America's future is, I feel, pure speculation. When mankind was in its infancy, steeped in uncertainty, ignorance, and error, was it possible to foresee what system it would adopt for its preservation? Who could venture to say that a certain nation would be a republic or a monarchy; this nation great, that nation small? To my way of thinking, such is our own situation. We are a young people. We inhabit a world apart, separated by broad seas. We are young in the ways of almost all the arts and sciences, although, in a certain manner, we are old in the ways of civilized society. I look upon the present state of America as similar to that of Rome after its fall. Each part of Rome adopted a political system conforming to its interest and situation or was led by the individual ambitions of certain chiefs, dynasties, or associations. But this important difference exists: those dispersed parts later reestablished their ancient nations, subject to the changes imposed by circumstances or events. But we scarcely retain a vestige of what once was; we are, moreover, neither Indian nor European, but a species midway between the legitimate proprietors of this country and the Spanish usurpers. In short, though Americans by birth we derive our rights from Europe, and we have to assert these rights against the rights of the natives, and at the same time we must defend ourselves against the invaders. This places us in a most extraordinary and involved situation. Notwithstanding that it is a type of divination to predict the result of the political course which America is pursuing, I shall venture some conjectures which, of course, are colored by my enthusiasm and dictated by rational desires rather than by reasoned calculations.

The rôle of the inhabitants of the American hemisphere has for centuries been purely passive. Politically they were non-existent. We are still in a position lower than slavery, and therefore it is more difficult for us to rise to the enjoyment of freedom. Permit me these transgressions in order to establish the issue. States are slaves because of either the nature or the misuse of their constitutions; a people is therefore enslaved when the government, by its nature or its vices, infringes on and usurps the rights of the citizen or subject. Applying these principles, we find that America was denied not only its freedom but even an active and effective tyranny. Let me explain. Under absolutism there are no recognized limits to the exercise of governmental powers. The will of the great sultan, khan, bey, and other despotic rulers is the supreme law, carried out more or less arbitrarily by the lesser pashas, khans, and satraps of Turkey and Persia, who have an organized system of oppression in which inferiors participate according to the authority vested in them. To them is entrusted the administration of civil, military, political, religious, and tax matters. But, after all is said and done, the rulers of Ispahan are Persians; the viziers of the Grand Turk are Turks; and the sultans of Tartary are Tartars. China does not bring its military leaders and scholars from the land of Genghis Khan, her conqueror, notwithstanding that the Chinese of today are the lineal descendants of those who were reduced to subjection by the ancestors of the present-day Tartars.

How different is our situation! We have been harassed by a conduct which has not only deprived us of our rights but has kept us in a sort of permanent infancy with regard to public affairs. If we could at least have managed our domestic affairs and our internal administration, we could have acquainted ourselves with the processes and mechanics of public affairs. We should also have enjoyed a personal consideration, thereby commanding a certain unconscious respect from the people, which is so necessary to preserve amidst revolutions. That is why I say we have even been deprived of an active tyranny, since we have not been permitted to exercise its functions.

Americans today, and perhaps to a greater extent than ever before, who live within the Spanish system occupy a position in society no better than that of serfs destined for labor, or at best they have no more status than that of mere consumers. Yet even this status is surrounded with galling restrictions, such as being forbidden to grow European crops, or to store products which are royal monopolies, or to establish factories of a type the Peninsula itself does not possess. To this add the exclusive trading privileges, even in articles of prime necessity, and the barriers between American provinces, designed to prevent all exchange of trade, traffic, and understanding. In short, do you wish to know what our future held?—simply the cultivation of the fields of indigo, grain, coffee, sugar cane, cacao, and cotton; cattle raising on the broad plains; hunting wild game in the jungles; digging in the earth to mine its gold—but even these limitations could never satisfy the greed of Spain.

So negative was our existence that I can find nothing comparable in any other civilized society, examine as I may the entire history of time and the politics of all nations. Is it not an outrage and a violation of human rights to expect a land so splendidly endowed, so vast, rich, and populous, to remain merely passive?

As I have just explained, we were cut off and, as it were, removed from the world in relation to the science of government and administration of the state. We were never viceroys or governors, save in the rarest of instances; seldom archbishops and bishops; diplomats never; as military men, only subordinates; as nobles, without royal privileges. In brief, we were neither magistrates nor financiers and seldom merchants—all in flagrant contradiction to our institutions.

Emperor Charles V made a pact with the discoverers, conquerors, and settlers of America, and this, as Guerra puts it, is our social contract. The monarchs of Spain made a solemn agreement with them, to be carried out on their own account and at their own risk, expressly prohibiting them from drawing on the royal treasury. In return, they were made the lords of the land, entitled to organize the public administration and act as the court of last appeal, together with many other exemptions and privileges that are too numerous to mention. The King committed himself never to alienate the American provinces, inasmuch as he had no jurisdiction but that of sovereign domain. Thus, for themselves and their descendants, the *conquistadores* possessed what were tantamount to feudal holdings. Yet there are explicit laws respecting employment in civil, ecclesiastical, and tax-raising establishments. These laws favor, almost exclusively, the natives of the country who are of Spanish extraction. Thus, by an outright violation of the laws and the existing agreements, those born in America have been despoiled of their constitutional rights as embodied in the code. . . .

III. The Enlightenment and the French Revolution

The English poet Alexander Pope once considered the impact of Newton on the intellectual life of his time. He wrote:

> Nature and Nature's laws lay hid in the Night. God said, "Let Newton be," and all was light.

These lines powerfully convey the awe that eighteenth-century intellectuals felt about Newton's achievement. In four elegant laws, he seemed to explain the underlying principles of all matter and motion. The secrets of the universe had been unlocked; and if Newton was not God himself, he was surely one of his appointed messengers.

Eighteenth-century thinkers believed that what Newton had achieved for physical nature could also be accomplished for 'human nature,' that is, in the social sciences. By fusing abstract reasoning and empirical investigation in the manner of Newton, they could discover the laws underpinning human society and consequently refashion political and social institutions in accordance with them. The intellectual movement embodying this viewpoint is the Enlightenment, arguably the first modern movement in Western thought. Enlightenment thinkers wanted to uproot (what they perceived as) hundreds of years of darkness—centuries of superstition, arbitrary custom, and church tyranny—and create a society grounded in rational principles. Many were not philosophers in the usual sense, but social critics and writers interested in reaching an expanding, frequently middle-class audience with a growing interest in public affairs. Enlightenment thinkers were as likely to write novels as philosophical treatises. They acted as advisers to monarchs and emperors, although their advice was not necessarily followed. Their views were spread through the growing eighteenth-century publishing business and the thriving literary societies, clubs, and salons of the time. Given the wider public role that they fashioned for themselves, Enlightenment thinkers have sometimes been described as *philosophes*, writers and social critics who were as interested in transforming the world as understanding it.

Though often associated with France, the Enlightenment was a European wide movement with important manifestations in Germany and Great Britain. The German philosopher Immanuel Kant (1724–1804) was arguably the most important philosopher of the eighteenth century, enormously influential on the history of aesthetics, ethics, and epistemology (the theory of knowledge). In "What is Enlightenment?" he attempts to define the principal characteristics of his age. Kant's reflections are reminiscent of Pope's contrast between darkness and light quoted at the beginning of this introduction. He suggests that motto of the period is "Have courage to use your own reason." It is an age distinguished from previous historical epochs by its refusal to accept traditional authority at face-value. Though Kant advocates the open discussions necessary to advance enlightenment, he is worried that they could possibly undermine state authority and as a result social stability. Such concerns are voiced in his second motto: "Argue as much as you will, and about what you will, only obey!" It is well worth considering whether these two mottos represent compatible aims.

Kant's fellow countryman, the critic and dramatist Gotthold Lessing (1729–1781), explores a theme close to the heart of Enlightenment thought—the nature of religious truth— in the selection from his play, *Nathan the Wise*. There was no single Enlightenment position on religion. Enlightenment thinkers attacked the church as it was constituted, yet recognized its value in terms of ethical teaching. Wearied by the religious divisions of the previous two centuries, more skeptical about there being a philosophical justification for one true religion, they emphasized the right of individuals to practice the religion of their choice and advocated that states with national churches embrace the idea of "religious toleration." While in the 1700s this was more of an idea than a reality, in the 1800s it began to take hold. The idea of religious toleration is the allegorical substance of the "tale of the three rings" from *Nathan the Wise*. Nathan, a wise Jew from Jerusalem, tells the story in response to the pleas of Saladin, the Sultan, who wants to know how to tell a true religion from a false one. The three rings in Nathan's tale represent Christianity, Judaism, and Islam.

The two writers representing Britain in this chapter are John Locke (1632–1704) and Adam Smith (1723–1790). Locke is not, strictly speaking, part of the Enlightenment. He is more properly viewed as a harbinger of the movement and one of its formative influences. Locke is perhaps best known for his influence on political thought. His contention that people have the right to change their government when their liberty and property are threatened is one of the ideas that influenced the American founding fathers, especially Thomas Jefferson. Yet Locke also played a central role in shaping eighteenth-century epistemological debates. His *An Essay Concerning Human Understanding* represents a refutation of Descartes's notion that innate ideas in the mind exist independently of experience. He argues that the mind at birth is a *tabula rasa*, a blank slate devoid of any content or ideas. According to Locke, ideas do not originate inside the mind but result from 'experience'— either through 'sensation,' sensory perception of the world, or 'reflection,' the process whereby the mind reflects on its own operations.

Adam Smith is, of course, well known as one of the founders of economics. Less known is his connection to the Enlightenment. Just as Newton sought to understand the laws of motion, Smith attempted to uncover the laws of economic behavior. Like other Enlightenment thinkers, he believed that knowledge of these laws was a precondition for bringing the world into harmony with them. Smith extended the thought of the eighteenth-century French *physiocrats*, a group of economic thinkers who advocated the ending of feudal or "artificial" controls on land use in order to liberate productive capacity. In *An Inquiry into the Nature and Causes of the Wealth of Nations*, Smith argues that restrictions on agriculture, manufacture, and trade in the form of monopolies, tariffs, and other controls are an impediment to maximizing productive capacity; and he believes that the verdict of the market is ultimately the best economic policy. In Smith's view, individuals in isolation, seeking to satisfy their own passions and desires, would ultimately produce the best social result as if "led by an invisible hand."

The Enlightenment thinkers, especially in France, used the tools of rational critique to campaign for the reform of political and social institutions. Yet probably few of them imagined that their ideas would inspire the French Revolution, a tumultuous event which overthrew the monarchy, redrew the political map, and plunged Europe into war for nearly a generation. The Enlightenment did not cause the French Revolution, but it is hard to picture it without it. The English historian Christopher Hill once wrote: "Revolutions are not made without ideas, but they are not made by intellectuals. Steam is essential to driving a railway engine; but neither a locomotive nor a permanent way can be built without steam." The Enlightenment was the steam of the revolutionary engine of France.

Historians continue to disagree why there was a French Revolution, but it is clear that by 1788 France was bankrupt, a result of nearly a century of wars with its chief rival Britain, and could not continue in its existing form. Backed to the wall, the monarchy called the Estates-General, a representative assembly of the three French estates—the clergy, the nobility, and everyone else (comprising the bourgeoisie and the peasantry). The leaders of the three estates disagreed about how the assembly should be structured. The representatives of the first two estates—the clergy and the nobility—argued that each estate should vote separately and receive one vote. This was of great benefit to them, since the leaders of the clergy were largely from the nobility, and thus they could always veto the will of the Third Estate. The leaders of the Third Estate, which had the same number of representatives as the other two combined, wanted the assembly to meet as a single body which voted by 'head' rather than by 'order.'

It is at this point that Emmanuel (Abbe) Sieyès (1748–1836), a clergyman and political theorist, entered the debate. In "What Is the Third Estate?" Sieyès argues that the Third Estate's demands are too timid. Insofar as it represents more than 90% of the French people, it comprises the nation: not only because it is the vast majority of the population, but because it is responsible for the material and intellectual output of France. He advocates that the Third Estate constitute itself as a national assembly. While it would be an exaggeration to say that Sieyès was responsible for starting the French Revolution, his political vision was realized in June 1789. When Louis XVI attempted to bar the Estates-General from meeting, the representatives of the Third Estate gathered together at the tennis courts of Versailles, declared themselves a national assembly, and pledged to meet as a body until France had a written constitution. The French Revolution had begun.

The Revolution was a French event, but its impact resonated throughout Europe. In England it gave rise to a major political debate between those who supported it and those who were its critics, a debate which had implication for English politics as well. For the Irish-born politician Edmund Burke (1729–1797) the Revolution was a colossal blunder. In one of the classic statements of conservative political theory, *Reflections on the French Revolution*, Burke rejects the idea that a political system could be recast on the basis of Enlightenment rationality. He argues that a nation is like a body. It develops over time, is continually changing and evolving, and could reform itself only in terms of its own historical traditions. He does not deny that France faces a crisis, but he believes that a revolution is a breach of faith with all those who had lived before it and all those who were yet to be born.

Implicit in Burke's argument is a defense of the English constitution which is not a written document but an accumulation of centuries of legal tradition.

Burke's attack on revolutionary France inspired the English writer and teacher Mary Wollstonecraft (1757–1797) to respond in not one but two political tracts refuting him. One of these, *A Vindication of the Rights of Woman*, is one of the first classics of feminist thought. For Wollstonecraft, the problem with the French Revolution is not that it takes place, but that it does not go far enough. The Revolution proclaims "the rights of man," but what it really means is the rights of men. Where previously the great majority of the population had been oppressed by the privileged classes, in revolutionary France one half of the population now dominates the other half. Wollstonecraft, drawing upon Enlightenment rationalism, argues that only if men and women are political and social equals can they develop the mutual respect that is necessary to create universal harmony. Observing a tendency for bourgeois women and men to imitate the manners of aristocracy, Wollstonecraft urges them to become educated citizens rather than creatures of sensation. Until both sexes are freed, they will both remain enslaved.

Immanuel Kant

What Is Enlightenment? (1784)

Enlightenment is man's release from his self-incurred tutelage. Tutelage is man's inability to make use of his understanding without direction from another. Self-incurred is this tutelage when its cause lies not in lack of reason but in lack of resolution and courage to use it without direction from another. *Sapere aude!* "Have courage to use your own reason!"—that is the motto of enlightenment.

Laziness and cowardice are the reasons why so great a portion of mankind, after nature has long since discharged them from external direction (*naturaliter maiorennes*), nevertheless remains under lifelong tutelage, and why it is so easy for others to set themselves up as their guardians. It is so easy not to be of age. If I have a book which understands for me, a pastor who has a conscience for me, a physician who decides my diet, and so forth, I need not trouble myself. I need not think, if I can only pay—others will readily undertake the irksome work for me.

That the step to competence is held to be very dangerous by the far greater portion of mankind (and by the entire fair sex)—quite apart from its being arduous—is seen to by those guardians who have so kindly assumed superintendence over them. After the guardians have first made their domestic cattle dumb and have made sure that these placid creatures will not dare take a single step without the harness of the cart to which they are tethered, the guardians then show them the danger which threatens if they try to go alone. Actually, however, this danger is not so great, for by falling a few times they would finally learn to walk alone. But an example of this failure makes them timid and ordinarily frightens them away from all further trials.

For any single individual to work himself out of the life under tutelage which has become almost his nature is very difficult. He has come to be fond of this state, and he is for the present really incapable of making use of his reason, for no one has ever let him try it out. Statutes and formulas, those mechanical tools of the rational employment or rather misemployment of his natural gifts, are the fetters of an everlasting tutelage. Whoever throws them off makes only an uncertain leap over the narrowest ditch because he is not accustomed to that kind of free motion. Therefore, there are few who have succeeded by their own exercises of mind both in freeing themselves from incompetence and in achieving a steady pace.

But that the public should enlighten itself is more possible; indeed, if only freedom is granted, enlightenment is almost sure to follow. For there will always be some independent thinkers, even among the established guardians of the great masses, who, after throwing off the yoke of tutelage from their own shoulders, will disseminate the spirit of the rational appreciation of both their own worth and every man's vocation for thinking for himself. But be it noted that the public, which has first been brought under this yoke by their guardians, forces the guardians themselves to remain bound when it is incited to do so by some of the guardians who are themselves capable of some enlightenment—so harmful is it to implant prejudices, for they later take vengeance on their cultivators or on their descendants. Thus the public can only slowly attain enlightenment. Perhaps a fall of personal despotism or of avaricious or tyrannical oppression may be accomplished by revolution, but never a true reform in ways of thinking. Rather, new prejudices will serve as well as old ones to harness the great unthinking masses.

For this enlightenment, however, nothing is required but freedom, and indeed the most harmless among all the things to which this term can properly be applied. It is the freedom to make public use of one's reason at every point. But I hear on all sides, "Do not argue!" The officer says: "Do not argue but drill!" The tax collector: "Do not argue but pay!" The cleric: "Do not argue but believe!" Only one prince in the world says, "Argue as much as you will, and about what you will, but obey!" Everywhere there is restriction on freedom.

Which restriction is an obstacle to enlightenment, and which is not an obstacle but a promoter of it? I answer: The public use of one's reason must always be free, and it alone can bring about enlightenment among men. The private use of reason, on the other hand, may often be very narrowly restricted without particularly hindering the progress of enlightenment. By the public use of one's reason I understand the use which a person makes of it as a scholar before the reading public. Private use I call that which one may make of it in a particular civil post or office which is entrusted to him. Many affairs which are conducted in the interest of the community require a certain mechanism through which some members of the community must passively conduct themselves with an artificial unanimity, so that the government may direct them to public ends, or at least prevent them from destroying those ends. Here argument is certainly not allowed—one must obey. But so far as a part of the mechanism regards himself at the same time as a member of the whole community or of a society of world citizens, and thus in the role of a scholar who addresses the public (in the proper sense of the word) through his writings, he certainly can argue without hurting the affairs for which he is in part responsible as a passive member. Thus it would be ruinous for an officer in service to debate about the suitability or utility of a command given to him by his superior; he must obey. But the right to make remarks on errors in the military service and to lay them before the public for judgment cannot equitably be refused him as a scholar. The citizen cannot refuse to pay the taxes imposed on him; indeed, and impudent complaint at those levied on him can be punished as a scandal (as it could occasion general refractoriness). But the same person nevertheless does not act contrary to his duty as a citizen when, as a scholar, he publicly expresses his thoughts on the inappropriateness or even the injustice of these levies. Similarly a clergyman is obligated to make his sermon to his pupils in catechism and his congregation conform to the symbol of the church which he serves, for he has been accepted on this condition. But as a scholar he has complete freedom, even the calling, to communicate to the public all his carefully tested and well-meaning thoughts on that which is erroneous in the symbol and to make suggestions for the better organization of the religious body and church. In doing this there is nothing that could be laid as a burden on his conscience. For what he teaches as a consequence of his office as a representative of the church, this he considers something about which he has no freedom to teach according to his own lights; it is something which he is appointed to propound at the dictation of and in the name of another. He will say, "Our church teaches this or that; those are the proofs which it adduces." He thus extracts all practical uses for his congregation from statutes to which he himself would not subscribe with full conviction but to the enunciation of which he can very well pledge himself because it is not impossible that truth lies hidden in them, and, in any case, there is at least nothing in them contradictory to inner religion. For if he believed he had found such in them, he could not conscientiously discharge the duties of his office; he would have to give it up. The use, therefore, which an appointed teacher makes of his reason before his congregation is merely private, because this congregation is only a domestic one (even if it be a large gathering); with respect to it, as a priest, he is not free, nor can he be free, because he carries out the orders of another. But as a scholar, whose writings speak to his public, the world, the clergyman in the public use of his reason enjoys an unlimited freedom to use his own reason and to speak in his own person. That the guardians of the people (in spiritual things) should themselves be incompetent is an absurdity which amounts to the eternalization of absurdities.

But would not a society of clergymen, perhaps a church conference or venerable classis (as they call themselves among the Dutch), be justified in obligating itself by oath to a certain unchangeable symbol in order to enjoy an unceasing guardianship over each of its members and thereby over the people as a whole, and even to make it eternal? I answer that this is altogether impossible. Such a contract, made to shut off all further enlightenment from the human race, is absolutely null and void even if confirmed by the supreme power, by parliaments, and by the most ceremonious of peace treaties. An age cannot bind itself and ordain to put the succeeding one into such a condition that it cannot extend its (at best very occasional) knowledge, purify itself of errors, and progress in general enlightenment. That would be a crime against human nature, the proper destination of which lies precisely in this progress; and the descendants would be fully justified in rejecting those decrees as having been made in an unwarranted and malicious manner.

The touchstone of everything that can be concluded as a law for a people lies in the question whether the people could have imposed such a law on itself. Now such a religious compact might be possible for a short and definitely limited time, as it were, in expectation of a better. One might let every citizen, and especially the clergyman, in the role of scholar, make his comments freely and publicly, i.e., through writing, on the erroneous aspects of the present institution. The newly introduced order might last until insight into the nature of these things had become so general and widely approved that through uniting their voices (even if not unanimously) they could bring a proposal to the throne to take those congregations under protection which had united into a changed religious organization according to their better ideas, without, however, hindering others who wish to remain in the order. But to unite in permanent religious institution which is not to be subject to doubt before the public even in the lifetime of one man, and thereby to make a period of time fruitless in the progress of mankind toward improvement, thus working to the disadvantage of posterity—that is absolutely forbidden. For himself (and only for a short time) a man may postpone enlightenment in what he ought to know, but to renounce it for himself and even more to renounce it for posterity is to injure and trample on the rights of mankind.

And what a people may not decree for itself can even less be decreed for them by a monarch, for his lawgiving authority rests on his uniting the general public will in his own. If he only sees to it that all true or alleged improvements stand together with civil order, he can leave it to his subjects to do what they find necessary for their spiritual welfare. This is not his concern, though it is incumbent on him to prevent one of them from violently hindering another in determining and promoting this welfare to the best of his ability. To meddle in these matters lowers his own majesty, since by the writings in which his subjects seek to present their views he may evaluate his own governance. He can do this when, with deepest understanding, he lays upon himself the reproach, *Caesar non est supra grammaticos*. Far more does he injure his own majesty when he degrades his supreme power by supporting the ecclesiastical despotism of some tyrants in his state over his other subjects.

If we are asked, "Do we now live in an *enlightened age*?" the answer is, "No," but we do live in an *age of enlightenment*. As things now stand, much is lacking which prevents men from being, or easily becoming, capable of correctly using their own reason in religious matters with assurance and free from outside direction. But, on the other hand, we have clear indications that the field has not been opened wherein men may freely deal with these things and that the obstacles to general enlightenment or the release from self-imposed tutelage are gradually being reduced. In this respect, this is the age of enlightenment, or the century of Frederick.

A prince who does not find it unworthy of himself to say that he holds it to be his duty to prescribe nothing to men in religious matters but to give them complete freedom while renouncing the haughty name of *tolerance*, is himself enlightened and deserves to be esteemed by the grateful world and posterity as the first, at least from the side of government, who divested the human race of its tutelage and left each man free to make use of his reason in matters of conscience. Under him venerable ecclesiastics are allowed, in the role of scholars, and without infringing on their official duties, freely to submit for public testing their judgments and views which here and there diverge from the established symbol. And an even greater freedom is enjoyed by those who are restricted by no official duties. This spirit of freedom spreads beyond this land, even to those in which it must struggle with external obstacles erected by a government which misunderstands its own interest. For an example gives evidence to such a government that in freedom there is not the least cause for concern about public peace and the stability of the community. Men work themselves gradually out of barbarity if only intentional artifices are not made to hold them in it.

I have placed the main point of enlightenment—the escape of men from their self-incurred tutelage—chiefly in matters of religion because our rulers have no interest in playing the guardian with respect to the arts and sciences and also because religious incompetence is not only the most harmful but also the most degrading of all. But the manner of thinking of the head of a state who favors religious enlightenment goes further, and he sees that there is no danger to his lawgiving in allowing his subjects to make public use of their reason and to publish their thoughts on a better formulation of his legislation and even their open-minded criticisms of the laws already made. Of this we have a shining example wherein no monarch is superior to him whom we honor.

But only one who is himself enlightened, is not afraid of shadows, and has a numerous and well-disciplined army to assure public peace, can say: "Argue as much as you will, and about what you will, only obey!" A republic could not dare say such a thing. Here is shown a strange and unexpected trend in human affairs in which almost everything, looked at in the large, is paradoxical. A greater degree of civil freedom appears advantageous to the freedom of mind of the people, and yet it places inescapable limitations upon it; a lower degree of civil freedom, on the contrary, provides the mind with room for each man to extend himself to his full capacity. As nature has uncovered from under this hard shell the seed for which she most tenderly cares—the propensity and vocation to free thinking—this gradually works back upon the character of the people, who thereby gradually become capable of managing freedom; finally, it affects the principles of government, which finds it to its advantage to treat men, who are now more than machines, in accordance with their dignity.

GOTTHOLD LESSING

from Nathan the Wise (1779)

Nathan. There lived a man in a far Eastern clime
In hoar antiquity, who from the hand
Of his most dear beloved received a ring
Of priceless estimate. An opal 'twas
Which split a hundred lovely radiances
And had a magic power, that whoso wore it,
Trusting therein, found grace with God and man.
What wonder therefore that this man o' the East
Let it not from his finger, and took pains
To keep it to his household for all time.
Thus he bequeathed the jewel to the son
Of all his sons he loved best, and provided
That he in turn bequeath it to the son
Who was to him the dearest; evermore
The best-beloved, without respect of birth,
But right o' the ring alone should be the head,
The house's prince. You understand me, Sultan.

Saladin. I understand: continue!

Nathan.   Well, this ring,
From son to son descending, came at last
Unto a father of three sons, who all
To him, all three, were dutiful alike,
And whom, all three, in natural consequence,
He loved alike. Only from time to time
Now this; now that one; now the third, as each
Might be alone with him, the other twain
Not sharing his o'erflowing heart, appeared
Worthiest the ring; and then, piously weak,
He promised it to each. And so things went
Long as they could. But dying hour drawn near

74

Brought the good father to perplexity.
It pained him, the two sons, trusting his word,
Should thus be wounded. What was he to do?
Quickly he sends for an artificer,
To make him on the model of his ring
Two others, bidding spare nor cost nor pains
To make them in all points identical;
And this the artist did. When they are brought
Even the father scarcely can distinguish
His pattern-ring. So, full of joy, he calls
His sons, and each one to him separately;
And gives to each son separately his blessing,
Gives each his ring; and dies. Still hear you, Sultan?

Saladin. [*Who has turned away perplexed.*] I hear, I hear—Only
bring you the tale
To speedy end. Is't done?

Nathan.   The tale is finished.
For what still follows, any man may guess.
Scarce was the father dead, but each one comes
And shows his ring, and each one claims to be
True prince o' the house. Vainly they search, strive, argue,
The true ring was not proved or provable—
[*After a pause, during which he waits the Sultan's reply.*
Almost as hard to prove as to us now
What the true creed is.

Saladin.   How? is this to be
The answer to my question?

Nathan.   Nay, it merely
Makes my excuse that I don't trust myself
Exactly to distinguish twixt the rings
The Sire with express purpose had bade make
So that no probing might distinguish them—

Saladin. The rings! You play with me! It was my thought
That the religions I have named to you
Were plainly, easily distinguishable,
Down even to clothing, down to meat and drink!

Nathan. Only not so in questions of foundation—
For base not all their creeds on history,

Written or handed down? And history
Must be received in faith implicitly.
Is't not so? Then on whom rest we this faith
Implicit, doubting not? Surely on our own?
Them from whose blood we spring? Surely on them
Who from our childhood gave us proofs of love?
Who never have deceived us, saving when
'Twere happier, safer so to be deceived?
How, then, shall I my fathers less believe
Than you your own? or in the other case,
Can I demand that you should give the lie
To your forefathers, that mine be not gainsaid?
And, yet again, the same holds of the Christians.
Is't not so?

Saladin. (By high God! The man is right; I must be dumb.)

Nathan.   Then let us come again
Back to our rings. As we have said—the sons
Appealed to law; and swore before the Judge
Out of the father's hand, immediately,
To have received the ring—and this was true—
After for long he had the promise sure
One day to enjoy the privilege of the ring—
And this no less was true. Each cried the father
Could not be false towards him, and ere he might
Let such suspicion stain him, must believe,
Glad as he were to think the best of them,
His brothers played him false, and he should soon
Expose the traitors, justify himself.

Saladin. And now, the Judge? I'm waiting, fain to hear
What you will make him say. What was his verdict?

Nathan. Thus spake the Judge: Bring me the father here
To witness; I will hear him; and if not
Leave then my judgment seat. Think you this chair
Is set for reading of riddles? Do you wait,
Expecting the true ring to open mouth?
Yet halt! I hear, the genuine ring possesses
The magic power to bring its wearer love
And grace with God and man. That must decide;
For never can the false rings have this virtue.
Well, then; say whom do two of you love best?

Come, speak! What! silent? Is the rings' effect
But backward and not outward? Is it so
That each one loves himself most? Then I judge
All three of you are traitors and betrayed!
Your rings all three are false. The genuine ring
Perchance the father lost, and to replace it
And hide the loss, had three rings made for one.

Saladin. O, splendid! splendid!

Nathan.   So, went on the Judge,
You may not seek my counsel, but my verdict;
But go! My counsel is, you take the thing
Exactly as it lies. If each of you
Received his ring from his good father's hand,
Then each of you believe his ring the true one—
'Tis possible the father would not suffer
Longer the one ring tyrannise in 's house,
Certain, he loved all three, and equal loved,
And would not injure two to favour one.
Well, then, let each one strive most zealously
To show a love untainted by self-care.
Each with his might vie with the rest to bring
Into the day the virtue of the jewel
His finger wears, and help this virtue forth
By gentleness, by spirit tractable,
By kind deeds and true piety towards God;
And when in days to come the magic powers
Of these fair rings among your children's children
Brighten the world, I call you once again,
After a thousand thousand years are lapsed,
Before this seat of judgment. On that day
A wiser man shall sit on it and speak.
Depart! So spake the modest Judge.

JOHN LOCKE

from An Essay on Human Understanding (1690)

Chapter 2. No Innate Principles in the Mind

1. *The way shown how we come by any knowledge, sufficient to prove it not innate.*—It is an established opinion amongst some men, that there are in the understanding certain *innate principles;* some primary notions, *(koinai ennoiai),* characters, as it were stamped upon the mind of man, which the soul receives in its very first being, and brings into the world with it. It would be sufficient to convince unprejudiced readers of the falseness of this supposition, if I should only show (as I hope I shall in the following parts of this discourse) how men, barely by the use of their natural faculties, may attain to all the knowledge they have, without the help of any innate impressions; and may arrive at certainty, without any such original notions or principles. For I imagine any one will easily grant, that it would be impertinent to suppose the ideas of colours innate in a creature to whom God hath given sight, and a power to receive them by the eyes from external objects; and no less unreasonable would it be to attribute several truths to the impressions of nature and innate characters, when we may observe in ourselves faculties fit to attain as easy and certain knowledge of them as if they were originally imprinted on the mind.

But because a man is not permitted without censure to follow his own thoughts in the search of truth, when they lead him ever so little out of the common road, I shall set down the reasons that made me doubt of the truth of that opinion, as an excuse for my mistake, if I be in one; which I leave to be considered by those who, with me, dispose themselves to embrace truth wherever they find it.

2. *General assent the great argument.*—There is nothing more commonly taken for granted, than that there are certain *principles,* both *speculative* and *practical* (for they speak of both), universally agreed upon by all mankind; which therefore, they argue, must needs be the constant impressions which the souls of men receive in their first beings and which they bring into the world with them, as necessarily and really as they do any of their inherent faculties.

3. *Universal consent proves nothing innate.*—This argument, drawn from universal consent, has this misfortune in it, that if it were true in matter of fact, that there were certain truths wherein all mankind agreed, it would not prove them innate, if there can be any other way shown, how men may come to that universal agreement in the things they do consent in; which I presume may be done.

4. *"What is, is,"* and *"It is impossible for the same Thing to be and not to be," not universally assented to.*—But, which is worse, this argument of universal consent which is made use of to prove innate principles, seems to me a demonstration that there are none such; because there are none to which all mankind give an universal assent. I shall begin with the speculative, and instance in those magnified principles of demonstration, "Whatsoever is, is," and "It is impossible for the same thing to be and not to be"; which, of all others, I think have the most allowed title to innate. These have so settled a reputation of maxims universally received, that it will no doubt be thought strange if any one should seem to question it. But yet I take liberty to say, that these propositions are so far from having an universal assent, that there are a great part of mankind to whom they are not so much as known.

5. *Not on the mind naturally imprinted, because not known to children, idiots, &c.*—For, first, it is evident, that all children and idiots have not the least apprehension or thought of them: and the want of that is enough to destroy that universal assent, which must needs be the necessary concomitant of all innate truths: it seeming to me near a contradiction to say, that there are truths imprinted on the soul which it perceives or understands not; imprinting, if it signify anything, being nothing else but the making certain truths to be perceived. No proposition can be said to be in the mind which it never yet knew, which it was never yet conscious of. For if any one may, then, by the same reason, all propositions that are true, and the mind is capable ever of assenting to, may be said to be in the mind, and to be imprinted; since if any one can be said to be in the mind, which it never yet knew, it must be only because it is capable of knowing it; and so the mind is of all truths it ever shall know. Nay, thus truths may be imprinted on the mind which it never did, nor ever shall know: for a man may live long, and die at last in ignorance of many truths which his mind was capable of knowing, and that with certainty. So that if the capacity of knowing be the natural impression contended for, all the truths a man ever comes to know will, by this account, be every one of them innate: and this great point will amount to no more, but only to a very high improper way of speaking. But then, to what end such contest for certain innate maxims? If truths can be imprinted on the understanding without being perceived, I can see no difference there can be between any truths the mind is *capable* of knowing in respect of their original: they must all be innate, or all adventitious; in vain shall a man go about to distinguish them. He therefore that talks of innate notions in the understanding, cannot (if he intend thereby any distinct sort of truths) mean such truths to be in the understanding as it never perceived, and is yet wholly ignorant of. For if these words "to be in the understanding" have any propriety, they signify to be understood. If therefore these two propositions: "Whatsoever is, is," and, "It is impossible for the same thing to be, and not to be," are by nature imprinted, children cannot be ignorant of them; infants, and all that have souls, must necessarily have them in their understandings, know the truth of them, and assent to it. . . .

Book II
Chapter 1. Of Ideas in General and Their Original

1. *Idea is the object of thinking.*—Every man being conscious to himself that he thinks, and that which his mind is applied about whilst thinking being the ideas that are there, it is

past doubt that men have in their minds several ideas, such as are those expressed by the words, "whiteness, hardness, sweetness, thinking, motion, man, elephant, army, drunkenness," and others. It is in the first place then to be enquired, How he comes by them?

I know it is a received doctrine, that men have native ideas and original characters stamped upon their minds in their very first being. This opinion I have at large examined already; and, I suppose, what I have said in the foregoing Book will be much more easily admitted, when I have shown whence the understanding may get all the ideas it has, and by what ways and degrees they may come into the mind; for which I shall appeal to every one's own observation and experience.

2. *All ideas come from sensation or reflection.*—Let us then suppose the mind to be, as we say, white paper, void of all characters, without any ideas; how comes it to be furnished? Whence comes it by that vast store, which the busy and boundless fancy of man has painted on it with an almost endless variety? Whence has it all the materials of reason and knowledge? To this I answer, in one word, from EXPERIENCE; in that all our knowledge is founded, and from that it ultimately derives itself. Our observation, employed either about external sensible objects, or about the internal operations of our minds, perceived and reflected on by ourselves, is that which supplies our understandings with all the materials of thinking. These two are the foundations of knowledge, from whence all the ideas we have or can naturally have, do spring.

3. *The objects of sensation one source of ideas.*—First, our senses, conversant about particular sensible objects, do convey into the mind several distinct perceptions of things, according to those various ways wherein those objects do affect them; and thus we come by those *ideas* we have of yellow, white, heat, cold, soft, hard, bitter, sweet, and all those which we call sensible qualities; which when I say the senses convey into the mind, I mean, they from external objects convey into the mind what produces there those perceptions. This great source of most of the ideas we have, depending wholly upon our senses, and derived by them to the understanding, I call, SENSATION.

4. *The operations of our minds the other source of them.*—Secondly, the other fountain, from which experience furnishes the understanding with ideas, is the perception of the operations of our mind within us, as it is employed about the ideas it has got: which operations, when the soul comes to reflect on and consider, do furnish the understanding with another set of ideas which could not be had from things without: and such are perception, thinking, doubting, believing, reasoning, knowing, willing, and all the different actings of our own minds; which we being conscious of, and observing in ourselves, do from these receive into our understanding as distinct ideas, as we do from bodies affecting our senses. This source of ideas every man has wholly in himself: and though it be not sense, as having nothing to do with external objects, yet it is very like it, and might properly enough be called internal sense. But as I call the other Sensation, so I call this REFLECTION, the ideas it affords being such only as the mind gets by reflecting on its own operations within itself. By Reflection, then, in the following part of this discourse, I would be understood to mean that notice which the mind takes of its own operations, and the manner of them, by reason whereof there come to be ideas of these operations in the understanding. These two, I say, viz., external material things as the objects of Sensation, and the operations of our own minds within as the objects of Reflection are, to me, the only originals from whence

all our ideas take their beginnings. The term *operations* here, I use in a large sense, as comprehending not barely the actions of the mind about its ideas, but some sort of passions arising sometimes from them, such as is the satisfaction or uneasiness arising from any thought.

5. *All our ideas are of the one or the other of these.*—The understanding seems to me not to have the least glimmering of any ideas which it doth not receive from one of these two. *External objects* furnish the mind with the ideas of sensible qualities, which are all those different perceptions they produce in us; and *the mind* furnishes the understanding with ideas of its own operations. These, when we have taken a full survey of them, and their several modes, combinations, and relations, we shall find to contain all our whole stock of ideas; and that we have nothing in our minds which did not come in one of these two ways. Let any one examine his own thoughts, and thoroughly search into his understanding, and then let him tell me, whether all the original ideas he has there, are any other than of the objects of his senses, or of the operations of his mind considered as objects of his reflection; and how great a mass of knowledge soever he imagines to be lodged there, he will, upon taking a strict view, see that he has not any idea in his mind but what one of these two have imprinted, though perhaps with infinite variety compounded and enlarged by the understanding, as we shall see hereafter.

6. *Observable in children.*—He that attentively considers the state of a child at his first coming into the world, will have little reason to think him stored with plenty of ideas that are to be the matter of his future knowledge. It is by degrees he comes to be furnished with them: and though the ideas of obvious and familiar qualities themselves before the memory begins to keep a register of time and order, yet it is often so late before some unusual qualities come in the way, that there are few men that cannot recollect the beginning of their acquaintance with them: and if it were worth while, no doubt a child might be so ordered as to have but a very few even of the ordinary ideas till he were grown up to a man. But all that are born into the world being surrounded with bodies that perpetually and diversely affect them, variety of ideas, whether care be taken about it or no, are imprinted on the minds of children. Light and colours are busy and at hand everywhere when the eye is but open; sounds and some tangible qualities fail not to solicit their proper senses, and force an entrance to the mind; but yet I think it will be granted easily, that if a child were kept in a place where he never saw any other but black and white till he were a man, he would have no more ideas of scarlet or green, than he that from his childhood never tasted an oyster or a pineapple has of those particular relishes.

7. *Men are differently furnished with these according to the different objects they converse with.*—Men then come to be furnished with fewer or more simple ideas from without, according as the objects they converse with afford greater or less variety; and from the operations of their minds within, according as they more or less reflect on them. For, though he that contemplates the operations of his mind cannot but have plain and clear ideas of them; yet, unless he turn his thoughts that way, and considers them *attentively*, he will no more have clear and distinct ideas of all the operations of his mind, and all that may be observed therein, than he will have all the particular ideas of any landscape, or of the parts and motions of a clock, who will not turn his eyes to it, and with attention heed all the parts of it. The picture or clock may be so placed, that they may come in his way every day;

but yet he will have but a confused idea of all the parts they are made up of, till he applies himself with attention to consider them each in particular.

8. *Ideas of reflection later, because they need attention.*—And hence we see the reason why it is pretty late before most children get ideas of the operations of their own minds; and some have not any very clear or perfect ideas of the greatest part of them all their lives. Because, though they pass there continually, yet, like floating visions, they make not deep impressions enough to leave in the mind clear, distinct, lasting ideas, till the understanding turns inward upon itself, reflects on its own operations, and makes them the object of its own contemplation. Children, when they come first into it, are surrounded with a world of new things, which, by a constant solicitation of their senses, draw the mind constantly to them, forward to take notice of new, and apt to be delighted with the variety of changing objects. Thus the first years are usually employed and diverted in looking abroad. Men's business in them is to acquaint themselves with what is to be found without; and so, growing up in a constant attention to outward sensations, seldom make any considerable reflection on what passes within them till they come to be of riper years; and some scarce ever at all.

9. *The soul begins to have ideas when it begins to perceive.*—To ask, at what time a man has first any ideas, is to ask when he begins to perceive; having ideas, and perception, being the same thing. I know it is an opinion, that the soul always thinks; and that it has the actual perception of ideas in itself constantly, as long as it exists; and that actual thinking is as inseparable from the soul, as actual extension is from the body; which if true, to enquire after the beginning of a man's ideas is the same as to enquire after the beginning of his soul. For by this account, soul and its ideas, as body and its extension, will begin to exist both at the same time.

Adam Smith

from An Inquiry Into the Nature and Causes of the Wealth of Nations (1776)

Chapter VII

Of the Natural and Market Price of Commodities

There is in every society or neighbourhood an ordinary or average rate both of wages and profit in every different employment of labour and stock. This rate is naturally regulated, as I shall show hereafter, partly by the general circumstances of the society, their riches or poverty, their advancing, stationary, or declining condition; and partly by the particular nature of each employment.

There is likewise in every society or neighbourhood an ordinary or average rate of rent, which is regulated too, as I shall shew hereafter, partly by the general circumstances of the society or neighbourhood in which the land is situated, and partly by the natural or improved fertility of the land.

These ordinary or average rates may be called the natural rates of wages, profit, and rent, at the time and place in which they commonly prevail.

When the price of any commodity is neither more nor less than what is sufficient to pay the rent of the land, the wages of the labour, and the profits of the stock employed in raising, preparing, and bringing it to market, according to their natural rates, the commodity is then sold for what may be called its natural price.

The commodity is then sold precisely for what it is worth, or for what it really costs the person who brings it to market; for though in common language what is called the prime cost of any commodity does not comprehend the profit of the person who is to sell it again, yet if he sells it at a price which does not allow him the ordinary rate of profit in his neighborhood, he is evidently a loser by the trade; since by employing his stock in some other way he might have made that profit. His profit, besides, is his revenue, the proper fund of his subsistence. As, while he is preparing and bringing the goods to market, he advances to his workmen their wages, or their subsistence; so he advances to himself, in the same manner, his own subsistence, which is generally suitable to the profit which he may reasonably expect from the sale of his goods. Unless they yield him this profit, therefore, they do not repay him what they may very properly be said to have really cost him.

Though the price, therefore, which leaves him this profit, is not always the lowest at which a dealer may sometimes sell his goods, it is the lowest at which he is likely to sell them for any considerable time; at least where there is perfect liberty, or where he may change his trade as often as he pleases.

The actual price at which any commodity is commonly sold is called its market price. It may either be above, or below, or exactly the same with its natural price.

The market price of every particular commodity is regulated by the proportion between the quantity which is actually brought to market, and the demand of those who are willing to pay the natural price of the commodity, or the whole value of the rent, labour, and profit, which must be paid in order to bring it thither. Such people may be called the effectual demanders, and their demand the effectual demand; since it may be sufficient to effectuate the bringing of the commodity to market. It is different from the absolute demand. A very poor man may be said in some sense to have a demand for a coach and six; he might like to have it; but his demand is not an effectual demand, as the commodity can never be brought to market in order to satisfy it.

When the quantity of any commodity which is brought to market falls short of the effectual demand, all those who are willing to pay the whole value of the rent, wages, and profit, which must be paid in order to bring it thither, cannot be supplied with the quantity which they want. Rather than want it altogether, some of them will be willing to give more. A competition will immediately begin among them, and the market price will rise more or less above the natural price, according as either the greatness of the deficiency, or the wealth and wanton luxury of the competitors, happen to animate more or less the eagerness of the competition. Among competitors of equal wealth and luxury the same deficiency will generally occasion a more or less eager competition, according as the acquisition of the commodity happens to be of more or less importance to them. Hence the exorbitant price of the necessities of life during the blockade of a town or in a famine.

When the quantity brought to market exceeds the effectual demand, it cannot be all sold to those who are willing to pay the whole value of the rent, wages and profit, which must be paid in order to bring it thither. Some part must be sold to those who are willing to pay less, and the low price which they give for it must reduce the price of the whole. The market price will sink more or less below the natural price, according as the greatness of the excess increases more and less the competition of the sellers, or according as it happens to be more or less important to them to get immediately rid of the commodity. The same excess in the importation of perishable, will occasion a much greater competition than in that of durable commodities; in the importation of oranges, for example, than in that of old iron.

When the quantity brought to market is just sufficient to supply the effectual demand and no more, the market price naturally comes to be either exactly, or as nearly as can be judged of, the same with the natural price. The whole quantity upon hand can be disposed of for this price, and cannot be disposed of for more. The competition of the different dealers obliges them all to accept of this price, but does not oblige them to accept of less. . . .

Chapter II

Of Restraints Upon the Importation from
Foreign Countries of Such Goods as Can Be Produced at Home

. . . every individual who employs his capital in the support of domestic industry, necessarily endeavours so to direct that industry, that its produce may be of the greatest possible value.

The produce of industry is what it adds to the subject or materials upon which it is employed. In proportion as the value of this produce is great or small, so will likewise be the profits of the employer. But it is only for the sake of profit that any man employs a capital in the support of industry; and he will always, therefore, endeavour to employ it in the support of that industry of which the produce is likely to be of the greatest value, or to exchange for the greatest quantity either of money or of other goods.

But the annual revenue of every society is always precisely equal to the exchangeable value of the whole annual produce of its industry, or rather is precisely the same thing with that exchangeable value. As every individual, therefore, endeavours as much as he can both to employ his capital in the support of domestic industry, and so to direct that industry that its produce may be of the greatest value; every individual necessarily labours to render the annual revenue of the society as great as he can. He generally, indeed, neither intends to promote the public interest, nor knows how much he is promoting it. By preferring the support of domestic to that of foreign industry, he intends only his own security; and by directing that industry in such a manner as its produce may be of the greatest value, he intends only his own gain, and he is in this, as in many other cases, led by an invisible hand to promote an end which was no part of his intention. Nor is it always the worse for the society that it was no part of it. By pursuing his own interest he frequently promotes that of the society more effectually than when he really intends to promote it. I have never known much good done by those who affected to trade for the public good. It is an affectation, indeed, not very common among merchants, and very few words need be employed in dissuading them from it. . . .

It is thus that every system which endeavours, either, by extraordinary encouragements, to draw towards a particular species of industry a greater share of the capital of the society than what would naturally go to it; or, by extraordinary restraints, to force from a particular species of industry some share of the capital which would otherwise be employed in it; is in reality subversive of the great purpose which it means to promote. It retards, instead of accelerating, the progress of the society towards real wealth and greatness: and diminishes, instead of increasing, the real value of the annual produce of its land and labour.

All systems either of preference or of restraint, therefore, being thus completely taken away, the obvious and simple system of natural liberty establishes itself of its own accord. Every man, as long as he does not violate the laws of justice, is left perfectly free to pursue his own interest his own way, and to bring both his industry and capital into competition with those of any other man, or order of men. The sovereign is completely discharged from a duty, in the attempting to perform which he must always be exposed to innumerable delusions, and for the proper performance of which no human wisdom or knowledge could ever be sufficient; the duty of superintending the industry of private people, and of directing it towards the employments most suitable to the interest of the society. According to the system of natural liberty, the sovereign has only three duties to attend to; three duties of great importance, indeed, but plain and intelligible to common understandings; first, the duty of protecting the society from the violence and invasion of other independent societies; secondly, the duty of protecting, as far as possible, every member of the society from the injustice or oppression of every other member of it, or the duty of establishing an exact administration of justice; and, thirdly, the duty of erecting and maintaining certain public works and certain public institutions, which it can never be for the interest of any individual, or small number of individuals, to erect and maintain; because the profit could never repay the expence to any individual or small number of individuals, though it may frequently do much more than repay it to a great society. . . .

Emmanuel Sieyès

from What Is the Third Estate? (1789)

The plan of this pamphlet is very simple. We have three questions to ask:

1st.   What is the third estate? Everything.

2nd.   What has it been heretofore in the political order? Nothing.

3rd.   What does it demand? To become something therein.

   We shall see if the answers are correct. Then we shall examine the measures that have been tried and those which must be taken in order that the third estate may in fact become *something*. Thus we shall state:

4th.   What the ministers have *attempted,* and what the privileged classes themselves *propose* in its favor.

5th.   What *ought* to have been done.

6th.   Finally, what *remains* to be done in order that the third estate may take its rightful place.

Chapter I The Third Estate Is a Complete Nation

What are the essentials of national existence and prosperity? *Private* enterprise and *public* functions.

Private enterprise may be divided into four classes: 1st. Since earth and water furnish the raw material for man's needs, the first class will comprise all families engaged in agricultural pursuits. 2nd. Between the original sale of materials and their consumption or use, further workmanship, more or less manifold, adds to these materials a second value, more or less compounded. Human industry thus succeeds in perfecting the benefits of nature and in increasing the gross produce twofold, tenfold, one hundredfold in value. Such is the work of the second class. 3rd. Between production and consumption, as well as among the different degrees of production, a group of intermediate agents, useful to producers as well as to consumers, comes into being; these are the dealers and merchants. . . . 4th. In addition to these three classes of industrious and useful citizens concerned with goods for consumption and use, a society needs many private undertakings and endeavors which are *directly* useful or agreeable to the *individual.* This fourth class includes from the most distinguished scientific and liberal professions to the least esteemed domestic services. Such are the labors which sustain society. Who performs them? The third estate.

Public functions likewise under present circumstances may be classified under four well known headings: the Sword, the Robe, the Church, and the Administration. It is unnecessary to discuss them in detail in order to demonstrate that the third estate everywhere constitutes nineteen-twentieths of them, except that it is burdened with all that is really arduous, with all the tasks that the privileged order refuses to perform. Only the lucrative and honorary positions are held by members of the privileged order. . . . nevertheless they have dared lay the order of the third estate under an interdict. They have said to it: "Whatever be your services, whatever your talents, you shall go thus far and no farther. It is not fitting that you be honored."

It suffices here to have revealed that the alleged utility of a privileged order to public service is only a chimera; that without it, all that is arduous in such service is performed by the third estate; that without it, the higher positions would be infinitely better filled; that they naturally ought to be the lot of and reward for talents and recognized services; and that if the privileged classes have succeeded in usurping all the lucrative and honorary positions, it is both an odious injustice to the majority of citizens and a treason to the commonwealth.

Who, then, would dare to say that the third estate has not within itself all that is necessary to constitute a complete nation? It is the strong and robust man whose one arm remains enchained. If the privileged order were abolished, the nation would be not something less but something more. Thus, what is the third estate? Everything; but an everything shackled and oppressed. What would it be without the privileged order? Everything; but an everything free and flourishing. Nothing can progress without it; everything would proceed infinitely better without the others. It is not sufficient to have demonstrated that the privileged classes, far from being useful to the nation, can only enfeeble and injure it; it is necessary, moreover, to prove that the nobility does not belong to the social organization at all; that, indeed, it may be a *burden* upon the nation, but that it would not know how to constitute a part thereof. . . .

What is a nation? a body of associates living under a *common* law and represented by the same *legislature.*

Is it not exceedingly clear that the noble order has privileges, exemptions, even rights separate from the rights of the majority of citizens? Thus it deviates from the common order, from the common law. Thus its civil rights already render it a people apart in a great nation. It is indeed *imperium in imperio.*

Also, it enjoys its political rights separately. It has its own representatives, who are by no means charged with representing the people. Its deputation sits apart; and when it is assembled in the same room with the deputies of ordinary citizens, it is equally true that its representation is essentially distinct and separate; it is foreign to the nation in principle, since its mandate does not emanate from the people, and in aim, since its purpose is to defend not the general but a special interest.

The third estate, then, comprises everything appertaining to the nation; and whatever is not the third estate may not be regarded as being of the nation. What is the third estate? Everything!

Chapter III
What Does the Third Estate Demand? To Become Something

... The true petitions of this order may be appreciated only through the authentic claims directed to the government by the large municipalities of the kingdom. What is indicated therein? That the people wishes to be *something*, and, in truth, the very least that is possible. It wishes to have real representatives in the Estates General, that is to say, deputies *drawn from its order*, who are competent to be interpreters of its will and defenders of its interests. But what will it avail it to be present at the Estates General if the predominating interest there is contrary to its own! Its presence would only consecrate the oppression of which it would be the eternal victim. Thus, it is indeed certain that it cannot come to vote at the Estates General unless it is to have in that body *an influence at least equal to that of the privileged classes*; and it demands a number of representatives equal to that of the first two orders together. Finally, this equality of representation would become completely illusory if every chamber voted separately. The third estate demands, then, that votes be taken *by head and not by order*. This is the essence of those claims so alarming to the privileged classes, because they believed that thereby the reform of abuses would become inevitable. The real intention of the third estate is to have an influence in the Estates General equal to that of the privileged classes. I repeat, can it ask less? And is it not clear that if its influence therein is less than equality, it cannot be expected to emerge from its political nullity and become *something*?

But what is indeed unfortunate is that the three articles constituting the demand of the third estate are insufficient to give it this equality of influence which it cannot, in reality, do without. In vain will it obtain an equal number of representatives drawn from its order; the influence of the privileged classes will establish itself and dominate even in the sanctuary of the third estate. . . .

Chapter VI
What Remains to be Done. Development of Some Principles

... The third estate must perceive in the trend of opinions and circumstances that it can hope for nothing except from its own enlightenment and courage. Reason and justice are in its favor; . . . there is no longer time to work for the conciliation of parties. What accord can be anticipated between the energy of the oppressed and the rage of the oppressors?

They have dared pronounce the word secession. They have menaced the King and the people. Well! Good God! How fortunate for the nation if this so desirable secession might be made permanently! How easy it would be to dispense with the privileged classes! How difficult to induce them to be citizens! . . .

In vain would they close their eyes to the revolution which time and force of circumstances have effected; it is none the less real. Formerly the third estate was serf, the noble order everything. Today the third estate is everything, the nobility but a word. . . .

In such a state of affairs, what must the third estate do if it wishes to gain possession of its political rights in a manner beneficial to the nation? There are two ways of attaining this objective. In following the first, the third estate must assemble apart: it will not meet with the nobility and the clergy at all; it will not remain with them, either by *order* or by *head*. I pray that they will keep in mind the enormous difference between the assembly of the third estate and that of the other two orders. The first represents 25,000,000 men, and deliberates concerning the interests of the nation. The two others, were they to unite, have the powers of only about 200,000 individuals, and think only of their privileges. The third estate alone, they say, cannot constitute the *Estates General*. Well! So much the better! It will form a *National Assembly*. . . .

Edmund Burke

from Reflections on the French Revolution (1790)

. . . You will observe, that from Magna Charta to the Declaration of Right, it has been the uniform policy of our constitution to claim and assert our liberties, as an *entailed inheritance* derived to us from our forefathers, and to be transmitted to our posterity; as an estate specially belonging to the people of this kingdom, without any reference whatever to any other more general or prior right. By this means our constitution preserves a unity in so great a diversity of its parts. We have an inheritable crown; an inheritable peerage; and a House of Commons and a people inheriting privileges, franchises, and liberties, from a long line of ancestors.

This policy appears to me to be the result of profound reflection; or rather the happy effect of following nature, which is wisdom without reflection, and above it. A spirit of innovation is generally the result of a selfish temper, and confined views. People will not look forward to posterity, who never look backward to their ancestors. Besides, the people of England well know, that the idea of inheritance furnishes a sure principle of conservation, and a sure principle of transmission; without at all excluding a principle of improvement. It leaves acquisition free; but it secures what it acquires. Whatever advantages are obtained by a state proceeding on these maxims, are locked fast as in a sort of family settlement; grasped as in a kind of mortmain for ever. By a constitutional policy, working after the pattern of nature, we receive, we hold, we transmit our government and our privileges, in the same manner in which we enjoy and transmit our property and our lives. The institutions of policy, the goods of fortune, the gifts of providence, are handed down to us, and from us, in the same course and order. Our political system is placed in a just correspondence and symmetry with the order of the world, and with the mode of existence decreed to a permanent body composed of transitory parts; wherein, by the disposition of a stupendous wisdom, moulding together the great mysterious incorporation of the human race, the whole, at one time, is never old, or middle-aged, or young, but, in a condition of unchangeable constancy, moves on through the varied tenor of perpetual decay, fall, renovation, and progression. Thus, by preserving the method of nature in the conduct of the state, in what we improve, we are never wholly new; in what we retain, we are never wholly obsolete. By adhering in this manner and on those principles to our forefathers, we are guided not by the superstition of antiquarians, but by the spirit of philosophic analogy.

In this choice of inheritance we have given to our frame of polity the image of a relation in blood; binding up the constitution of our country with our dearest domestic ties; adopting our fundamental laws into the bosom of our family affections; keeping inseparable, and cherishing with the warmth of all their combined and mutually reflected charities, our state, our hearths, our sepulchres, and our altars. . . .

You might, if you pleased, have profited of our example, and have given to your recovered freedom a correspondent dignity. Your privileges, though discontinued, were not lost to memory. Your constitution, it is true, whilst you were out of possession, suffered waste and dilapidation; but you possessed in some parts the walls, and, in all, the foundations, of a noble and venerable castle. You might have repaired those walls; you might have built on those old foundations. Your constitution was suspended before it was perfected; but you had the elements of a constitution very nearly as good as could be wished. In your old states you possessed that variety of parts corresponding with the various descriptions of which your community was happily composed; you had all that combination, and all that opposition of interests, you had that action and counteraction, which, in the natural and in the political world, from the reciprocal struggle of discordant power, draws out the harmony of the universe. These opposed and conflicting interests, which you considered as so great a blemish in your old and in our present constitution, interpose a salutary check to all precipitate resolutions. They render deliberation a matter not of choice, but of necessity; they make all change a subject of *compromise*, which naturally begets moderation; they produce *temperaments* preventing the sore evil of harsh, crude, unqualified reformations; and rendering all the headlong exertions of arbitrary power, in the few or in the many for ever impracticable. Through that diversity of members and interests, general liberty had as many securities as there were separate views in the several orders; whilst by pressing down the whole by the weight of a real monarchy, the separate parts would have been prevented from warping, and starting from their allotted places.

You had all these advantages in your ancient states; but you chose to act as if you had never been moulded into civil society, and had everything to begin anew. You began ill, because you began by despising everything that belonged to you. You set up your trade without a capital. If the last generations of your country appeared without much lustre in your eyes, you might have passed them by, and derived your claims from a more early race of ancestors. Under a pious predilection for those ancestors, your imaginations would have realized in them a standard of virtue and wisdom, beyond the vulgar practice of the hour: and you would have risen with the example to whose imitation you aspired. Respecting your forefathers, you would have been taught to respect yourselves. You would not have chosen to consider the French as a people of yesterday, as a nation of low-born servile wretches until the emancipating year of 1789. . . .

Compute your gains: see what is got by those extravagant and presumptuous speculations which have taught your leaders to despise all their predecessors, and all their contemporaries, and even to despise themselves, until the moment in which they became truly despicable. By following those false lights, France has bought undisguised calamities at a higher price than any nation has purchased the most unequivocal blessings! France has bought poverty by crime! France has not sacrificed her virtue to her interest, but she has abandoned her interest, that she might prostitute her virtue. All other nations have begun the fabric of a new government, or the reformation of an old, by establishing originally, or by enforcing with greater exactness, some rites or other of religion. All other people have laid the foundations of civil freedom in severer manners, and a system of a more austere and masculine morality. France, when she let loose the reins of regal authority, doubled the license of a ferocious dissoluteness in manners, and of an insolent irreligion in opinions and practices; and has extended through all ranks of life, as if she were communicating some privilege, or laying open some secluded benefit, all the unhappy corruptions that usually were the disease of wealth and power. This is one of the new principles of equality in France. . . .

It is said, that twenty-four millions ought to prevail over two hundred thousand. True; if the constitution of a kingdom be a problem of arithmetic. This sort of discourse does well enough with the lamp-post for its second: to men who *may* reason calmly, it is ridiculous. The will of the many, and their interest, must very often differ; and great will be the difference when they make an evil choice. A government of five hundred country attornies and obscure curates is not good for twenty-four millions of men, though it were chosen by eight and forty million; nor is it the better for being guided by a dozen of persons of quality, who have betrayed their trust in order to obtain that power. At present, you seem in everything to have strayed out of the high road of nature. The property of France does not govern it. Of course property is destroyed, and rational liberty has no existence. All you have got for the present is a paper circulation, and a stock-jobbing constitution: and, as to the future, do you seriously think that the territory of France, upon the republican system of eighty-three independent municipalities, (to say nothing of the parts that compose them,) can ever be governed as one body, or can ever be set in motion by the impulse of one mind? . . .

It is now sixteen or seventeen years since I saw the queen of France, then the dauphiness, at Versailles; and surely never lighted on this orb, which she hardly seemed to touch, a more delightful vision. I saw her just above the horizon, decorating and cheering the elevated sphere she just began to move in,—glittering like the morning-star, full of life, and splendour, and joy. Oh! what a revolution! and what a heart must I have to contemplate without emotion that elevation and that fall! Little did I dream when she added titles of veneration to those of enthusiastic, distant, respectful love, that she should ever be obliged to carry the sharp antidote against disgrace concealed in that bosom; little did I dream that I should have lived to see such disasters fallen upon her in a nation of gallant men, in a nation of men of honour, and of cavaliers. I thought ten thousand swords must have leaped from their scabbards to avenge even a look that threatened her with insult. But the age of chivalry is gone. That of sophisters, economists, and calculators, has succeeded; and the glory of Europe is extinguished for ever. Never, never more shall we behold that generous loyalty to rank and sex, that proud submission, that dignified obedience, that subordination of the heart, which kept alive, even in servitude itself, the spirit of an exalted freedom. The unbought grace of life, the cheap defence of nations, the nurse of manly sentiment and heroic enterprise, is gone! It is gone, that sensibility of principle, that charity of honor, which felt a stain like a wound, which inspired courage whilst it mitigated ferocity, which ennobled whatever it touched, and under which vice itself lost half its evil, by losing all its grossness.

This mixed system of opinion and sentiment had its origin in the ancient chivalry; and the principle, though varied in its appearance by the varying state of human affairs, subsisted and influenced through a long succession of generations, even to the time we live in.

If it should ever be totally extinguished, the loss I fear will be great. It is this which has given its character to modern Europe. It is this which has distinguished it under all its forms of government, and distinguished it to its advantage, from the states of Asia, and possibly from those states which flourished in the most brilliant periods of the antique world. It was this, which, without confounding ranks, had produced a noble equality, and handed it down through all the gradations of social life. It was this opinion which mitigated kings into companions, and raised private men to be fellows with kings. Without force or opposition, it subdued the fierceness of pride and power; it obliged sovereigns to submit to the soft collar of social esteem, compelled stern authority to submit to elegance, and gave a dominating vanquisher of laws to be subdued by manners.

But now all is to be changed. All the pleasing illusions, which made power gentle and obedience liberal, which harmonized the different shades of life, and which, by a bland assimilation, incorporated into politics the sentiments which beautify and soften private society, are to be dissolved by this new conquering empire of light and reason. All the decent drapery of life is to be rudely torn off. All the superadded ideas, furnished from the wardrobe of a moral imagination, which the heart owns, and the understanding ratifies, as necessary to cover the defects of our naked, shivering nature, and to raise it to dignity in our own estimation, are to be exploded as a ridiculous, absurd, and antiquated fashion.

On this scheme of things, a king is but a man, a queen is but a woman; a woman is but an animal, and an animal not of the highest order. All homage paid to the sex in general as such, and without distinct views, is to be regarded as romance and folly. Regicide, and parricide, and sacrilege, are but fictions of superstition, corrupting jurisprudence by destroying its simplicity. The murder of a king, or a queen, or a bishop, or a father, are only common homicide; and if the people are by any chance, or in any way, gainers by it, a sort of homicide much the most pardonable, and into which we ought not to make too severe a scrutiny.

On the scheme of this barbarous philosophy, which is the offspring of cold hearts and muddy understandings, and which is as void of solid wisdom as it is destitute of all taste and elegance, laws are to be supported only by their own terrors, and by the concern which each individual may find in them from his own private speculations, or can spare to them from his own private interests. . . .

MARY WOLLSTONECRAFT

from Vindication of the Rights of Woman (1792)

To account for, and excuse the tyranny of man, many ingenious arguments have been brought forward to prove, that the two sexes, in the acquirement of virtue, ought to aim at attaining a very different character; or, to speak explicitly, women are not allowed to have sufficient strength of mind to acquire what really deserves the name of virtue. Yet it should seem, allowing them to have souls, that there is but one way appointed by Providence to lead *mankind* to either virtue or happiness.

If then women are not a swarm of ephemeron triflers, why should they be kept in ignorance under the specious name of innocence? Men complain, and with reason, of the follies and caprices of our sex, when they do not keenly satirise our headstrong passions and grovelling vices. Behold, I should answer, the natural effect of ignorance! The mind will ever be unstable that has only prejudices to rest on, and the current will run with destructive fury when there are no barriers to break its force. Women are told from their infancy, and taught by the example of their mothers, that a little knowledge of human weakness, justly termed cunning, softness of temper, *outward* obedience, and a scrupulous attention to a puerile kind of propriety, will obtain for them the protection of man; and should they be beautiful, everything else is needless, for at least twenty years of their lives. . . . .

How grossly do they insult us who thus advise us only to render ourselves gentle, domestic brutes! For instance, the winning softness so warmly and frequently recommended, that governs by obeying. What childish expressions, and how insignificant is the being—can it be an immortal one?—who will condescend to govern by such sinister methods? "Certainly," says Lord Bacon, "man is of kin to the beasts by his body; and if he be not of kin to God by his spirit, he is a base and ignoble creature!" Men, indeed, appear to me to act in a very unphilosophical manner, when they try to secure the good conduct of women by attempting to keep them always in a state of childhood. Rousseau was more consistent when he wished to stop the progress of reason in both sexes, for if men eat of the tree of knowledge, women will come in for a taste; but, from the imperfect cultivation which their understandings now receive, they only attain a knowledge of evil. . . .

. . . the most perfect education, in my opinion, is such an exercise of the understanding as is best calculated to strengthen the body and form the heart. Or, in other words, to enable the individual to attain such habits of virtue as will render it independent. In fact, it is a farce to call any being virtuous whose virtues do not result from the exercise of its own

95

reason. This was Rousseau's opinion respecting men; I extend it to women, and confidently assert that they have been drawn out of their sphere by false refinement, and not by an endeavour to acquire masculine qualities. Still the regal homage which they receive is so intoxicating, that until the manners of the times are changed, and formed on more reasonable principles, it may be impossible to convince them that the illegitimate power which they obtain by degrading themselves is a curse, and that they must return to nature and equality if they wish to secure the placid satisfaction that unsophisticated affections impart. But for this epoch we must wait—wait perhaps till kings and nobles, enlightened by reason, and, preferring the real dignity of man to childish state, throw off their gaudy hereditary trappings; and if then women do not resign the arbitrary power of beauty—they will prove that they have *less* mind than man.

I may be accused of arrogance; still I must declare what I firmly believe, that all the writers who have written on the subject of female education and manners, from Rousseau to Dr. Gregory, have contributed to render women more artificial, weak characters, than they would otherwise have been; and consequently, more useless members of society. I might have expressed this conviction in a lower key, but I am afraid it would have been the whine of affectation, and not the faithful expression of my feelings, of the clear result which experience and reflection have led me to draw. When I come to that division of the subject, I shall advert to the passages that I more particularly disapprove of, in the works of the authors I have just alluded to; but it is first necessary to observe that my objection extends to the whole purport of those books, which tend, in my opinion, to degrade one-half of the human species, and render women pleasing at the expense of every solid virtue. . . .

Many are the causes that, in the present corrupt state of society, contribute to enslave women by cramping their understandings and sharpening their senses. One, perhaps, that silently does more mischief than all the rest, is their disregard of order.

To do everything in an orderly manner is a most important precept, which women, who, generally speaking, receive only a disorderly kind of education, seldom attend to with that degree of exactness that men, who from their infancy are broken into method, observe. This negligent kind of guesswork—for what other epithet can be used to point out the random exertions of a sort of instinctive common sense never brought to the test of reason?—prevents their generalizing matters of fact; so they do today what they did yesterday, merely because they did it yesterday.

This contempt of the understanding in early life has more baneful consequences than is commonly supposed; for the little knowledge which women of strong minds attain is, from various circumstances, of a more desultory kind than the knowledge of men, and it is acquired more by sheer observations on real life than from comparing what has been individually observed with the results of experience generalized by speculation. Led by their dependent situation and domestic employments more into society, what they learn is rather by snatches; and as learning is with them in general only a secondary thing, they do not pursue any one branch with that persevering ardour necessary to give vigour to the faculties and clearness to the judgment. In the present state of society a little learning is required to support the character of a gentleman, and boys are obliged to submit to a few years of discipline. But in the education of women, the cultivation of the understanding is always subordinate to the acquirement of some corporeal accomplishment. Even when enervated by confinement and false notions of modesty, the body is prevented from attaining that grace and beauty which relaxed half-formed limbs never exhibit. Besides, in youth, their faculties are not brought forward by emulation; and having no serious scientific study, if they have natural sagacity, it is turned too soon on life and manners. They dwell on effects and modifications, without tracing them back to causes; and complicated rules to adjust behaviour are a weak substitute for simple principles.

As a proof that education gives this appearance of weakness to females, we may instance the example of military men, who are, like them, sent into the world before their minds have been stored with knowledge, or fortified by principles. The consequences are similar; soldiers acquire a little superficial knowledge, snatched from the muddy current of conversation, and from continually mixing with society, they gain what is termed a knowledge of the world; and this acquaintance with manners and customs has frequently been confounded with a knowledge of the human heart. But can the crude fruit of casual observation, never brought to the test of judgment, formed by comparing speculation and experience, deserve such a distinction? Soldiers, as well as women, practise the minor virtues with punctilious politeness. Where is then the sexual difference, when the education has been the same? All the difference that I can discern arises from the superior advantage of liberty which enables the former to see more of life.

It is wandering from my present subject, perhaps, to make a political remark; but as it was produced naturally by the train of my reflections, I shall not pass it silently over.

Standing armies can never consist of resolute robust men; they may be well-disciplined machines, but they will seldom contain men under the influence of strong passions, or with very vigorous faculties; and as for any depth of understanding, I will venture to affirm that it is as rarely to be found in the army as amongst women. And the cause, I maintain, is the same. It may be further observed that officers are also particularly attentive to their persons, fond of dancing, crowded rooms, adventures, and ridicule. Like the *fair* sex, the business of their lives is gallantry; they were taught to please, and they only live to please. Yet they do not lose their rank in the distinction of sexes, for they are still reckoned superior to women, though in what their superiority consists, beyond what I have just mentioned, it is difficult to discover.

The great misfortune is this, that they both acquire manners before morals, and a knowledge of life before they have from reflection any acquaintance with the grand ideal outline of human nature. The consequence is natural. Satisfied with common nature, they become a prey to prejudices, and taking all their opinions on credit, they blindly submit to authority. So that if they have any sense, it is a kind of instinctive glance that catches proportions, and decides with respect to manners, but fails when arguments are to be pursued below the surface, or opinions analysed.

May not the same remark be applied to women? Nay, the argument may be carried still further, for they are both thrown out of a useful station by the unnatural distinctions established in civilized life. Riches and hereditary honours have made cyphers of women to give consequence to the numerical figure; and idleness has produced a mixture of gallantry and despotism into society, which leads the very men who are the slaves of their mistresses to tyrannize over their sisters, wives, and daughters. This is only keeping them in rank and file, it is true. Strengthen the female mind by enlarging it, and there will be an end to blind obedience; but as blind obedience is ever sought for by power, tyrants and sensualists are in the right when they endeavour to keep woman in the dark, because the former only want slaves, and the latter a plaything. The sensualist, indeed, has been the most dangerous of tyrants, and women have been duped by their lovers, as princes by their ministers, whilst dreaming that they reigned over them. . . .

Youth is the season for love in both sexes; but in those days of thoughtless enjoyment provision should be made for the more important years of life, when reflection takes place of sensation. But Rousseau, and most of the male writers who have followed his steps, have warmly indicated that the whole tendency of female education ought to be directed to one point—to render them pleasing.

Let me reason with the supporters of this opinion who have any knowledge of human nature. Do they imagine that marriage can eradicate the habitude of life? The woman who has only been taught to please will soon find that her charms are oblique sunbeams, and that they cannot have much effect on her husband's heart when they are seen every day, when the summer is passed and gone. Will she then have sufficient native energy to look into herself for comfort, and cultivate her dormant faculties? or is it not more rational to expect that she will try to please other men, and, in the emotions raised by the expectation of new conquests, endeavour to forget the mortification her love or pride has received? When the husband ceases to be a lover, and the time will inevitably come, her desire of pleasing will then grow languid, or become a spring of bitterness; and love, perhaps, the most evanescent of all passions, gives place to jealousy or vanity. . . .

. . . How then can the great art of pleasing be such a necessary study? it is only useful to a mistress. The chaste wife and serious mother should only consider her power to please as the polish of her virtues, and the affection of her husband as one of the comforts that render her task less difficult, and her life happier. But, whether she be loved or neglected, her first wish should be to make herself respectable, and not to rely for all her happiness on a being subject to like infirmities with herself.

The worthy Dr. Gregory fell into a similar error. I respect his heart, but entirely disapprove of his celebrated *Legacy to his Daughters*.

He advises them to cultivate a fondness for dress, because a fondness for dress, he asserts, is natural to them. I am unable to comprehend what either he or Rousseau mean when they frequently use this indefinite term. If they told us that in a pre-existent state the soul was fond of dress, and brought this inclination with it into a new body, I should listen to them with a half-smile, as I often do when I hear a rant about innate elegance. But if he only meant to say that the exercise of the faculties will produce this fondness, I deny it. It is not natural; but arises, like false ambition in men, from a love of power.

Dr. Gregory goes much further; he actually recommends dissimulation, and advises an innocent girl to give the lie to her feelings, and not dance with spirit, when gaiety of heart would make her feet eloquent without making her gestures immodest. In the name of truth and common sense, why should not one woman acknowledge that she can take more exercise than another? or, in other words, that she has a sound constitution; and why, to damp innocent vivacity, is she darkly to be told that men will draw conclusions which she little thinks of? Let the libertine draw what inference he pleases; but, I hope, that no sensible mother will restrain the natural frankness of youth by instilling such indecent cautions. . . .

Women ought to endeavour to purify their hearts; but can they do so when their uncultivated understandings make them entirely dependent on their senses for employment and amusement, when no noble pursuits set them above the little vanities of the day, or enable them to curb the wild emotions that agitate a reed, over which every passing breeze has power? To gain the affections of a virtuous man, is affectation necessary? Nature has given woman a weaker frame than man; but, to ensure her husband's affections, must a wife, who, by the exercise of her mind and body whilst she was discharging the duties of a daughter, wife, and mother, has allowed her constitution to retain its natural strength, and her nerves a healthy tone,—is she, I say, to condescend to use art, and feign a sickly delicacy, in order to secure her husband's affection? Weakness may excite tenderness, and gratify the arrogant pride of man; but the lordly caresses of a protector will not gratify a noble mind that pants for and deserves to be respected. Fondness is a poor substitute for friendship!

In a seraglio, I grant, that all these arts are necessary; the epicure must have his palate tickled, or he will sink into apathy; but have women so little ambition as to be satisfied with such a condition? Can they supinely dream life away in the lap of pleasure, or the languor of weariness, rather than assert their claim to pursue reasonable pleasures, and render themselves conspicuous by practising the virtues which dignify mankind? . . .

Besides, the woman who strengthens her body and exercises her mind will, by managing her family and practising various virtues, become the friend, and not the humble dependent of her husband; and if she, by possessing such substantial qualities, merit his regard, she will not find it necessary to conceal her affection, nor to pretend to an unnatural coldness of constitution to excite her husband's passions. . . .

Nature, or, to speak with strict propriety, God, has made all things right; but man has sought him out many inventions to mar the work. . . .

If, I say, for I would not impress by declamation when Reason offers her sober light, if they be really capable of acting like rational creatures, let them not be treated like slaves; or, like the brutes who are dependent on the reason of man, when they associate with him; but cultivate their minds, give them the salutary sublime curb of principle, and let them attain conscious dignity by feeling themselves only dependent on God. Teach them, in common with man, to submit to necessity, instead of giving, to render them more pleasing, a sex to morals.

Further, should experience prove that they cannot attain the same degree of strength of mind, perseverance, and fortitude, let their virtues be the same in kind, though they may vainly struggle for the same degree; and the superiority of man will be equally clear, if not clearer; and truth, as it is a simple principle, which admits of no modification, would be common to both. Nay the order of society, as it is at present regulated, would not be inverted, for woman would then only have the rank that reason assigned her, and arts could not be practised to bring the balance even, much less to turn it.

These may be termed Utopian dreams. Thanks to that Being who impressed them on my soul, and gave me sufficient strength of mind to dare to exert my own reason, till, becoming dependent only on Him for the support of my virtue, I view, with indignation, the mistaken notions that enslave my sex.

I love man as my fellow; but his sceptre, real or usurped, extends not to me, unless the reason of an individual demands my homage; and even then the submission is to reason, and not to man. In fact, the conduct of an accountable being must be regulated by the operations of its own reason; or on what foundation rests the throne of God?

It appears to me necessary to dwell on these obvious truths, because females have been insulated, as it were; and while they have been stripped of the virtues that should clothe humanity, they have been decked with artificial graces that enable them to exercise a short-lived tyranny. Love, in their bosoms, taking place of every nobler passion, their sole ambition is to be fair, to raise emotion instead of inspiring respect; and this ignoble desire, like the servility in absolute monarchies, destroys all strength of character. Liberty is the mother of virtue, and if women be, by their very constitution, slaves, and not allowed to breathe the sharp invigorating air of freedom, they must ever languish like exotics, and be reckoned beautiful flaws in nature. Let it also be remembered, that they are the only flaw.

As to the argument respecting the subjection in which the sex has ever been held, it retorts on man. The many have always been enthralled by the few; and monsters, who scarcely have shown any discernment of human excellence, have tyrannized over thousands of their fellow-creatures. Why have men of superior endowments submitted to such degradation? For, is it not universally acknowledged that kings, viewed collectively, have ever been inferior, in abilities and virtue, to the same number of men taken from the common mass of mankind—yet have they not, and are they not still treated with a degree of reverence that is an insult to reason? China is not the only country where a living man has been made a God. . . .

I shall not pursue this argument any further than to establish an obvious inference, that as sound politics diffuse liberty, mankind, including woman, will become more wise and virtuous.

. . . A man when he enters any profession has his eye steadily fixed on some future advantage (and the mind gains great strength by having all its efforts directed to one point), and, full of his business, pleasure is considered as mere relaxation; whilst women seek for pleasure as the main purpose of existence. In fact, from the education, which they receive from society, the love of pleasure may be said to govern them all; but does this prove that there is a sex in souls? It would be just as rational to declare that the courtiers in France, when a destructive system of despotism had formed their character, were not men, because liberty, virtue, and humanity, were sacrificed to pleasure and vanity. Fatal passions, which have ever domineered over the *whole* race! . . .

In short, women, in general, as well as the rich of both sexes, have acquired all the follies and vices of civilization, and missed the useful fruit. It is not necessary for me always to premise, that I speak of the condition of the whole sex, leaving exceptions out of the question. Their senses are inflamed, and their understandings neglected, consequently they become the prey of their senses, delicately termed sensibility, and are blown about by every momentary gust of feeling. Civilized women are, therefore, so weakened by false refinement, that, respecting morals, their condition is much below what it would be were they left in a state nearer to nature. Ever restless and anxious, their over-exercised sensibility not only renders them uncomfortable themselves, but troublesome, to use a soft phrase, to others. All their thoughts turn on things calculated to excite emotion and feeling, when they should reason, their conduct is unstable, and their opinions are wavering—not the wavering produced by deliberation or progressive views, but by contradictory emotions. By fits and starts, they are warm in many pursuits; yet this warmth, never concentrated into perseverance, soon exhausts itself; exhaled by its own heat, or meeting with some other fleeting passion, to which reason has never given any specific gravity, neutrality ensues. Miserable, indeed, must be that being whose cultivation of mind has only tended to inflame its passions! A distinction should be made between inflaming and strengthening them. The passions thus pampered, whilst the judgment is left unformed, what can be expected to ensue? Undoubtedly, a mixture of madness and folly!

This observation should not be confined to the *fair* sex; however, at present, I only mean to apply it to them.

Novels, music, poetry, and gallantry, all tend to make women the creatures of sensation, and their character is thus formed in the mould of folly during the time they are acquiring accomplishments, the only improvement they are excited, by their station in society, to acquire. This overstretched sensibility naturally relaxes the other powers of the mind, and prevents intellect from attaining that sovereignty which it ought to attain to render a rational creature useful to others, and content with its own station; for the exercise of the understanding, as life advances, is the only method pointed out by nature to calm the passions.

Satiety has a very different effect, and I have often been forcibly struck by an emphatical description of damnation; when the spirit is represented as continually hovering with abortive eagerness round the defiled body, unable to enjoy anything without the organs of sense. Yet, to their senses, are women made slaves, because it is by their sensibility that they obtain present power.

And will moralists pretend to assert that this is the condition in which one-half of the human race should be encouraged to remain with listless inactivity and stupid acquiescence? Kind instructors! what were we created for? To remain, it may be said, innocent; they mean in a state of childhood. We might as well never have been born, unless it were necessary that we should be created to enable man to acquire the noble privilege of reason, the power of discerning good from evil, whilst we lie down in the dust from whence we were taken, never to rise again.

It would be an endless task to trace the variety of meannesses, cares, and sorrows, into which women are plunged by the prevailing opinion, that they were created rather to feel than reason, and that all the power they obtain must be obtained by their charms and weakness:

Fine by defect, and amiably weak!

And, made by this amiable weakness entirely dependent, excepting what they gain by illicit sway, on man, not only for protection, but advice, is it surprising that, neglecting the duties that reason alone points out, and shrinking from trials calculated to strengthen their minds, they only exert themselves to give their defects a graceful covering, which may serve to heighten their charms in the eye of the voluptuary, though it sink them below the scale of moral excellence.

Fragile in every sense of the word, they are obliged to look up to man for every comfort. In the most trifling danger they cling to their support, with parasitical tenacity, piteously demanding succour; and their *natural* protector extends his arm, or lifts up his voice, to guard the lovely trembler—from what? Perhaps the frown of an old cow, or the jump of a mouse; a rat would be a serious danger. In the name of reason, and even common sense, what can save such beings from contempt; even though they be soft and fair.

These fears, when not affected, may produce some pretty attitudes; but they show a degree of imbecility which degrades a rational creature in a way women are not aware of—for love and esteem are very distinct things.

I am fully persuaded that we should hear of none of these infantine airs, if girls were allowed to take sufficient exercise, and not confined in close rooms till their muscles are relaxed, and their powers of digestion destroyed. To carry the remark still further, if fear in girls, instead of being cherished, perhaps, created, were treated in the same manner as cowardice in boys, we should quickly see women with more dignified aspects. It is true, they could not then with equal propriety be termed the sweet flowers that smile in the walk of man; but they would be more respectable members of society, and discharge the important duties of life by the light of their own reason. "Educate women like men," says Rousseau, "and the more they resemble our sex the less power will they have over us." This is the very point I aim at. I do not wish them to have power over men; but over themselves.

In the same strain have I heard men argue against instructing the poor; for many are the forms that aristocracy assumes. "Teach them to read and write," say they, "and you take them out of the station assigned them by nature." An eloquent Frenchman has answered them, I will borrow his sentiments. "But they know not, when they make man a brute, that they may expect every instant to see him transformed into a ferocious beast. Without knowledge there can be no morality."

Ignorance is a frail base for virtue! Yet, that it is the condition for which woman was organized, has been insisted upon by the writers who have most vehemently argued in favour of the superiority of man; a superiority not in degree, but offence; though, to soften the argument, they have laboured to prove, with chivalrous generosity, that the sexes ought not to be compared; man was made to reason, woman to feel: and that together, flesh and spirit, they make the most perfect whole, by blending happily reason and sensibility into one character. . . .

I come round to my old argument: if woman be allowed to have an immortal soul, she must have, as the employment of life, an understanding to improve. And when, to render the present state more complete, though everything proves it to be but a fraction of a mighty sum, she is incited by present gratification to forget her grand destination, nature is counteracted, or she was born only to procreate and rot. Or, granting brutes of every description a soul, though not a reasonable one, the exercise of instinct and sensibility may be the step which they are to take, in this life, towards the attainment of reason in the next; so that through all eternity they will lag behind man, who, why we cannot tell, had the power given him of attaining reason in his first mode of existence. . . .

IV. Romanticism and Industrial Transformation

The several decades following the French Revolution found Europe in the midst of social, economic, and political transformations more profound, and profoundly hurried, than anything in historical memory. While these transformations reshaped societies and governments across Europe, Great Britain, the first nation to become industrialized, serves as a prototype—and harbinger of things to come—for other nations. The growth of industry and spread of its attendant social consequences in Britain were debated impassionedly among politicians, philosophers, writers, and advocates for the poor in the British Isles and on the continent. Rapid urbanization resulted in unsanitary slums and increased crime, while the shift to large factories from smaller workplaces left workers with less and less say concerning the conditions in which they worked. At the same time, industrialization was providing an increasingly comfortable life for the growing middle classes, particularly for those with capital, who could become extremely wealthy through manufacturing, railroads, shipping, and banking. And in England, as elsewhere, male members of the propertied middle class could vote, unlike working-class men; women did not begin to have access to the vote in most European nations until after the Great War.

The contradictions of industrial transformation in Britain are accentuated by the contemporaneous movement in the arts known as Romanticism. Romanticism had its beginnings in opposition to the pre-eminence of reason, science, and logic—and denigration of feeling and imagination—in Enlightenment thinking. Inspired by the ideals of the French Revolution and the philosophies of Rousseau and Kant, Romantic writers in Germany, England, and other nations turned to organic rather than mechanical categories for understanding, focused on spiritual insight and emotion in place of 'factual' knowledge, and venerated genius rather than reason and empirical study. Where eighteenth-century rationalists had imagined God as a watchmaker, the Romantics envisioned deity as a cosmic poet and artist. Abandoning the eighteenth-century emphasis on classical aesthetic forms, reason, and restraint, the Romantics turned to nature, the exotic, and the supernatural, finding in them a greater creative freedom necessary for the full expression of human nature.

Romanticism's heady emphasis on nature, individual experience, and the imagination thus occurs historically in a time when each seems threatened by social change. William Blake (1757–1827) and William Wordsworth (1770–1850), writing in the 1790s, celebrate poetic genius and use poetry as a medium for examining contemporary social contradictions and philosophical issues. For Wordsworth, the natural world functions as a site in which poets can reflect upon themselves and their society, often seeing in rural life a truthfulness that seems uncorrupted by the hurried pace and hypocrisy of the cities. In the decades that follow, writers turn their attention to the practical and philosophical realities of the new, bourgeois, industrialized, urban society. From very divergent vantage points, poets and philosophers in the first half of the nineteenth century considered what society was, might become, and ought to be.

The overwhelming social and cultural consequences of economic and political transformation inspired everything from fiery political debate to books defining how women and men in different social classes should behave and what they ought to read. As the middle classes became increasingly prosperous, their interests began to be allied with those of the aristocracy; as the working classes struggled with desperate poverty, crowded living conditions, and dangerous workplaces, they became increasingly restless and politicized. Benjamin Disraeli, a man of letters and politician who later became prime minister, warned in his 1846 novel *Sybil* that Britain was becoming "Two Nations."

Some saw these developments as dangerous, others as evidence of Britain's greatness—a range of responses is evident in the selections that follow. Sarah Stickney Ellis (1799–1872), who was widely read by members of England's middle classes, sees in the separate private and public spheres of Victorian England evidence of the nation's industriousness and moral character. Middle-class women, she argues, now less burdened by the work necessary for day-to-day existence, should turn their attention from frivolous diversions or public affairs to the creation of domestic comforts; it is their duty to serve as exemplars of virtue and moral excellence. Like Ellis, educator and cultural critic Matthew Arnold (1822–1888) wrote about the middle classes, but for very different reasons. Where Ellis celebrated them for their virtue, Arnold criticized them as materialistic, narrow-minded, and uninformed "Philistines." In *Culture and Anarchy* and other works, he argued in effect that the Victorian middle classes needed civilization and enlightenment, and that it would be not through industry, but culture, that their society would be improved.

The condition of the poor in industrialized nations was a subject of much debate, first in England and then on the continent. Great cities, busy factories, railroads, and empires made some men wealthy, but their wealth came from the work of thousands of working men and women in conditions that many found appalling. Civilization had always required people to surrender some freedoms, but many now asked if modernization cost too many too much. Andrew Ure (1778–1857), a Scottish scientist, found "the scene of industry . . . always exhilarating" and argued that workers benefitted from factories more than they suffered. For others, such as Friedrich Engels (1820–1895), the human costs of industrialization were horrific: "One realizes," he observed, "that these Londoners have been forced to sacrifice the best qualities of their human nature, to bring to pass all the marvels of civilisation which crowd their city." Writing largely for middle-class audiences, both English writers such as Charles Dickens (1812–1870) and Elizabeth Gaskell and visitors from abroad such as Engels (son of a prosperous cotton manufacturer) described working-class existence in detail, finding in it grounds for moral indignation and social reform, even a workers' revolution.

The Lamb (1789)

Little Lamb who made thee
Dost thou know who made thee
Gave thee life & bid thee feed.
By the stream & o'er the mead;
Gave thee clothing of delight,
Softest clothing wooly bright;
Gave thee such a tender voice,
Making all the vales rejoice!
Little Lamb who made thee
Dost thou know who made thee

Little Lamb I'll tell thee,
Little Lamb I'll tell thee!
He is called by thy name,
For he calls himself a Lamb:
He is meek & he is mild,
He became a little child:
I a child & thou a lamb,
We are called by his name.
Little Lamb God bless thee.
Little Lamb God bless thee.

The Tyger (1794)

Tyger Tyger, burning bright,
In the forests of the night;
What immortal hand or eye,
Could frame thy fearful symmetry?

In what distant deeps or skies
Burnt the fire of thine eyes!
On what wings dare he aspire?
What the hand, dare sieze the fire?

And what shoulder, & what art,
Could twist the sinews of thy heart?
And when thy heart began to beat,
What dread hand? & what dread feet?

What the hammer? what the chain,
In what furnace was they brain?
What the anvil? what dread grasp,
Dare its deadly terrors clasp?

When the stars threw down their spears
And water'd heaven with their tears:
Did he smile his work to see?
Did he who made the Lamb make thee?

Tyger, Tyger burning bright,
In the forests of the night:
What immortal hand or eye,
Dare frame thy fearful symmetry?

London (1794)

I wander thro' each charter'd street,
Near where the charter'd Thames does flow.
And mark in every face I meet
Marks of weakness, marks of woe.

In every cry of every Man,
In every Infants cry of fear,
In every voice: in every ban,
The mind-forg'd manacles I hear

How the Chimney-sweepers cry
Every blackning Church appalls,
And the hapless Soldiers sigh,
Runs in blood down Palace walls

But most thro' midnight streets I hear
How the youthful Harlots curse
Blasts the new-born Infants tear
And blights with plagues the Marriage hearse

Mock on, mock on, Voltaire, Rousseau (ca. 1800)

Mock on, mock on, Voltaire, Rousseau;
Mock on, mock on: 'tis all in vain!
You throw the sand against the wind,
And the wind blows it back again.

And every sand becomes a gem
Reflected in the beams divine;
Blown back they blind the mocking eye,
But still in Israel's paths they shine.

The atoms of Democritus
And Newton's particles of light
Are sands upon the Red Sea shore,
Where Israel's tents do shine so bright.

WILLIAM WORDSWORTH

Selected Poems (1798)
from Preface *to* Lyrical Ballads (1800)

The Tables Turned

An Evening Scene
on the Same Subject

Up! up! my friend, and quit your books;
Or surely you'll grow double:
Up! up! my friend, and clear your looks;
Why all this toil and trouble?

The sun, above the mountain's head,
A freshening lustre mellow
Through all the long green fields has spread,
His first sweet evening yellow.

Books! 'tis a dull and endless strife:
Come, hear the woodland linnet,
How sweet his music! on my life,
There's more of wisdom in it.

And hark! how blithe the throstle sings!
He, too, is no mean preacher:
Come forth into the light of things,
Let nature be your teacher.

She has a world of ready wealth,
Our minds and hearts to bless—
Spontaneous wisdom breathed by health,
Truth breathed by cheerfulness.

One impulse from a vernal wood
May teach you more of man,
Of moral evil and of good,
Than all the sages can.

Sweet is the lore which nature brings;
Our meddling intellect
Mis-shapes the beauteous forms of things:—
We murder to dissect.

Enough of science and of art;
Close up those barren leaves;
Come forth, and bring with you a heart
That watches and receives.

Lines

Composed a Few Miles Above Tintern Abbey on Revisiting
    the Banks of the Wye During a Tour, July 13, 1798

Five years have past; five summers, with the length
Of five long winters! and again I hear
These waters, rolling from their mountain-springs
With a soft inland murmur.—Once again
Do I behold these steep and lofty cliffs,
That on a wild secluded scene impress
Thoughts of more deep seclusion; and connect
The landscape with the quiet of the sky.
The day is come when I again repose
Here, under this dark sycamore, and view
These plots of cottage-ground, these orchard-tufts,
Which at this season, with their unripe fruits,
Are clad in one green hue, and lose themselves
'Mid groves and copses. Once again I see
These hedge-rows, hardly hedge-rows, little lines
Of sportive wood run wild: these pastoral farms,
Green to the very door; and wreaths of smoke
Sent up, in silence, from among the trees!
With some uncertain notice, as might seem
Of vagrant dwellers in the houseless woods,
Or of some hermit's cave, where by his fire
The hermit sits alone.

These beauteous forms,
Through a long absence, have not been to me
As is a landscape to a blind man's eye:
But oft, in lonely rooms, and 'mid the din
Of towns and cities, I have owed to them
In hours of weariness, sensations sweet,
Felt in the blood, and felt along the heart;
And passing even into my purer mind,
With tranquil restoration:—feelings too
Of unremembered pleasure: such, perhaps,
As have no slight or trivial influence
On that best portion of a good man's life,
His little, nameless, unremembered, acts
Of kindness and of love. Nor less, I trust,
To them I may have owed another gift,
Of aspect more sublime; that blessed mood,
In which the burthen of the mystery,
In which the heavy and the weary weight
Of all this unintelligible world,
Is lightened:—that serere and blessed mood,
In which the affections gently lead us on,—
Until, the breath of this corporeal frame
And even the motion of our human blood
Almost suspended, we are laid asleep
In body, and become a living soul:
While with an eye made quiet by the power
Of harmony, and the deep power of joy,
We see into the life of things.
                              If this
Be but a vain belief, yet, oh! how oft—
In darkness and amid the many shapes
Of joyless daylight; when the fretful stir
Unprofitable, and the fever of the world,
Having hung upon the beatings of my heart—
How oft, in spirit, have I turned to thee,
O sylvan Wye! thou wanderer thro' the woods,
How often has my spirit turned to thee!
   And now, with gleams of half-extinguished thought,
With many recognitions dim and faint,
And somewhat of a sad perplexity,
The picture of the mind revives again:
While here I stand, not only with the sense
Of present pleasure, but with pleasing thoughts
That in this moment there is life and food

For future years. And so I dare to hope,
Though changed, no doubt, from what I was when first
I came among these hills; when like a roe
I bounded o'er the mountains, by the sides
Of the deep rivers, and the lonely streams,
Wherever nature led: more like a man
Flying from something that he dreads, than one
Who sought the thing he loved. For nature then
(The coarser pleasures of my boyish days,
And their glad animal movements all gone by)
To me was all in all.—I cannot paint
What then I was. The sounding cataract
Haunted me like a passion: the tall rock,
The mountain, and the deep and gloomy wood,
Their colours and their forms, were then to me
An appetite; a feeling and a love,
That had no need of a remoter charm,
By thought supplied, nor any interest
Unborrowed from the eye.—That time is past,
And all its aching joys are now no more,
And all its dizzy raptures. Not for this
Faint I, nor mourn nor murmur; other gifts
Have followed; for such loss, I would believe,
Abundant recompense. For I have learned
To look on nature, not as in the hour
Of thoughtless youth; but hearing oftentimes
The still, sad music of humanity,
Nor harsh nor grating, though of ample power
To chasten and subdue. And I have felt
A presence that disturbs me with the joy
Of elevated thoughts; a sense sublime
Of something far more deeply interfused,
Whose dwelling is the light of setting suns,
And the round ocean and the living air,
And the blue sky, and in the mind of man:
A motion and a spirit, that impels
All thinking things, all objects of all thought,
And rolls through all things. Therefore am I still
A lover of the meadows and the woods,
And mountains; and of all that we behold
From this green earth; of all the mighty world
Of eye, and ear,—both what they half create,
And what perceive; well pleased to recognise
In nature and the language of the sense

The anchor of my purest thoughts, the nurse,
The guide, the guardian of my heart, and soul
Of all my moral being.
                              Nor perchance,
If I were not thus taught, should I the more
Suffer my genial spirits to decay:
For thou art with me here upon the banks
Of this fair river; thou my dearest Friend,
My dear, dear friend; and in thy voice I catch
The language of my former heart, and read
My former pleasures in the shooting lights
Of thy wild eyes. Oh! yet a little while
May I behold in thee what I was once,
My dear, dear sister! and this prayer I make,
Knowing that nature never did betray
The heart that loved her; 'tis her privilege,
Through all the years of this our life, to lead
From joy to joy: for she can so inform
The mind that is within us, so impress
With quietness and beauty, and so feed
With lofty thoughts, that neither evil tongues,
Rash judgments, nor the sneers of selfish men,
Nor greetings where no kindness is, nor all
The dreary intercourse of daily life,
Shall e'er prevail against us, or disturb
Our cheerful faith, that all which we behold
Is full of blessings. Therefore let the moon
Shine on thee in thy solitary walk;
And let the misty mountain-winds be free
To blow against thee: and, in after years,
When these wild ecstasies shall be matured
Into a sober pleasure; when thy mind
Shall be a mansion for all lovely forms,
Thy memory be as a dwelling-place
For all sweet sounds and harmonies; oh! then,
If solitude, or fear, or pain, or grief,
Should be thy portion, with what healing thoughts
Of tender joy wilt thou remember me,
And these my exhortations! Nor, perchance—
If I should be where I no more can hear
Thy voice, nor catch from thy wild eyes these gleams
Of past existence—wilt thou then forget
That on the banks of this delightful stream
We stood together; and that I, so long

A worshipper of nature, hither came
Unwearied in that service: rather say
With warmer love—oh! with far deeper zeal
Of holier love. Nor wilt thou then forget
That after many wanderings, many years
Of absence, these steep woods and lofty cliffs,
And this green pastoral landscape, were to me
More dear, both for themselves and for thy sake!

from Preface *to* Lyrical Ballads

Taking up the subject, then, upon general grounds, let me ask, what is meant by the word Poet? What is a Poet? To whom does he address himself? And what language is to be expected from him?—He is a man speaking to men: a man, it is true, endowed with more lively sensibility, more enthusiasm and tenderness, who has a greater knowledge of human nature, and a more comprehensive soul, than are supposed to be common among mankind; a man pleased with his own passions and volitions, and who rejoices more than other men in the spirit of life that is in him; delighting to contemplate similar volitions and passions as manifested in the goings-on of the Universe, and habitually impelled to create them where he does not find them. To these qualities he has added a disposition to be affected more than other men by absent things as if they were present; an ability of conjuring up in himself passions, which are indeed far from being the same as those produced by real events, yet (especially in those parts of the general sympathy which are pleasing and delightful) do more nearly resemble the passions produced by real events, than anything which, from the motions of their own minds merely, other men are accustomed to feel in themselves:—whence, and from practice, he has acquired a greater readiness and power in expressing what he thinks and feels, and especially those thoughts and feelings which, by his own choice, or from the structure of his own mind, arise in him without immediate external excitement.

But whatever portion of this faculty we may suppose even the greatest Poet to possess, there cannot be a doubt that the language which it will suggest to him must often, in liveliness and truth, fall short of that which is uttered by men in real life, under the actual pressure of those passions, certain shadows of which the Poet thus produces, or feels to be produced, in himself.

However exhalted a notion we would wish to cherish of the character of a Poet, it is obvious, that while he describes and imitates passions, his employment is in some degree mechanical, compared with the freedom and power of real and substantial action and suffering. So that it will be the wish of the Poet to bring his feelings near to those of the persons whose feelings he describes, nay, for short spaces of time, perhaps, to let himself slip into an entire delusion, and even confound and identify his own feelings with theirs; modifying only the language which is thus suggested to him by a consideration that he describes for a particular purpose, that of giving pleasure. Here, then, he will apply the principle of selection which has been already insisted upon. He will depend upon this for removing what would otherwise be painful or disgusting in the passion; he will feel that there is no necessity to trick out or to elevate nature: and, the more industriously he applies this principle, the deeper will be his faith that no words, which *his* fancy or imagination can suggest, will be to be compared with those which are the emanations of reality and truth.

But it may be said by those who do not object to the general spirit of these remarks, that, as it is impossible for the Poet to produce upon all occasions language as exquisitely fitted for the passion as that which the real passion itself suggests, it is proper that he should consider himself as in the situation of a translator, who does not scruple to substitute excellencies of another kind for those which are unattainable by him; and endeavours occasionally to surpass his original, in order to make some amends for the general inferiority to which he feels that he must submit. But this would be to encourage idleness and unmanly despair. Further, it is the language of men who speak of what they do not understand; who talk of Poetry as of a matter of amusement and idle pleasure; who will converse with us as gravely about a *taste* for Poetry, as they express it, as if it were a thing as indifferent as a taste for rope-dancing, or Frontiniac or Sherry. Aristotle, I have been told, has said, that Poetry is the most philosophic of all writing: it is so: its object is truth, not individual and local, but general, and operative; not standing upon external testimony, but carried alive into the heart by passion; truth which is its own testimony, which gives competence and confidence to the tribunal to which it appeals, and receives them from the same tribunal. Poetry is the image of man and nature. The obstacles which stand in the way of the fidelity of the Biographer and Historian, and of their consequent utility, are incalculably greater than those which are to be encountered by the Poet who comprehends the dignity of his art. The Poet writes under one restriction only, namely, the necessity of giving immediate pleasure to a human Being possessed of that information which may be expected from him, not as a lawyer, a physician, a mariner, an astronomer, or a natural philosopher, but as a Man. Except this one restriction, there is no object standing between the Poet and the image of things; between this, and the Biographer and Historian, there are a thousand.

Nor let this necessity of producing immediate pleasure be considered as a degradation of the Poet's art. It is far otherwise. It is an acknowledgment of the beauty of the universe, an acknowledgment the more sincere, because not formal, but indirect; it is a task light and easy to him who looks at the world in the spirit of love: further, it is a homage paid to the native and naked dignity of man, to the grand elementary principle of pleasure, by which he knows, and feels, and lives, and moves. We have no sympathy but what is propagated by pleasure: I would not be misunderstood; but wherever we sympathise with pain, it will be found that the sympathy is produced and carried on by subtle combinations with pleasure. We have no knowledge, that is, no general principles drawn from the contemplation of particular facts, but what has been built up by pleasure, and exists in us by pleasure alone. The Man of science, the Chemist and Mathematician, whatever difficulties and disgusts they may have had to struggle with, know and feel this. However painful may be the objects with which the Anatomist's knowledge is connected, he feels that his knowledge is pleasure; and where he has no pleasure he has no knowledge. What then does the Poet? He considers man and the objects that surround him as acting and re-acting upon each other, so as to produce an infinite complexity of pain and pleasure; he considers man in his own nature and in his ordinary life as contemplating this with a certain quantity of immediate knowledge, with certain convictions, intuitions, and deductions, which from habit acquire the quality of intuitions; he considers him as looking upon this complex scene of ideas and sensations, and finding everywhere objects that immediately excite in him sympathies which, from the necessities of his nature, are accompanied by an overbalance of enjoyment.

To this knowledge which all men carry about with them, and to these sympathies in which, without any other discipline than that of our daily life, we are fitted to take delight, the Poet principally directs his attention. He considers man and nature as essentially adapted to each other, and the mind of man as naturally the mirror of the fairest and most interesting properties of nature. And thus the Poet, prompted by this feeling of pleasure, which accompanies him through the whole course of his studies, converses with general nature, with affections akin to those, which, through labour and length of time, the Man of science has raised up in himself, by conversing with those particular parts of nature which are the objects of his studies. The knowledge both of the Poet and the Man of science is pleasure; but the knowledge of the one cleaves to us as a necessary part of our existence, our natural and unalienable inheritance; the other is a personal and individual acquisition, slow to come to us, and by no habitual and direct sympathy connecting us with our fellow-beings. The Man of science seeks truth as a remote and unknown benefactor; he cherishes and loves it in his solitude: the Poet, singing a song in which all human beings join with him, rejoices in the presence of truth as our visible friend and hourly companion. Poetry is the breath and finer spirit of all knowledge; it is the impassioned expression which is in the countenance of all Science. Emphatically may it be said of the Poet, as Shakspeare hath said of man, "that he looks before and after." He is the rock of defence for human nature; an upholder and preserver, carrying everywhere with him relationship and love. In spite of difference of soil and climate, of language and manners, of laws and customs: in spite of things silently gone out of mind, and things violently destroyed; the Poet binds together by passion and knowledge the vast empire of human society, as it is spread over the whole earth, and over all time. The objects of the Poet's thoughts are everywhere; though the eyes and senses of man are, it is true, his favourite guides, yet he will follow wheresoever he can find an atmosphere of sensation in which to move his wings. Poetry is the first and last of all knowledge—it is as immortal as the heart of man. If the labours of Men of science should ever create any material revolution, direct or indirect, in our condition, and in the impressions which we habitually receive, the Poet will sleep then no more than at present; he will be ready to follow the steps of the Man of science, not only in those general indirect effects, but he will be at his side, carrying sensation into the midst of the objects of the science itself. The remotest discoveries of the Chemist, the Botanist, or Mineralogist, will be as proper objects of the Poet's art as any upon which it can be employed, if the time should ever come when these things shall be familiar to us, and the relations under which they are contemplated by the followers of these respective sciences shall be manifestly and palpably material to us as enjoying and suffering beings. If the time should ever come when what is now called science, thus familiarised to men, shall be ready to put on, as it were, a form of flesh and blood, the Poet will lend his divine spirit to aid the transfiguration, and will welcome the Being thus produced, as a dear and genuine inmate of the household of man.—It is not, then, to be supposed that any one, who holds that sublime notion of Poetry which I have attempted to convey, will break in upon the sanctity and truth of his pictures by transitory and accidental ornaments, and endeavour to excite admiration of himself by arts, the necessity of which must manifestly depend upon the assumed meanness of his subject.

What has been thus far said applies to Poetry in general; but especially to those parts of composition where the Poet speaks through the mouths of his characters; and upon this point it appears to authorise the conclusion that there are few persons of good sense, who would not allow that the dramatic parts of composition are defective, in proportion as they deviate from the real language of nature, and are coloured by a diction of the Poet's own, either peculiar to him as an individual Poet or belonging simply to Poets in general; to a body of men who, from the circumstance of their compositions being in metre, it is expected will employ a particular language.

It is not, then, in the dramatic parts of composition that we look for this distinction of language; but still it may be proper and necessary where the Poet speaks to us in his own person and character. To this I answer by referring the Reader to the description before given of a Poet. Among the qualities there enumerated as principally conducing to form a Poet, is implied nothing differing in kind from other men, but only in degree. The sum of what was said is, that the Poet is chiefly distinguished from other men by a greater promptness to think and feel without immediate external excitement, and a greater power in expressing such thoughts and feelings as are produced in him in that manner. But these passions and thoughts and feelings are the general passions and thoughts and feelings of men. And with what are they connected? Undoubtedly with our moral sentiments and animal sensations, and with the causes which excite these; with the operations of the elements, and the appearances of the visible universe; with storm and sunshine, with the revolutions of the seasons, with cold and heat, with loss of friends and kindred, with injuries and resentments, gratitude and hope, with fear and sorrow. These, and the like, are the sensations and objects which the Poet describes, as they are the sensations of other men, and the objects which interest them. The Poet thinks and feels in the spirit of human passions. How, then, can his language differ in any material degree from that of all other men who feel vividly and see clearly? It might be *proved* that it is impossible. But supposing that this were not the case, the Poet might then be allowed to use a peculiar language when expressing his feelings for his own gratification, or that of men like himself. But Poets do not write for Poets alone, but for men. Unless therefore we are advocates for that admiration which subsists upon ignorance, and that pleasure which arises from hearing what we do not understand, the Poet must descend from this supposed height; and, in order to excite rational sympathy, he must express himself as other men express themselves. To this it may be added, that while he is only selecting from the real language of men, or, which amounts to the same thing, composing, accurately in the spirit of such selection, he is treading upon safe ground, and we know what we are to expect from him. Our feelings are the same with respect to metre; for, as it may be proper to remind the Reader, the distinction of metre is regular and uniform, and not, like that which is produced by what is usually called POETIC DICTION, arbitrary, and subject to infinite caprices upon which no calculation whatever can be made. In the one case, the Reader is utterly at the mercy of the Poet, respecting what imagery or diction he may choose to connect with the passion; whereas, in the other, the metre obeys certain laws, to which the Poet and Reader both willingly submit because they are certain, and because no interference is made by them with the passion, but such as the concurring testimony of ages has shown to heighten and improve the pleasure which co-exists with it.

SARAH STICKNEY ELLIS

from The Women of England:
Their Social Duties and Domestic Habits (1838)

Every country has its peculiar characteristics, not only of climate and scenery, of public institutions, government, and laws; but every country has also its *moral characteristics*, upon which is founded its true title to a station, either high or low, in the scale of nations. . . .

. . . It is not . . . from the aristocracy of the land that the characteristics of English women should be taken. . . . Neither is it entirely amongst the indigent and most laborious of the community, that we can with propriety look for those strong features of nationality, which stamp the moral character of different nations. . . .

In looking around, then, upon our "nation of shop-keepers," we readily perceive that by dividing society into three classes, as regards what is commonly called rank, the middle class must include so vast a portion of the intelligence and moral power of the country at large, that it may not improperly be designated the pillar of our nation's strength, its base being the important class of the laborious poor, and its rich and highly ornamental capital, the ancient nobility of the land. In no other country is society thus beautifully proportioned, and England should beware of any deviation from the order and symmetry of her national column. . . .

. . . It is, then, strictly speaking, to those who belong to that great mass of the population of England which is connected with trade and manufactures;—or, in order to make the application more direct, to that portion of it who are restricted to the services of from one to four domestics,—who, on the one hand, enjoy the advantages of a liberal education, and, on the other, have no pretension to family rank. . . .

It is from the class of females above described, that we naturally look for the highest tone of moral feeling, because they are at the same time removed from the pressing necessities of absolute poverty, and admitted to the intellectual privileges of the great: and thus, while they enjoy every facility in the way of acquiring knowledge, it is their still higher privilege not to be exempt from the domestic duties which call forth the best energies of the female character. . . .

It is perhaps the nearest approach we can make toward any thing like a definition of what is most striking in the characteristics of the women of England, to say, that the nature of their domestic circumstances is such as to invest their characters with the threefold recommendation of *promptitude in action, energy of thought, and benevolence of feeling*. With

118

all the responsibilities of family comfort and social enjoyment resting upon them, and unaided by those troops of menials who throng the halls of the affluent and the great, they are kept alive to the necessity of making their own personal exertions conducive to the great end of promoting the happiness of those around them. . . .

"What shall I do to gratify myself—to be admired—or to vary the tenor of my existence?" are not the questions which a woman of right feelings asks on first awaking to the avocations of the day. Much more congenial to the highest attributes of woman's character, are inquiries such as these: "How shall I endeavor through this day to turn the time, the health, and the means permitted me to enjoy, to the best account? Is anyone sick, I must visit their chamber without delay, and try to give their apartment an air of comfort, by arranging such things as the wearied nurse may not have thought of. Is any one about to set off on a journey, I must see that the early meal is spread, to prepare it with my own hands, in order that the servant, who was working late last night, may profit by unbroken rest. Did I fail in what was kind or considerate to any of the family yesterday; I will meet her this morning with a cordial welcome, and show, in the most delicate way I can, that I am anxious to atone for the past. Was any one exhausted by the last day's exertion, I will be an hour before them this morning, and let them see that their labor is so much in advance. Or, if nothing extraordinary occurs to claim my attention, I will meet the family with a consciousness that, being the least engaged of any member of it, I am consequently the most at liberty to devote myself to the general good of the whole, by cultivating cheerful conversation, adapting myself to the prevailing tone of feeling, and leading those who are least happy, to think and speak of what will make them more so."

. . . Good household management, conducted on this plan, is indeed a science well worthy of attention. It comprises so much, as to invest it with an air of difficulty on the first view; but no woman can reasonably complain of incapability, because nature has endowed the sex with perceptions so lively and acute, that where benevolence is the impulse, and principle the foundation upon which they act, experience will soon teach them by what means they may best accomplish the end they have in view. . . .

The domestic woman, moving in a comparatively limited circle, is not necessarily confined to a limited number of ideas, but can often expatiate upon subjects of mere local interest with a vigor of intellect, a freshness of feeling, and a liveliness of fancy, which create in the mind of the uninitiated stranger, a perfect longing to be admitted into the home associations from whence are derived such a world of amusement, and so unfailing a relief from the severer duties of life. . . .

Above all other characteristics of the women of England, the strong moral feeling pervading even their most trifling and familiar actions, ought to be mentioned as most conducive to the maintenance of that high place which they so justly claim in the society of their native land. . . . The women of England are not surpassed by those of any other country for their clear perception of the right and the wrong of common and familiar things, for their reference to principle in the ordinary affairs of life, and for their united maintenance of that social order, sound integrity, and domestic peace, which constitute the foundation of all that is most valuable in the society of our native land.

Much as I have said of the influence of the domestic habits of my country-women, it is, after all, to the prevalence of religious instruction, and the operation of religious principle upon the heart, that the consistent maintenance of their high tone of moral character is to be attributed. . . . Women are said to be more easily brought under this influence than men; and we consequently see, in places of public worship, and on all occasions in which religious object is the motive for exertion, a greater proportion of women than men. . . .

If . . . all was confusion and neglect at home—filial appeals unanswered—domestic comforts uncalculated—husbands, sons, and brothers referred to servants for all the little offices of social kindness, in order that the ladies of the family might hurry away at the appointed time to some committee-room, scientific lecture, or public assembly: however laudable the object for which they met, there would be sufficient cause why their cheeks should be mantled with the blush of burning shame . . . which those whose charity has not begun at home, ought never to appropriate to themselves.

It is a widely mistaken notion to suppose that the sphere of usefulness recommended here, is a humiliating and degraded one. . . . With [some women] it is a favorite plea, brought forward in extenuation of their own uselessness, that they have no influence—that they are not leading women—that society takes no note of them. . . .

It is an important consideration, that from such women as these, myriads of immortal beings derive that early bias of character, which under Providence decides their fate, not only in this world, but in the world to come. And yet they flutter on, and say they have no influence—they do not aspire to be leading women—they are in society but as grains of sand on the sea-shore. Would they but pause one moment to ask how will this plea avail them, when as daughters without gratitude, friends without good faith, wives without consideration, and mothers without piety, they stand before the bar of judgment, to render an account of the talents committed to their trust! . . .

Amongst this unpretending class are found striking and noble instance of women, who apparently feeble and insignificant, when called into action by pressing and peculiar circumstances, can accomplish great and glorious purposes, supported and carried forward by that most valuable of all faculties—*moral power*. And just in proportion as women cultivate this faculty (under the blessing of heaven) . . . is their influence over their fellow-creatures, and consequently their power of doing good.

It is not to be presumed that women *possess* more moral power than men, but happily for them, such are their early impressions, associations, and general position in the world, that their moral feelings are less liable to be impaired by the pecuniary objects which too often constitute the chief end of man, and which, even under the limitations of better principle, necessarily engage a large portion of his thoughts. . . .

How often has man returned to his home with a mind confused by the many voices, which in the mart, the exchange, or the public assembly, have addressed themselves to his inborn selfishness or his worldly pride; and while his integrity was shaken, and his resolution gave way beneath the pressure of apparent necessity, or the insidious pretences of expediency, he has stood corrected before the clear eye of woman, as it looked directly to the naked truth, and detected the lurking evil of the specious act he was about to commit. Nay, so potent may have become this secret influence, that he may have borne it about with him like a kind of second conscience, for mental reference, and spiritual counsel, in moments of trial: and when the snares of the world were around him, and temptations from within and without have bribed over the witness in his own bosom, he has thought of the humble monitress who sat alone, guarding the fireside comforts of his distant home; and the remembrance of her character, clothed in moral beauty, has scattered the clouds before his mental vision, and sent him back to that beloved home, a wiser and a better man. . . .

MATTHEW ARNOLD

from Culture and Anarchy (1869)

. . . Now, having first saluted free-trade and its doctors with all respect, let us see whether even here, too, our Liberal friends do not pursue their operations in a mechanical way, without reference to any firm intelligible law of things, to human life as a whole, and human happiness; and whether it is not more for our good, at this particular moment at any rate, if, instead of worshipping free-trade with them Hebraistically, as a kind of fetish, and helping them to pursue it as an end in and for itself, we turn the free stream of our thought upon their treatment of it, and see how this is related to the intelligible law of human life, and to national well-being and happiness. In short, suppose we Hellenise a little with free-trade, . . .

But first let us understand how the policy of free-trade really shapes itself for our Liberal friends, and how they practically employ it as an instrument of national happiness and salvation. . . . so it seems clearly right that the poor man should eat untaxed bread, and, generally, that restrictions and regulations which, for the supposed benefit of some particular person or class of persons, make the price of things artificially high here, or artificially low there, and interfere with the natural flow of trade and commerce, should be done away with. But in the policy of our Liberal friends free-trade means more than this, and is specially valued as a stimulant to the production of wealth, as they call it, and to the increase of the trade, business, and population of the country. We have already seen how these things,—trade, business, and population,—are mechanically pursued by us as ends precious in themselves, and are worshipped as what we call fetishes; and Mr. Bright, I have already said, when he wishes to give the working class a true sense of what makes glory and greatness, tells it to look at the cities it has built, the railroads it has made, the manufactures it has produced. So to this idea of glory and greatness the free-trade which our Liberal friends extol so solemnly and devoutly has served,—to the increase of trade, business, and population; and for this it is prized. Therefore, the untaxing of the poor man's bread has, with this view of national happiness, been used not so much to make the existing poor man's bread cheaper or more abundant, but rather to create more poor men to eat it; so that we cannot precisely say that we have fewer poor men than we had before free-trade, but we can say with truth that we have many more centres of industry, as they are called, and much more business, population, and manufactures. And if we are sometimes a little troubled by our multitude of poor men, yet we know the increase of manufactures and population to be such a salutary thing in itself, and our free-trade policy begets such an admirable movement, creating fresh centres of industry and fresh poor men here, while we were thinking about our poor men there, that we are quite dazzled and borne away, and more and more industrial movement is called for, and our social progress seems to become one triumphant and enjoyable course of what is sometimes called, vulgarly, outrunning the constable.

If, however, taking some other criterion of man's well-being than the cities he has built and the manufactures he has produced, we persist in thinking that our social progress would be happier if there were not so many of us so very poor, and in busying ourselves with notions of in some way or other adjusting the poor man and business one to the other, and not multiplying the one and the other mechanically and blindly, then our Liberal friends, the appointed doctors of free-trade, take us up very sharply. "Art is long," says the *Times*, "and life is short; for the most part we settle things first and understand them afterwards. Let us have as few theories as possible; what is wanted is not the light of speculation. If nothing worked well of which the theory was not perfectly understood, we should be in sad confusion. The relations of labour and capital, we are told, are not understood, yet trade and commerce, on the whole, work satisfactorily." I quote from the *Times* of only the other day. But thoughts like these, as I have often pointed out, are thoroughly British thoughts, and we have been familiar with them for years.

Or, if we want more of a philosophy of the matter than this, our free-trade friends have two axioms for us, axioms laid down by their justly esteemed doctors, which they think ought to satisfy us entirely. One is, that, other things being equal, the more population increases, the more does production increase to keep pace with it; because men by their numbers and contact call forth all manner of activities and resources in one another and in nature, which, when men are few and sparse, are never developed. The other is, that, although population always tends to equal the means of subsistence, yet people's notions of what subsistence is enlarge as civilisation advances, and take in a number of things beyond the bare necessaries of life; and thus, therefore, is supplied whatever check on population is needed. But the error of our friends is, perhaps, that they apply axioms of this sort as if they were self-acting laws which will put themselves into operation without trouble or planning on our part, if we will only pursue free-trade, business, and population zealously and staunchly. Whereas the real truth is, that, however the case might be under other circumstances, yet in fact, as we now manage the matter, the enlarged conception of what is included in *subsistence* does not operate to prevent the bringing into the world of numbers of people who but just attain to the barest necessaries of life or who even fail to attain to them; while, again, though production may increase as population increases, yet it seems that the production may be of such a kind, as so related, or rather non-related, to population, that the population may be little the better for it.

For instance, with the increase of population since Queen Elizabeth's time the production of silk-stockings has wonderfully increased, and silk-stockings have become much cheaper, and procurable in greater abundance by many more people, and tend perhaps, as population and manufactures increase, to get cheaper and cheaper, and at last to become, according to Bastiat's favourite image, a common free property of the human race, like light and air. But bread and bacon have not become much cheaper with the increase of population since Queen Elizabeth's time, nor procurable in much greater abundance by many more people; neither do they seem at all to promise to become, like light and air, a common free property of the human race. And if bread and bacon have not kept pace with our population, and we have many more people in want of them now than in Queen Elizabeth's time, it seems vain to tell us that silk-stockings have kept pace with our population, or even more than kept pace with it, and that we are to get our comfort out of that.

In short, it turns out that our pursuit of free-trade, as of so many other things, has been too mechanical. We fix upon some object, which in this case is the production of wealth, and the increase of manufactures, population, and commerce through free-trade, as a kind of one thing needful or end in itself; and then we pursue it staunchly and mechanically, and say that it is our duty to pursue it staunchly and mechanically, not to see how it is related to the whole intelligible law of things and to full human perfection, or to treat it as the piece of machinery, of varying value as its relations to the intelligible law of things vary, which it really is. . . .

I remember, only the other day, a good man looking with me upon a multitude of children who were gathered before us in one of the most miserable regions of London,— children eaten up with disease, half-sized, half-fed, half-clothed, neglected by their parents, without health, without home, without hope,—said to me: "The one thing really needful is to teach these little ones to succour one another, if only with a cup of cold water; but now, from one end of the country to the other, one hears nothing but the cry for knowledge, knowledge, knowledge!" And yet surely, so long as these children are there in these festering masses, without health, without home, without hope, and so long as their multitude is perpetually swelling, charged with misery they must still be for themselves, charged with misery they must still be for us, whether they help one another with a cup of cold water or no; and the knowledge how to prevent their acculumating is necessary, even to give their moral life and growth a fair chance!

May we not, therefore, say, that neither the true Hebraism of this good man, willing to *spend* and be spent for these sunken multitudes, nor what I may call the spurious Hebraism of our free-trading Liberal friends,—mechanically worshipping their fetish of the production of wealth and of the increase of manufactures and population, and looking neither to the right nor left so long as this increase goes on,—avail us much here; and that here, again, what we want is Hellenism, the letting our consciousness play freely and simply upon the facts before us, and listening to what it tells us of the intelligible law of things as concerns them? And surely what it tells us is, that a man's children are not really *sent*, any more than the pictures upon his wall, or the horses in his stable are *sent*; and that to bring people into the world, when one cannot afford to keep them and oneself decently and not too precariously, or to bring more of them into the world than one can afford to keep thus, is, whatever the *Times* . . . may say, by no means an accomplishment of the divine will or a fulfilment of Nature's simplest laws, but is just as wrong, just as contrary to reason and the will of God, as for a man to have horses, or carriages, or pictures, when he cannot afford them, or to have more of them than he can afford; and that, in the one case as in the other, the larger the scale on which the violation of reason's law is practised, and the longer it is persisted in, the greater must be the confusion and final trouble. Surely no laudations of free-trade, no meetings of bishops and clergy in the East End of London, no reading of papers and processions in the streets and forcible irruptions into the parks, even in professed support of this good design, ought to be unflinchingly forbidden and repressed; and that far more is lost than is gained by permitting them. Because a State in which law is authoritative and sovereign, a firm and settled course of public order, is requisite if man is to bring to maturity anything precious and lasting now, or to found anything precious and lasting for the future.

Thus, in our eyes, the very framework and exterior order of the State, whoever may administer the State, is sacred; and culture is the most resolute enemy of anarchy, because of the great hopes and designs for the State which culture teaches us to nourish. But as, believing in right reason, and having faith in the progress of humanity towards perfection, and ever labouring for this end, we grow to have clearer sight of the ideas of right reason, and of the elements and helps of perfection, and come gradually to fill the framework of the State with them, to fashion its internal composition and all its laws and institutions conformably to them, and to make the State more and more the expression, as we say, of our best self, which is not manifold, and vulgar, and unstable, and contentious, and ever-varying, but one, and noble, and secure, and peaceful, and the same for all mankind,—with what aversion shall we not *then* regard anarchy, with what firmness shall we not check it, when there is so much that is so precious which it will endanger! . . .

Andrew Ure

from The Philosophy of Manufactures (1835)

. . . When the wandering savage becomes a citizen, he renounces many of his dangerous pleasures in return for tranquility and protection. He can no longer gratify at will a revengeful spirit upon his foes, nor seize with violence a neighbor's possessions. In like manner, when the handicraftsman exchanges hard work with fluctuating employment and pay, for continuous work of a lighter kind with steady wages, he must necessarily renounce his old prerogative of stopping when he pleases, because he would thereby throw the whole establishment into disorder. Of the amount of injury resulting from the violation of the rules of automatic labor he can hardly ever be the proper judge; just as mankind at large can never fully estimate the evils consequent upon an infraction of God's moral law. Yet the factory operative, little versant in the great operations of political economy, currency, and trade, and actuated too often by an invidious feeling toward the capitalist who animates his otherwise torpid talents, is easily persuaded by artful demagogues, that his sacrifice of time and skill is beyond proportion of his recompense, or that fewer hours of industry would be an ample equivalent for his wages. This notion seems to have taken an early and inveterate hold of the factory mind, and to have been riveted from time to time by the leaders of those secret combinations, so readily formed among a peculiar class of men, concentrated in masses within a narrow range of country.

Instead of repining as they have done at the prosperity of their employers, and concerting odious measures to blast it, they should, on every principle of gratitude and self-interest, have rejoiced at the success resulting from their labors, and by regularity and skill have recommended themselves to monied men desirous of engaging in a profitable concern, and of procuring qualified hands to conduct it. Thus good workmen would have advanced their condition to that of overlookers, managers, and partners in new mills, and have increased at the same time the demand for their companions' labor in the market. It is only by an undisturbed progression of this kind that the rate of wages can be permanently raised or upheld. Had it not been for the violent collisions and interruptions resulting from erroneous views among the operatives, the factory system would have developed still more rapidly and beneficially for all concerned than it has, and would have exhibited still more frequently gratifying examples of skilful workmen becoming opulent proprietors. Every misunderstanding either repels capital altogether, or diverts it from flowing, for a time, in the channels of trade liable to strikes.

No master would wish to have any wayward children to work within the walls of his factory, who do not mind their business without beating, and he therefore usually fines and turns away any spinners who are known to maltreat their assistants. Hence, ill-usage of any kind is a very rare occurrence. I have visited many factories, both in Manchester and in the surrounding districts, during a period of several months, entering the spinning rooms, unexpectedly, and often alone, at different times of day, and I never saw a single instance of corporal chastisement inflicted on a child, nor indeed did I ever see children in ill-humor. They seemed to be always cheerful and alert, taking pleasure in the light play of their muscles—enjoying the mobility natural to their age. The scene of industry, far from exciting sad emotions in my mind, was always exhilarating. It was delightful to observe the nimbleness with which they pieced the broken ends, as the mule-carriage began to recede from the fixed roller-beam, and to see them at leisure, after a few seconds' exercise of their tiny fingers, to amuse themselves in any attitude they chose, till the stretch and winding-on were once more completed. The work of these lively elves seemed to resemble a sport, in which habit gave them a pleasing dexterity. Conscious of their skill, they were delighted to show it off to any stranger. As to exhaustion by the day's work, they evinced no trace of it on emerging from the mill in the evening, for they immediately began to skip about any neighboring play-ground, and to commence their little amusements with the same alacrity as boys issuing from a school. It is moreover my firm conviction, that if children are not ill-used by bad parents or guardians, but receive in food and raiment the full benefit of what they earn, they would thrive better in our modern factories than if left alone in apartments too often ill-aired, damp and cold.

Of all the modern prejudices that exist with regard to factory labor, there is none more unfounded than that which ascribes to it excessive tedium and irksomeness above other occupations, owing to its being carried on in conjunction with the "unceasing motion of the steam-engine." In an establishment for spinning or weaving cotton, all the hard work is performed by the steam-engine, which leaves for the attendant no hard labor at all, and literally nothing to do in general; but at intervals to perform some delicate operation, such as joining threads that break, taking the cops off the spindles, etc. And it is so far from being true that the work in a factory is incessant, because the motion of the steam-engine is incessant, that the labor is not incessant on that very account, because it is performed in conjunction with the steam-engine. Of all manufacturing employments, those are by far the most irksome and incessant in which steam-engines are not employed, as in lace-running and stocking-weaving, and the way to prevent an employment from being incessant is to introduce a steam-engine into it. . . .

The factory system, then, instead of being detrimental to the comfort of the laboring population, is its grand Palladium; for the more complicated and extensive the machinery required for any manufacture, the less risk is there of its agents being injured by the competition of foreign manufactures, and the greater inducement and ability has the mill-owner to keep up the wages of his work-people. The main reason why they are so high is, that they form a small part of the value of the manufactured article, so that if reduced too low by a sordid master, they would render his operatives less careful, and thereby injure the quality of their work more than could be compensated by saving in wages. . . .

The most recent, and perhaps most convincing, evidence regarding the healthiness of factory children is that given in the official report of Mr. Harrison, the inspecting surgeon appointed for the mills of Preston and its vicinity. There are 1,656 under 18 years of age, of whom 952 are employed in spinning-rooms, 468 in carding rooms, 128 at power-looms, and 108 in winding, skewering cops, etc. "I have made very particular inquiries respecting the health of every child whom I have examined, and I find that the average annual sickness of each child is not more than four days; at least, that not more than four days on an average are lost by each child in a year, in consequence of sickness. This includes disorders of every kind, for the most part induced by causes wholly unconnected with factory labor. I have been not a little surprised to find so little sickness which can fairly be attributed to mill work. I have met with very few children who have suffered from injuries occasioned by machinery; and the protection, especially in new factories, is so complete, that accidents will, I doubt not, speedily become rare. I have not met with a single instance out of the 1,656 children whom I have examined, of deformity, that is referable to factory labor. It must be admitted, that factory children do not present the same blooming robust appearance as is witnessed among children who labor in the open air, but I question if they are not more exempt from acute diseases, and do not, on the average, suffer less sickness than those who are regarded as having more healthy employments. The average age at which the children of this district enter the factories is ten years and two months; and the average age of all the young persons together is fourteen years."...

Friedrich Engels

from The Condition of the Working Class in England (1844)

. . . Such, in brief, is the history of English industrial development in the past sixty years, a history, which has no counterpart in the annals of humanity. Sixty, eighty years ago, England was a country like every other, with small towns, few and simple industries, and a thin but *proportionally* large agricultural population. Today it is a country like no other, with a capital of two and a half million inhabitants; with vast manufacturing cities; with an industry that supplies the world, and produces almost everything by means of the most complex machinery; with an industrious, intelligent, dense population, of which two-thirds are employed in trade and commerce, and composed of classes wholly different; forming, in fact, with other customs and other needs, a different nation from the England of those days. The industrial revolution is of the same importance for England as the political revolution is for France, and the philosophical revolution for Germany; and the difference between England in 1760 and in 1844 is at least as great as that between France, under the *ancient régime* and during the revolution of July. But the mightiest result of this industrial transformation is the English proletariat.

. . . The rapid extension of manufacture demanded hands, wages rose, and troops of workmen migrated from the agricultural districts to the towns. Population multiplied enormously, and nearly all the increase took place in the proletariat. . . . Thus arose the great manufacturing and commercial cities of the British Empire, in which at least three-fourths of the population belong to the working-class, while the lower middle-class consists only of small shopkeepers, and very very few handicraftsmen. For, though the rising manufacture first attained importance by transforming tools into machines, work-rooms into factories, and consequently, the toiling lower middle-class into the toiling proletariat, and the former large merchants into manufacturers, though the lower middle-class was thus early crushed out, and the population reduced to the two opposing elements, workers and capitalists, this happened outside of the domain of manufacture proper, in the province of handicraft and retail trade as well. In the place of the former masters and apprentices, came great capitalists and working-men who had no prospect of rising above their class. Handiwork was carried on after the fashion of factory work, the division of labour was strictly applied, and small employers who could not compete with great establishments were forced down into the proletariat. At the same time the destruction of the former organization of handwork, and the disappearance of the lower middle-class deprived the working-man of all possibility of rising into the middle-class himself. Hitherto he had always had the prospect of establishing himself somewhere as master artificer, perhaps employing journeymen and apprentices; but now, when master artificers were crowded out by manufacturers, when large capital had become necessary for carrying on work independently, the working-class became, for the first time, an integral, permanent class of the population, whereas it had formerly often been merely a transition leading to the bourgeoisie. Now, he who was born to toil had no other prospect than that of remaining a toiler all his life. Now, for the first time, therefore, the proletariat was in a position to undertake an independent movement.

In this way were brought together those vast masses of working-men who now fill the whole British Empire, whose social condition forces itself every day more and more upon the attention of the civilized world. The condition of the working-class is the condition of the vast majority of the English people. The question: What is to become of those destitute millions, who consume today what they earned yesterday; who have created the greatness of England by their inventions and their toil; who become with every passing day more conscious of their might, and demand, with daily increasing urgency, their share of the advantages of society?—This, since the Reform Bill, has become the national question. All Parliamentary debates, of any importance, may be reduced to this; and, though the English middle-class will not as yet admit it, though they try to evade this great question, and to represent their own particular interests as the truly national ones, their action is utterly useless. With every session of Parliament, the working-class gains ground, the interests of the middle-class diminish in importance; and, in spite of the fact that the middle-class is the chief, in fact, the only power in Parliament, the last session of 1844 was a continuous debate upon subjects affecting the working-class, the Poor Relief Bill, the Factory Act, the Masters' and Servants' Act; . . .

In spite of all this, the English middle-class, especially the manufacturing class, which is enriched directly by means of the poverty of the workers, persists in ignoring this poverty. This class, feeling itself the mighty representative class of the nation, is ashamed to lay the sore spot of England bare before the eyes of the world; will not confess, even to itself, that the workers are in distress, because it, the property-holding, manufacturing class, must bear the moral responsibility for this distress. Hence the scornful smile which intelligent Englishmen (and they, the middle-class alone are known on the Continent) assume when any one begins to speak of the condition of the working-class; hence the utter ignorance on the part of the whole middle-class of everything which concerns the workers; hence the ridiculous blunders which men of this class, in and out of Parliament, make when the position of the proletariat comes under discussion; hence the absurd freedom from anxiety, with which the middle-class dwells upon a soil that is honeycombed, and may any day collapse, the speedy collapse of which is as certain as a mathematical or mechanical demonstration; hence the miracle that the English have as yet no single book upon the condition of their workers, although they have been examining and mending the old state of things no one knows how many years. Hence also the deep wrath of the whole working-class, from Glasgow to London, against the rich, by whom they are systematically plundered and mercilessly left to their fate, a wrath which before too long a time goes by, a time almost within the power of man to predict, must break out into a Revolution in comparison with which the French Revolution, and the year 1794, will prove to have been child's play.

CHARLES DICKENS

from Hard Times (1854)

Chapter V

The Key-Note

Coketown, to which Messrs. Bounderby and Gradgrind now walked, was a triumph of fact; it had no greater taint of fancy in it than Mrs. Gradgrind herself. Let us strike the key-note, Coketown, before pursuing our tune.

It was a town of red brick, or of brick that would have been red if the smoke and ashes had allowed it; but as matters stood it was a town of unnatural red and black like the painted face of a savage. It was a town of machinery and tall chimneys, out of which interminable serpents of smoke trailed themselves for ever and ever, and never got un-coiled. It had a black canal in it, and a river that ran purple with ill-smelling dye, and vast piles of building full of windows where there was a rattling and a trembling all day long, and where the piston of the steam-engine worked monotonously up and down, like the head of an elephant in a state of melancholy madness. It contained several large streets all very like one another, and many small streets still more like one another, inhabited by people equally like one another, who all went in and out at the same hours, with the same sound upon the same pavements, to do the same work, and to whom every day was the same as yesterday, and to-morrow and every year the counterpart of the last and the next.

These attributes of Coketown were in the main inseparable from the work by which it was sustained; against them were to be set off, comforts of life which found their way all over the world, and elegancies of life which made, we will not ask how much of the fine lady, who could scarcely bear to hear the place mentioned. The rest of its features were voluntary, and they were these.

You saw nothing in Coketown but what was severely workful. If the members of a religious persuasion built a chapel there,—as the member of eighteen religious persuasions had done,—they made it a pious warehouse of red brick, with sometimes (but this is only in highly ornamented examples) a bell in a bird-cage on the top of it. The solitary exception was the New Church; a stuccoed edifice with a square steeple over the door, terminating in four short pinnacles like florid wooden legs. All the public inscriptions in the town were painted alike, in severe characters of black and white. The jail might have been the infirmary, the infirmary might have been the jail, the town-hall might have been

132

either, or both, or anything else, for anything that appeared to the contrary in the graces of their construction. Fact, fact, fact, everywhere in the material aspect of the town; fact, fact, fact, everywhere in the immaterial. The M'Choakumchild school was all fact, and the school of design was all fact, and the relations between master and man were all fact, and everything was fact between the lying-in hospital and the cemetery, and what you couldn't state in figures, or show to be purchasable in the cheapest market and saleable in the dearest, was not, and never should be, world without end, Amen.

A town so sacred to fact, and so triumphant in its assertion, of course go on well? Why no, not quite well. No? Dear me!

V. Materialism, Evolution, Nationalism, Imperialism

Questions about human societies continued to preoccupy many people through the second half of the nineteenth century and into the twentieth. Faced with the profound social changes resulting from the French and industrial revolutions and influenced by Enlightenment rationalism, scientists and philosophers developed theories to explain the origins and functioning of human societies, to account for differences between various cultures and societies, and to improve them. In the eighteenth century, French thinkers had conceived the idea of the encyclopedia, a series of texts that would sum up human knowledge; in the early nineteenth century the German philosopher Hegel had constructed a universal theory of history in which all human history was understood as a dialectical progression from primitive to philosophically sophisticated cultures. Asking "what is the ultimate design of the World?" Hegel responded that "the History of the world is none other than the progress of the consciousness of Freedom; a process whose development according to the necessity of its nature, it is our business to investigate."

Hegel's terms provide a useful introduction to the varied, yet related, concerns of philosophers, scientists, and politicians in the nineteenth century. Some, such as Hegel, were primarily interested in explaining history and society in terms of abstract principles. Others, such as the French philosopher Auguste Comte, founder of Positivism, were primarily interested in using precise observation and description to obtain exact knowledge. Others, including Karl Marx (1818–1883), had more pressing purposes in mind. As Marx wrote in his *Theses on Feuerbach* in 1845: "The philosophers have only *interpreted* the world, in various ways; the point, however, is to *change* it." Each of these impulses—to understand the world, to know it precisely, and to transform it—can be traced through the selections that follow. One of the striking features of these writers is their confidence—both in their ideas and in the capacity of science and philosophy to explain the major dilemmas of human life and, in doing so, make it possible for men and women to change the world.

Marx, born into a middle-class, German Jewish family that had converted to Christianity, studied philosophy, history, and jurisprudence at the Universities of Bonn and Berlin. After completing his doctoral dissertation, he wrote for and edited an opposition newspaper and intellectual journals; some of his earliest essays were critical analyses of Hegel's philosophy. As Marx recounts in the Preface to *Toward a Critique of Political Economy*, a summary of his early work, the newspaper was soon suppressed under strict Prussian censorship laws and he moved to Paris and then, banished by the French government under Prussian influence, to Brussels. In Brussels Marx and Friedrich Engels, with whom he collaborated for nearly forty years, drafted early expositions of their materialist conception of history. Hegel and other idealists, they argued, had erred dramatically in supposing that ideas are the central force in human history. In effect, Marx and Engels turned Hegelian philosophy on its head, arguing that the real dialectic of human history is grounded in material reality instead:

> In direct contrast to German philosophy which descends from heaven to earth, here we ascend from earth to heaven. That is to say, we do not set out from what men say, imagine, conceive, nor from men as narrated, thought of, imagined, conceived, in order to arrive at men in the flesh. We set out from real, active men, and on the basis of their real life-process we demonstrate the development of the ideological reflexes and echoes of this life-process.

In 1849 Marx moved to London, where he lived until his death, working on an exhaustive analysis of political economy, writing for the *New York Daily Tribune,* and corresponding with participants in workers' movements across Europe.

While Marx's theories deal with man-made economic systems, those of his contemporary Charles Darwin (1809-1882) deal with the natural world. At 22 Darwin had traveled around the world on H.M.S. *Beagle,* helping to survey the coast of South America, taking detailed notes on animals and plants, and observing native cultures. At 50, he published what many would argue is the single most significant text of the nineteenth century: *The Origin of Species.* Drawing on over two decades of research, Darwin laid out in precise detail a theory of evolution, advancing the idea of natural selection to account for variation in nature and implying (though not saying directly, as he would later in *The Descent of Man)* that the human species too had evolved from more primitive forms. While he recognized the challenge evolution posed to many popular religious interpretations of the world, Darwin also suggested that evolution was compatible with the idea of a Creator. As the last sentence of *The Origin of Species* suggests, Darwin's theory proposed evolution as a grand narrative that could explain the development of the natural world and—presumably—that of the social world as well:

> There is grandeur in this view of life, with its several powers, having been originally breathed into a few forms or into one; and that, whilst this planet has gone cycling on according to the fixed law of gravity, from so simple a beginning endless forms most beautiful and most wonderful have been, and are being, evolved.

Anticipating something of the public uproar his theories would provoke, Darwin himself did not elaborate on implications his ideas might have for understanding human history. But both advocates and critics of his ideas were quick to extrapolate. Early sociologists, including Herbert Spencer in Britain and William Graham Sumner in the United States, applied evolutionary theory to human societies, an approach often referred to as social Darwinism. Some were attracted to the idea that certain human races or societies might be the superior product of natural selection because it suggested orderly new explanations for the differences between cultures and societies that philosophers had observed and discussed for centuries. To others, it also suggested scientific, even moral justifications for class societies and European imperialism: perhaps the rich were inherently superior to the poor, and perhaps Europeans were more evolved than peoples in other parts of the world. And for some, crude applications of evolutionary theory to contemporary ethnic and racial conflicts provided a pseudo-scientific veneer to racism.

Probably the most powerful political ideology in late nineteenth- and early twentieth-century Europe was nationalism. Through conquest, economic alliance, or dynastic marriage, nation-states had often linked together people who spoke different languages and had different histories. In the mid-nineteenth century, however, the idea that nations should be 'naturally' composed of people sharing a common language, culture, and history became immensely popular. Culturally, nationalism was in part an outgrowth of romanticism, which had celebrated folk art forms over more cosmopolitan practices. Politically, it was in part an after-effect of the domination of Europe by France under Napoleon. Nationalist sentiments were influential throughout Europe, taking different forms as circumstances varied. The power of the immense Habsburg Empire, for example, was seriously weakened both by conflict between the Magyar nobles of Hungary and the dominant Austrians, who spoke German, and by Pan-Slavic movements hoping to unite all Slavic peoples in a single nation. Irish resistance to British rule intensified, leading eventually to the partition of Ireland and establishment of the Irish Free State in 1922. In Italy and Germany—terms that until mid-century referred to geographic locations divided into numerous small states and principalities—nationalist fervor helped lead to a unified Kingdom of Italy in the 1860s and to the German Empire in the 1870s.

Nationalist sentiments also affected the ways imperialism was understood at home: part of Britain's sense of national pride, for example, rested on the fact that it was not simply a nation, but the British *Empire,* upon which the sun never set. While the primary motivations for imperialism were economic and political, notions of cultural superiority drawn from romantic nationalism, social Darwinism, religious ideology, and other sources served to explain and justify European rule abroad. Imperialism and colonialism were, however, the subject of much debate in Europe in the nineteenth and twentieth centuries. In the nineteenth century, disagreements about the purpose of empire tended to be between competing interests in support of imperialism and to focus on strategies and practices. Following the Great War, discussion turned to the very different matter of whether Europe should, or could, continue to rule most of the world.

Different points of view concerning the largest and most established overseas empire, that of Great Britain, are represented in this reader by three short texts. Edward Dicey (1832–1911), a journalist and writer, edited the London *Observer,* Britain's oldest national Sunday paper, in the 1870s and 1880s. Richard Burton (1821–1890) was one of the most celebrated travelers and writers in the nineteenth century. Fluent in over twenty languages, well-read in history and ethnography, and audacious, Burton wrote lengthy accounts of the peoples he visited and places he saw on his travels. The two-volume *Personal Narrative of a Pilgrimage to Al-Madinah and Meccah* (1855), for example, recounts his pilgrimage to Mecca disguised as a Moslem and contains extensive ethnographic and political information seldom accessible to Europeans. Though a supporter of imperialism, Burton was often very critical of Britain's colonial policy abroad, particularly when he saw it as the doing of politicians ill-informed about local cultures. Gertrude Bell (1868–1926), a graduate of Oxford and amateur archaeologist, traveled extensively in Persia, Syria, Iraq, and Arabia. *The Desert and the Sown* is an extensive account, with photographs, of her long journey into Syria in the last years of Ottoman rule. During the Great War, Bell worked for the British administration in Basra, advising on imperial policy in the region and helping to further British-Arab relations in anticipation of the division of the Ottoman Empire at the end of the war.

KARL MARX

Preface *to* Toward a Critique of Political Economy (1859)

I examine the system of bourgeois economy in the following order: *capital, landed property, wage-labour; the State, foreign trade, world market.* The economic conditions of existence of the three great classes into which modern bourgeois society is divided are analysed under the first three headings; the interconnection of the other three headings is self-evident. The first part of the first book, dealing with Capital, comprises the following chapters: 1. The commodity; 2. Money or simple circulation; 3. Capital in general. The present part consists of the first two chapters. The entire material lies before me in the form of monographs, which were written not for publication but for self-clarification at widely separated periods; their remoulding into an integrated whole according to the plan I have indicated will depend upon circumstances.

A general introduction, which I had drafted, is omitted, since on further consideration it seems to me confusing to anticipate results which still have to be substantiated, and the reader who really wishes to follow me will have to decide to advance from the particular to the general. A few brief remarks regarding the course of my study of political economy may, however, be appropriate here.

Although I studied jurisprudence, I pursued it as a subject subordinated to philosophy and history. In the year 1842–43, as editor of the *Rheinische Zeitung,* I first found myself in the embarrassing position of having to discuss what is known as material interests. The deliberations of the Rhenish Landtag on forest thefts and the division of landed property; the official polemic started by Herr von Schaper, then Oberpräsident of the Rhine Province, against the *Rheinische Zeitung* about the condition of the Moselle peasantry, and finally the debates on free trade and protective tariffs caused me in the first instance to turn my attention to economic questions. On the other hand, at that time when good intentions "to push forward" often took the place of factual knowledge, an echo of French socialism and communism, slightly tinged by philosophy, was noticeable in the *Rheinische Zeitung.* I objected to this dilettantism, but at the same time frankly admitted in a controversy with the *Allgemeine Augsburger Zeitung* that my previous studies did not allow me to express any opinion on the content of the French theories. When the publishers of the *Rheinische Zeitung* conceived the illusion that by a more compliant policy on the part of the paper it might be possible to secure the abrogation of the death sentence passed upon it, I eagerly grasped the opportunity to withdraw from the public stage to my study.

The first work which I undertook to dispel the doubts assailing me was a critical re-examination of the Hegelian philosophy of law; the introduction to this work being published in the *Deutsch-Französische Jahrbücher* issued in Paris in 1844. My inquiry led me to the conclusion that neither legal relations nor political forms could be comprehended whether by themselves or on the basis of a so-called general development of the human mind, but that on the contrary they originate in the material conditions of life, the totality of which Hegel, following the example of English and French thinkers of the eighteenth century, embraces within the term "civil society"; that the anatomy of this civil society, however, has to be sought in political economy. The study of this, which I began in Paris, I continued in Brussels, where I moved owing to an expulsion order issued by M. Guizot. The general conclusion at which I arrived and which, once reached, became the guiding principle of my studies can be summarised as follows. In the social production of their existence, men inevitably enter into definite relations, which are independent of their will, namely relations of production appropriate to a given stage in the development of their material forces of production. The totality of these relations of production constitutes the economic structure of society, the real foundation, on which arises a legal and political superstructure and to which correspond definite forms of social consciousness. The mode of production of material life conditions the general process of social, political and intellectual life. It is not the consciousness of men that determines their existence, but their social existence that determines their consciousness. At a certain stage of development, the material productive forces of society come into conflict with the existing relations of production or—this merely expresses the same thing in legal terms—with the property relations within the framework of which they have operated hitherto. From forms of development of the productive forces these relations turn into their fetters. Then begins an era of social revolution. The changes in the economic foundation lead sooner or later to the transformation of the whole immense superstructure. In studying such transformations it is always necessary to distinguish between the material transformation of the economic conditions of production, which can be determined with the precision of natural science, and the legal, political, religious, artistic or philosophic—in short, ideological forms in which men become conscious of this conflict and fight it out. Just as one does not judge an individual by what he thinks about himself, so one cannot judge such a period of transformation by its consciousness, but, on the contrary, this consciousness must be explained from the contradictions of material life, from the conflict existing between the social forces of production and the relations of production. No social order is ever destroyed before all the productive forces for which it is sufficient have been developed, and new superior relations of production never replace older ones before the material conditions for their existence have matured within the framework of the old society. Mankind thus inevitably sets itself only such tasks as it is able to solve, since closer examination will always show that the problem itself arises only when the material conditions for its solution are already present or at least in the course of formation. In broad outline, the Asiatic, ancient, feudal and modern bourgeois modes of production may be designated as epochs marking progress in the economic development of society. The bourgeois mode of production is the last antagonistic form of the social process of production—antagonistic not in the sense of individual antagonism but of an antagonism that emanates from the individuals' social conditions of existence—but the productive forces developing within bourgeois society create also the material conditions for a solution of this antagonism. The prehistory of human society accordingly closes with this social formation.

Frederick Engels, with whom I maintained a constant exchange of ideas by correspondence since the publication of his brilliant essay on the critique of economic categories (printed in the *Deutsch-Französische Jahrbücher*), arrived by another road (compare his *Lage der arbeitenden Klasse in England*) at the same result as I, and when in the spring of 1845 he too came to live in Brussels, we decided to set forth together our conception as opposed to the ideological one of German philosophy, in fact to settle accounts with our former philosophical conscience. The intention was carried out in the form of a critique of post-Hegelian philosophy. The manuscript, two large octavo volumes, had long ago reached the publishers in Westphalia when we were informed that owing to changed circumstances it could not be printed. We abandoned the manuscript to the gnawing criticism of the mice all the more willingly since we had achieved our main purpose—self-clarification. Of the scattered works in which at that time we presented one or another aspect of our views to the public, I shall mention only the *Manifesto of the Communist Party*, jointly written by Engels and myself, and a *Discours sur le libre échange*, which I myself published. The salient points of our conception were first outlined in an academic, although polemical, form in my *Misère de la philosophie . . .* , this book which was aimed at Proudnon appeared in 1847. The publication of an essay on *Wage-Labour* written in German in which I combined the lectures I had held on this subject at the German Workers' Association in Brussels, was interrupted by the February Revolution and my forcible removal from Belgium in consequence.

The publication of the *Neue Rheinische Zeitung* in 1848 and 1849 and subsequent events cut short my economic studies, which I could only resume in London in 1850. The enormous amount of material relating to the history of political economy assembled in the British Museum, the fact that London is a convenient vantage point for the observation of bourgeois society, and finally the new stage of development which this society seemed to have entered with the discovery of gold in California and Australia, induced me to start again from the very beginning and to work carefully through the new material. These studies led partly of their own accord to apparently quite remote subjects on which I had to spend a certain amount of time. But it was in particular the imperative necessity of earning my living which reduced the time at my disposal. My collaboration, continued now for eight years, with the *New York Tribune*, the leading Anglo-American newspaper, necessitated an excessive fragmentation of my studies, for I wrote only exceptionally newspaper correspondence in the strict sense. Since a considerable part of my contributions consisted of articles dealing with important economic events in Britain and on the Continent, I was compelled to become conversant with practical detail which, strictly speaking, lie outside the sphere of political economy.

This sketch of the course of my studies in the domain of political economy is intended merely to show that my views—no matter how they may be judged and how little they conform to the interested prejudices of the ruling classes—are the outcome of conscientious research carried on over many years. At the entrance to science, as at the entrance to hell, the demand must be made:

Qui si convien lasciare ogni sospetto
Ogni viltà convien che qui sia morta.
Karl Marx

Charles Darwin

from The Origin of Species (1859)
from The Descent of Man (1871)

from the Origin of Species

. . . Nothing is easier than to admit in words the truth of the universal struggle for life, or more difficult—at least I have found it so—than constantly to bear this conclusion in mind. Yet, unless it be thoroughly engrained in the mind, the whole economy of nature, with every fact on distribution, rarity, abundance, extinction, and variation, will be dimly seen or quite misunderstood. We behold the face of nature bright with gladness, we often see superabundance of food; we do not see or we forget, that the birds which are idly singing round us mostly live on insects or seeds, and are thus constantly destroying life; or we forget how largely these songsters, or their eggs, or their nestlings, are destroyed by birds and beasts of prey; we do not always bear in mind, that, though food may be now super-abundant, it is not so at all seasons of each recurring year. . . .

A struggle for existence inevitably follows from the high rate at which all organic beings tend to increase. Every being, which during its natural lifetime produces several eggs or seeds, must suffer destruction during some period of its life, and during some season or occasional year, otherwise, on the principle of geometrical increase, its numbers would quickly become so inordinately great that no country could support the product. Hence, as more individuals are produced than can possibly survive, there must in every case be a struggle for existence, either one individual with another of the same species, or with the individuals of distinct species, or with the physical conditions of life. It is the doctrine of Malthus applied with manifold force to the whole animal and vegetable kingdoms; for in this case there can be no artificial increase of food, and no prudential restraint from marriage. Although some species may be now increasing, more or less rapidly, in numbers, all cannot do so, for the world would not hold them.

There is no exception to the rule that every organic being naturally increases at so high a rate that, if not destroyed, the earth would soon be covered by the progeny of a single pair. Even slow-breeding man has doubled in twenty-five years, and at this rate, in less than a thousand years, there would literally not be standing-room for his progeny. Linnaeus has calculated that if an annual plant produced only two seeds—and there is no plant so unproductive as this—and their seedlings next year produced two, and so on, then in twenty years there would be a million plants. The elephant is reckoned the slowest breeder of all known animals, and I have taken some pains to estimate its probable minimum rate of natural increase; it will be safest to assume that it begins breeding when thirty years old, and goes on breeding till ninety years old, bringing forth six young in the interval, and surviving until one hundred years old; if this be so, after a period of from 740 to 750 years there would be nearly nineteen million elephants alive, descended from the first pair.

But we have better evidence on this subject than mere theoretical calculations, namely, the numerous recorded cases of the astonishingly rapid increase of various animals in a state of nature, when circumstances have been favourable to them during two or three following seasons. Still more striking is the evidence from our domestic animals of many kinds which have run wild in several parts of the world; if the statements of the rate of increase of slow-breeding cattle and horses in South America, and latterly in Australia, had not been well authenticated, they would have been incredible. So it is with plants; cases could be given of introduced plants which have become common throughout whole islands in a period of less than ten years. Several of the plants, such as the cardoon and a tall thistle, which are now the commonest over the wide plains of La Plata, clothing square leagues of surface almost to the exclusion of every other plant, have been introduced from Europe; and there are plants which now range in India, as I hear from Dr. Falconer, from Cape Comorin to the Himalaya, which have been imported from America since its discovery. In such cases, and endless others could be given, no one supposes, that the fertility of animals or plants has been suddenly and temporarily increased in any sensible degree. The obvious explanation is that the conditions of life have been highly favourable, and that there has consequently been less destruction of the old and young, and that nearly all the young have been enabled to breed. Their geometrical ratio of increase, the result of which never fails to be surprising, simply explains their extraordinarily rapid increase and wide diffusion in their new homes.

In a state of nature almost every full-grown plant annually produces seeds, and amongst animals there are very few which do not annually pair. Hence we may confidently assert, that all plants and animals are tending to increase at a geometrical ratio,—that all would rapidly stock every station in which they could anyhow exist—and that this geometrical tendency to increase must be checked by destruction at some period of life. Our familiarity with the larger domestic animals tends, I think, to mislead us: we see no great destruction falling on them, but we do not keep in mind that thousands are annually slaughtered for food, and that in a state of nature an equal number would have somehow to be disposed of.

The only difference between organisms which annually produce eggs or seeds by the thousand, and those which produce extremely few, is, that the slow-breeders would re-quire a few more years to people, under favourable conditions, a whole district, let it be ever so large. The condor lays a couple of eggs and the ostrich a score, and yet in the same country the condor may be the more numerous of the two; the Fulmar petrel lays but one egg, yet it is believed to be the most numerous bird in the world. One fly deposits hun-dreds of eggs, and another, like the hippobosca, a single one; but this difference does not determine how many individuals of the two species can be supported in a district. A large number of eggs is of some importance to those species which depend on a fluctuating amount of food, for it allows them rapidly to increase in number. But the real importance of a large number of eggs or seeds is to make up for much destruction at some period of life; and this period in the great majority of cases is an early one. If an animal can in any way protect its own eggs or young, a small number may be produced, and yet the average stock be fully kept up; but if many eggs or young are destroyed, many must be produced, or the species will become extinct. It would suffice to keep up the full number of a tree, which lived on an average for a thousand years, if a single seed were produced once in a thousand years, supposing that this seed were never destroyed, and could be ensured to germinate in a fitting place. So that, in all cases, the average number of any animal or plant depends only indirectly on the number of its eggs or seeds.

In looking at Nature, it is most necessary to keep the foregoing considerations always in mind—never to forget that every single organic being may be said to be striving to the utmost to increase in numbers; that each lives by a struggle at some period of its life; that heavy destruction inevitably falls either on the young or old, during each generation or at recurrent intervals. Lighten any check, mitigate the destruction ever so little, and the number of the species will almost instantaneously increase to any amount.

The causes which check the natural tendency of each species to increase are most obscure. Look at the most vigorous species; by as much as it swarms in numbers, by so much will it tend to increase still further. We know not exactly what the checks are even in a single instance. Nor will this surprise any one who reflects how ignorant we are on this head, even in regard to mankind, although so incomparably better known than any other animal. This subject of the checks to increase has been ably treated by several authors, and I hope in a future work to discuss it at considerable length, more especially in regard to the feral animals of South America. Here I will make only a few remarks, just to recall to the reader's mind some of the chief points. Eggs or very young animals seem generally to suffer most, but this is not invariably the case. With plants there is a vast destruction of seeds, but, from some observations which I have made it appears that the seedlings suffer most from germinating in ground already thickly stocked with other plants. Seedlings, also, are destroyed in vast numbers by various enemies; for instance, on a piece of ground three feet long and two wide, dug and cleared, and where there could be no choking from other plants, I marked all the seedlings of our native weeds as they came up, and out of 357 no less than 295 were destroyed, chiefly by slugs and insects. If turf which has long been mown, and the case would be the same with turf closely browsed by quadrupeds, be let to grow, the more vigorous plants gradually kill the less vigorous, though fully grown plants; thus out of twenty species growing on a little plot of mown turf (three feet by four) nine species perished, from the other species being allowed to grow up freely.

The amount of food for each species of course gives the extreme limit to which each can increase; but very frequently it is not the obtaining food, but the serving as prey to other animals, which determines the average number of species. Thus, there seems to be little doubt that the stock of partridges, grouse, and hares on any large estate depends chiefly on the destruction of vermin. If not one head of game were shot during the next twenty years in England, and, at the same time, if no vermin were destroyed, there would, in all probability, be less game than at present, although hundreds of thousands of game animals are now annually shot. On the other hand, in some cases, as with the elephant, none are destroyed by beasts of prey; for even the tiger in India most rarely dares to attack a young elephant protected by its dam. . . .

Many cases are on record showing how complex and unexpected are the checks and relations between organic beings, which have to struggle together in the same country. . . .

[I give an] instance showing how plants and animals, remote in the scale of nature, are bound together by a web of complex relations. I shall hereafter have occasion to show that the exotic Lobelia fulgens is never visited in my garden by insects, and consequently, from its peculiar structure, never sets a seed. Nearly all our orchidaceous plants absolutely require the visits of insects to remove their pollen-masses and thus to fertilise them. I find from experiments that humble-bees are almost indispensable to the fertilisation of the heartsease (Violo tricolor), for other bees do not visit this flower. I have also found that the visits of bees are necessary for the fertilisation of some kinds of clover; for instance, 20 heads of Dutch clover (Trifolium repens) yielded 2,290 seeds, but 20 other heads protected from bees produced not one. Again, 100 heads of red clover (T. pratense) produced 2,700 seeds, but the same number of protected heads produced not a single seed. Humble-bees alone visit red clover, as other bees cannot reach the nectar. It has been suggested that moths may fertilise the clovers; but I doubt whether they could do so in the case of the red clover, from their weight not being sufficient to depress the wing petals. Hence we may infer as highly probable that, if the whole genus of humble-bees became extinct or very rare in England, the heartsease and red clover would become very rare, or wholly disappear. The number of humble-bees in any district depends in a great measure upon the number of field-mice, which destroy their combs and nests; and Col. Newman, who has long attended to the habits of humble-bees, believes that "more than two-thirds of them are thus destroyed all over England." Now the number of mice is largely dependent, as every one knows, on the number of cats; and Col. Newman says, "Near villages and small towns I have found the nests of humble-bees more numerous than elsewhere, which I attribute to the number of cats that destroy the mice." Hence it is quite credible that the presence of a feline animal in large numbers in a district might determine, through the intervention first of mice and then of bees, the frequency of certain flowers in that district! . . .

If under changing conditions of life organic beings present individual differences in almost every part of their structure, and this cannot be disputed; if there be, owing to their geometrical rate of increase, a severe struggle for life at some age, season, or year, and this certainly cannot be disputed; then, considering the infinite complexity of the relations of all organic beings to each other and to their conditions of life, causing an infinite diversity in structure, constitution, and habits, to be advantageous to them, it would be a most extraordinary fact if no variations had ever occurred useful to each being's own welfare, in the same manner as so many variations have occurred useful to man. But if variations useful to any organic being ever do occur, assuredly individuals thus characterised will have the best chance of being preserved in the struggle for life; and from the strong principle of inheritance, these will tend to produce offspring similarly characterised. This principle of preservation, or the survival of the fittest, I have called Natural Selection. It leads to the improvement of each creature in relation to its organic and inorganic conditions of life; and consequently, in most cases, to what must be regarded as an advance in organisation. Nevertheless, low and simple forms will long endure if well fitted for their simple conditions of life.

Natural selection, on the principle of qualities being inherited at corresponding ages, can modify the egg, seed, or young, as easily as the adult. Amongst many animals, sexual selection will have given its aid to ordinary selection, by assuring to the most vigorous and best adapted males the greatest number of offspring. Sexual selection will also give characters useful to the males alone, in their struggles or rivalry with other males; and these characters will be transmitted to one sex or to both sexes, according to the form of inheritance which prevails.

Whether natural selection has really thus acted in adapting the various forms of life to their several conditions and stations, must be judged by the general tenor and balance of evidence given in the following chapters. But we have already seen how it entails extinction; and how largely extinction has acted in the world's history, geology plainly declares. Natural selection, also, leads to divergence of character; for the more organic beings diverge in structure, habits, and constitution, by so much the more can a large number be supported on the area—of which we see proof by looking to the inhabitants of any small spot, and to the productions naturalised in foreign lands. Therefore, during the modification of the descendants of any one species, and during the incessant struggle of all species to increase in numbers, the more diversified the descendants become, the better will be their chance of success in the battle for life. Thus the small differences distinguishing varieties of the same species, steadily tend to increase, till they equal the greater differences between species of the same genus, or even of distinct genera.

We have seen that it is the common, the widely-diffused and widely-ranging species, belonging to the larger genera within each class, which vary most; and these tend to transmit to their modified offspring that superiority which now makes them dominant in their own countries. Natural selection, as has just been remarked, leads to divergence of character and to much extinction of the less improved and intermediate forms of life. On these principles, the nature of the affinities, and the generally well-defined distinctions between the innumerable organic beings in each class throughout the world, may be explained. It is a truly wonderful fact—the wonder of which we are apt to overlook from familiarity—that all animals and all plants throughout all time and space should be related to each other in groups, subordinate to groups, in the manner which we everywhere behold—namely, varieties of the same species most closely related, species of the same genus less closely and unequally related, forming sections and subgenera, species of distinct genera much less closely related, and genera related in different degrees, forming subfamilies, families, orders, subclasses and classes. The several subordinate groups in any class cannot be ranked in a single file, but seem clustered round points, and these round other points, and so on in almost endless cycles. If species had been independently created, no explanation would have been possible of this kind of classification; but it is explained through inheritance and the complex action of natural selection, entailing extinction and divergence of character. . . .

The affinities of all the beings of the same class have sometimes been represented by a great tree. I believe this simile largely speaks the truth. The green and budding twigs may represent existing species; and those produced during former years may represent the long succession of extinct species. At each period of growth all the growing twigs have tried to branch out on all sides, and to overtop and kill the surrounding twigs and branches, in the same manner as species and groups of species have at all times overmastered other species in the great battle for life. The limbs divided into great branches, and these into lesser and lesser branches, were themselves once, when the tree was young, budding twigs; and this connection of the former and present buds by ramifying branches may well represent the classification of all extinct and living species in groups subordinate to groups. Of the many twigs which flourished when the tree was a mere bush, only two or three, now grown into great branches, yet survive and bear the other branches; so with the species which lived during long-past geological periods, very few have left living and modified descendants. From the first growth of the tree, many a limb and branch has decayed and dropped off; and these fallen branches of various sizes may represent those whole orders, families, and genera which have now no living representatives, and which are known to us only in a fossil state. As we here and there see a thin straggling branch springing from a fork low down in a tree, and which by some chance has been favoured and is still alive on its summit, so we occasionally see an animal like the Ornithorhynchus or Lepidosiren, which in some small degree connects by its affinities two large branches of life, and which has apparently been saved from fatal competition by having inhabited a protected station. As buds give rise by growth to fresh buds, and these, if vigorous, branch out and overtop on all sides many a feebler branch, so by generation I believe it has been with the Great Tree of Life, which fills with its dead and broken branches the crust of the earth, and covers the surface with its everbranching and beautiful ramifications. . . .

from The Descent of Man

Chapter XXI
General Summary and Conclusion

. . . The main conclusion arrived at in this work, and now held by many naturalists who are well competent to form a sound judgment, is that man is descended from some less highly-organized form. The grounds upon which this conclusion rests will never be shaken, for the close similarity between man and the lower animals in embryonic development, as well as in innumerable points of structure and constitution, both of high, and of the most trifling importance—the rudiments which he retains, and the abnormal reversions to which he is occasionally liable—are facts which cannot be disputed. They have long been known, but until recently they told us nothing with respect to the origin of man. Now, when viewed by the light of our knowledge of the whole organic world, their meaning is unmistakable. The great principle of evolution stands up clear and firm, when these groups of facts are considered in connection with others, such as the mutual affinities of the members of the same group, their geographical distribution in past and present times, and their geological succession. It is incredible that all these facts should speak falsely. He who is not content to look, like a savage, at the phenomena of Nature as disconnected, cannot any longer believe that man is the work of a separate act of creation. He will be forced to admit that the close resemblance of the embryo of man to that, for instance, of a dog—the construction of his skull, limbs, and whole frame, independently of the uses to which the parts may be put, on the same plan with that of other mammals—the occasional reappearance of various structures, for instance, of several distinct muscles, which man does not normally possess, but which are common to the Quadrumana—and a crowd of analogous facts—all point in the plainest manner to the conclusion that man is the co-descendant with other mammals of a common progenitor.

[This] conclusion . . . that man is descended from some lowly-organized form, will, I regret to think, be highly distasteful to many persons. But there can hardly be a doubt that we are descended from barbarians. The astonishment which I felt on first seeing a party of Fuegians on a wild and broken shore will never be forgotten by me, for the reflection at once rushed into my mind—such were our ancestors. These men were absolutely naked and bedaubed with paint, their long hair was tangled, their mouths frothed with excitement, and their expression was wild, startled, and distrustful. They possessed hardly any arts, and, like wild animals, lived on what they could catch; they had no government, and were merciless to every one not of their own small tribe. He who has seen a savage in his native land will not feel much shame, if forced to acknowledge that the blood of some more humble creature flows in his veins. For my own part, I would as soon be descended from that heroic little monkey, who braved his dreaded enemy in order to save the life of his keeper; or from that old baboon, who, descending from the mountains, carried away in triumph his young comrade from a crowd of astonished dogs—as from a savage who delights to torture his enemies, offers up bloody sacrifices, practises infanticide without remorse, treats his wives like slaves, knows no decency, and is haunted by the grossest superstitions.

Man may be excused for feeling some pride at having risen, though not through his own exertions, to the very summit of the organic scale; and the fact of his having thus risen, instead of having been aboriginally placed there, may give him hopes for a still higher destiny in the distant future. But we are not here concerned with hopes or fears, only with the truth as far as our reason allows us to discover it. I have given the evidence to the best of my ability; and we must acknowledge, as it seems to me, that man with all his noble qualities, with sympathy which feels for the most debased, with benevolence which extends not only to other men but to the humblest living creature, with his godlike intellect which has penetrated into the movements and constitution of the solar system—with all these exalted powers—Man still bears in his bodily frame the indelible stamp of his lowly origin.

Edward Dicey

from Mr. Gladstone and Our Empire (1877)

It does not logically follow that because a politician objects to any further extension of our Empire he should therefore be in favour of its dismemberment. But if once this country comes to the conclusion that we have had enough of empire, and that we should do wisely to reduce our Imperial liabilities as soon as we can do so consistently with the moral obligations we have undertaken, then the days of our rule as a great Power beyond the four seas are clearly numbered. Englishmen who live out their lives in these small islands, who give the best of their labour to the questions, conflicts, issues of our insular existence, are apt to forget what England is in truth. Take up any gazeteer and you will find there what every schoolboy is supposed to know, but what to scores of Englishmen out of every hundred will read like a new discovery, the dimensions of the Empire of Great Britain. The United Kingdom, with an area of 120,000 square miles and a population of thirty-three millions, rules over eight million square miles of the globe's surface and two hundred millions of the world's inhabitants. Open any map, and glance for one moment at the dominions in which the Union Jack is the standard of the ruling race! Canada, stretching from the Atlantic to the Pacific, the peninsula of India, the continent of Australia, the South of Africa, are only the largest blotches so to speak, in a world chart blurred and dotted over with the stamp marks of British rule. Spread-eagle declamation about the Empire over which the sun never sets is not in accordance with the taste of our day, or the tone of thought which prevails amidst our governing classes. Facts and not fancies are the cry of the age. But it is well to remember that, after all, the existence of the British Empire is a fact and not a fancy. . . . Wherever the Union Jack floats, there the English race rules; English laws prevail; English ideas are dominant: English speech holds the upper hand. Our Empire may or may not be a benefit to England or to the countries over which she holds dominion; but its reality is as certain as its magnitude. . . . All I do assert is that England, like Rome, is the corner-stone of an imperial fabric such as it has fallen to the lot of no other country to erect, or to uphold when erected. This being so—and that it is so even the most fanatical of anti-imperialists will admit—the burden of proof surely rests with those who would pull down this Greater Britain, or allow it to fall to pieces, not with those who would consolidate or, if need be, extend the inheritance handed down to us by the labour, self-sacrifice, and courage of bygone generations of Englishmen.

The general issue of Empire or no Empire is not affected by considerations as to individual augmentations or cessions of territory. I may admit, as a matter of argument, that

England gained, rather than lost, by the secession of her American colonies; that the cession of the Ionian Islands was a wise measure and the annexation of Fiji an unwise one. I may even acknowledge that the secession of Canada from the mother country is an event to be looked forward to without regret. Personally I should dissent from most of these conclusions but, even if I accepted them, I should see no cause to alter my view, that the maintenance of the Empire—that is of British authority over a vast outlying territory— ought to be one of the chief, if not the chief, object of British statesmanship. . . . What I want to point out is that our Empire is the result not so much of any military spirit as of a certain instinct of development inherent in our race. We have in us the blood of the Vikings; and the same impulse which sent the Norsemen forth to seek new homes in strange lands has, for century after century, impelled their descendants to wander forth in search of wealth, power, or adventure. 'To be fruitful, and multiply, and replenish the earth', seems to be the mission entrusted to us, as it was to the survivors of the deluge. The Wandering Jew of nations, it is forbidden to us to rest. The history of all our conquests, settlements, annexations, is, with rare exceptions, substantially the same. Attracted by the hope of gain, the love of excitement, or, more still, by the mere migratory instinct, English settlers pitch their tents in some foreign land, and obtain a footing in the country. But, unlike the colonists of other races, they carry England with them; they keep their own tongue, marry amidst their own people; dwell after their own fashion, and, though they may live and die in the land of their adoption, look to the mother country as their home. As their footing becomes established their interests clash with those of the native population. Whether with or without due cause, quarrels ensue; and then, sometimes by their own energy, sometimes by the aid of England, sometimes by both combined, they establish their own supremacy and become the ruling race in the regions which they entered as traders . . . [T]he point I wish to have placed in a clear light is that our Empire is due, not to the ambition of kings, not to the genius of generals, not even to the prevalence of one of those phases of military ardour through which most nations have to pass, but to the silent, constant operation of the instincts, laudable or otherwise, which have filled the world with the sound of the English tongue.

RICHARD BURTON

from Two Trips to Gorilla Land (1876)

After a languid conviction during the last half-century of owning some ground upon the West Coast of Africa, England has been rudely aroused by a little war which will have large consequences. The causes that led to the 'Ashantee Campaign' . . . may be broadly laid down as general incuriousness, local mismanagement, and the operation of unprincipled journalism.

It is not a little amusing to hear the complaints of the public that plain truth about the African has not been told. I could cite more than one name that has done so. But what was the result? We were all soundly abused by the negrophile; the multitude cared little about reading 'unpopular opinions'; and then, when the fullness of time came, it turned upon us, and rent us, and asked why we had not spoken freely concerning Ashanti and Fanti, and all the herd. My *Wanderings in West Africa* is a case in point: so little has it been read, that a President of the Royal Geographical Society could state, "If Fantees are cowardly and lazy, Krumen are brave"; the latter being the most notorious poltroons on the West African seaboard.

The hostilities on the Gold Coast might have been averted with honour to ourselves at any time between 1863 and 1870, by a Colonial Office mission and a couple of thousand pounds. I need hardly say what has been the case now. The first steps were taken with needless disasters, and the effect has been far different from what we intended or what was advisable. For a score of years we [travellers] have been advising the English statesman not to despise the cunning of barbarous tribes, never to attempt finessing with Asiatic or African; to treat these races with perfect sincerity and truthfulness. I have insisted, and it is now seen with what reason, that every attempt at deception, at asserting the 'thing which is not', will presently meet with the reward it deserves. I can only regret that my counsels have not made themselves heard.

Yet this ignoble war between barbarous tribes whom it has long been the fashion to pet, this poor scuffle between the breechloader and the Birmingham trade musket, may yet in one sense do good. It must perforce draw public attention to the West Coast of Africa, and raise the question, 'What shall we do with it?' My humble opinion, expressed early in 1865 to the Right Honourable Mr. Adderley, has ever been this. If we are determined not to follow the example of the French, the Dutch, the Portuguese, and the Spaniard, and not to use the country as a convict station, resolving to consume, as it were, our crime at home, we should also resolve to retain only a few ports and forts, without territory, at points commanding commerce, after the fashion of Lusitanians in the old heroic days. The export slave-trade is now dead and buried; the want of demand must prevent its revival; and free emigration has yet to be created. As Mr. Bright rightly teaches strong places and garrisons are not necessary to foster trade and to promote the success of missions. The best proof on the West African Coast is to be found in the so-called Oil Rivers, where we have never held a mile of ground, and where our commerce prospers most. The great 'Tribune' will forgive my agreeing in opinion with him when he finds that we differ upon one most important point. It is the merchant, not the garrison, that causes African wars. If the home authorities would avoid a campaign, let them commit their difficulty to a soldier, not to a civilian.

The chronic discontent of the so-called 'civilized' Africa, the contempt of the rulers if not of the rule, and the bitter hatred between the three races, white, black, and black-white, fomented by many an unprincipled print, which fills its pocket with coin of cant and Christian charity, will end in even greater scandals than the last disreputable war. If the *damnosa licentia* be not suppressed—and where are the strong hands to suppress it?—we may expect to see the scenes of Jamaica revived with improvements at Sierra Leone. However unwilling I am to cut off any part of our great and extended empire, to renew anywhere, even in Africa, the process of dismemberment . . . it is evident to me that English occupation of the West African Coast has but slightly forwarded the cause of humanity, and that upon the whole it has proved a remarkable failure.

GERTRUDE BELL

from The Desert and the Sown (1907)

Preface

Those who venture to add a new volume to the vast literature of travel, unless they be men of learning or politicians, must be prepared with an excuse. My excuse is ready, as specious and I hope as plausible as such things should be. I desired to write not so much a book of travel as an account of the people whom I met or who accompanied me on my way, and to show what the world is like in which they live and how it appears to them. And since it was better that they should, as far as possible, tell their own tale, I have strung their words upon the thread of the road, relating as I heard them the stories with which shepherd and man-at-arms beguiled the hours of the march, the talk that passed from lip to lip round the camp-fire, in the black tent of the Arab and the guest-chamber of the Druze, as well as the more cautious utterances of Turkish and Syrian officials. Their statecraft consists of guesses, often shrewd enough, at the results that may spring from the clash of unknown forces, of which the strength and the aim are but dimly apprehended; their wisdom is that of men whose channels of information and standards for comparison are different from ours, and who bring a different set of preconceptions to bear upon the problems laid before them. The Oriental is like a very old child. He is unacquainted with many branches of knowledge which we have come to regard as of elementary necessity; frequently, but not always, his mind is little preoccupied with the need of acquiring them, and he concerns himself scarcely at all with what we call practical utility. He is not practical in our acceptation of the word, any more than a child is practical, and his utility is not ours. On the other hand, his action is guided by traditions of conduct and morality that go back to the beginnings of civilisation, traditions unmodified as yet by any important change in the manner of life to which they apply and out of which they arose. These things apart, he is as we are; human nature does not undergo a complete change east of Suez, nor is it impossible to be on terms of friendship and sympathy with the dwellers in those regions. In some respects it is even easier than in Europe. You will find in the East habits of intercourse less fettered by artificial chains, and a wider tolerance born of greater diversity. Society is divided by caste and sect and tribe into an infinite number of groups, each one of which is following a law of its own, and however fantastic, to our thinking, that law may be, to the Oriental it is an ample and a satisfactory explanation of all peculiarities. A man may go about in public veiled up to the eyes, or clad if he please only in a girdle: he will excite no remark. Why should he? Like every one else he is merely obeying his own law. So too the European may pass up and down the wildest places, encountering little curiosity and of criticism even less. The news he brings will be heard with interest, his opinions will be listened to with attention, but he will not be thought odd or mad, nor even mistaken, because his practices and the ways of his thought are at variance with those of the people among whom he finds himself. "'Adat-hu:" it is his custom. And for this reason he will be the wiser if he does not seek to ingratiate himself with Orientals by trying to ape their habits, unless he is so skillful that he can pass as one of themselves. Let him treat the law of others respectfully, but he himself will meet with a far greater respect if he adheres strictly to his own. For a woman this rule is of the first importance, since a woman can never disguise herself effectually. That she should be known to come of a great and honoured stock, whose customs are inviolable, is her best claim to consideration.

None of the country through which I went is ground virgin to the traveller, though parts of it have been visited but seldom, and described only in works that are costly and often difficult to obtain. Of such places I have given a brief account, and as many photographs as seemed to be of value. I have also noted in the northern cities of Syria those vestiges of antiquity that catch the eye of a casual observer. There is still much exploration to be done in Syria and on the edge of the desert, and there are many difficult problems yet to be solved. The work has been well begun by de Vogüé, Wetzstein, Brünnow, Sachau, Dussaud, Puchstein and his colleagues, the members of the Princeton Expedition and others. To their books I refer those who would learn how immeasurably rich is the land in architectural monuments and in the epigraphic records of a far-reaching history.

My journey did not end at Alexandretta as this account ends. In Asia Minor I was, however, concerned mainly with archaeology; the results of what work I did there have been published in a series of papers in the *Revue Archeologique*, where, through the kindness of the editor, Monsieur Salomon Reinach, they have found a more suitable place than the pages of such a book as this could have offered them.

I do not know either the people or the language of Asia Minor well enough to come into anything like a close touch with the country, but I am prepared, even on a meagre acquaintance, to lay tokens of esteem at the feet of the Turkish peasant. He is gifted with many virtues, with the virtue of hospitality beyond all others.

I have been at some pains to relate the actual political conditions of unimportant persons. They do not appear so unimportant to one who is in their midst, and for my part I have always been grateful to those who have provided me with a clue to their relations with one another. But I am not concerned to justify or condemn the government of the Turk. I have lived long enough in Syria to realise that his rule is far from being the ideal of administration, and seen enough of the turbulent elements which he keeps more or less in order to know that his post is a difficult one. I do not believe that any government would give universal satisfaction; indeed, there are few which attain that desired end even in more united countries. Being English, I am persuaded that we are the people who could best have taken Syria in hand with the prospect of a success greater than that which might be attained by a moderately reasonable Sultan. We have long recognised that the task will not fall to us. We have unfortunately done more than this. Throughout the dominions of Turkey we have allowed a very great reputation to weaken and decline; reluctant to accept the responsibility of official interference, we have yet permitted the irresponsible protests, vehemently expressed, of a sentimentality that I make bold to qualify as ignorant, and our dealings with the Turk have thus presented an air of vacillation which he may be pardoned for considering perfidious and for regarding with animosity. These feelings, combined with the deep-seated dread of a great Asiatic Empire which is also mistress of Egypt and of the sea, have, I think, led the Porte to seize the first opportunity for open resistance to British demands, whether out of simple miscalculation of the spirit that would be aroused, or with the hope of foreign backing, it is immaterial to decide. The result is equally deplorable, and if I have gauged the matter at all correctly, the root of it lies in the disappearance of English influence at Constantinople. The position of authority that we occupied has been taken by another, yet it is and must be of far deeper importance to us than to any other that we should be able to guide when necessary the tortuous politics of Yildiz Kiosk. The greatest of all Mohammedan powers cannot afford to let her relations with the Khalif of Islam be regulated with so little consistency or firmness, and if the Sultan's obstinacy in the Tabah quarrel can prove to us how far the reins have slipped from our hands, it will have served its turn. Seated as we are upon the Mediterranean and having at our command, as I believe, a considerable amount of goodwill within the Turkish empire and the memories of an ancient friendship, it should not be impossible to recapture the place we have lost.

But these are matters outside the scope of the present book and my *apologia* had best end where every Oriental writer would have begun: "In the name of God, the Merciful, the Compassionate!"

from Chapter I

To those bred under an elaborate social order few such moments of exhilaration can come as that which stands at the threshold of wild travel. The gates of the enclosed garden are thrown open, the chain at the entrance of the sanctuary is lowered, with a wary glance to right and left you step forth, and, behold! the immeasurable world. The world of adventure and of enterprise, dark with hurrying storms, glittering in raw sunlight, an unanswered question and an unanswerable doubt hidden in the fold of every hill. Into it you must go alone, separated from the troops of friends that walk the rose alleys, stripped of the purple and fine linen that impede the fighting arm, roofless, defenceless, without possessions. The voice of the wind shall be heard instead of the persuasive voices of counsellors, the touch of the rain and the prick of the frost shall be spurs sharper than praise or blame, and necessity shall speak with an authority unknown to that borrowed wisdom which men obey or discard at will. So you leave the sheltered close, and, like the man in the fairy story, you feel the bands break that were riveted about your heart as you enter the path that stretches across the rounded shoulder of the earth.

VI. The Birth of the Modern and the First World War

In the late nineteenth and first half of the twentieth centuries, there was a second industrial revolution whose impact was greater and whose effects were more widespread than the first one a hundred years before. Germany and the United States displaced Britain as the most innovative and advanced industrial powers. The age of steam was supplanted by the age of electricity. The telephone, the phonograph, the bicycle, the cinema, the sewing machine, the airplane, the typewriter, and the automobile transformed the way that people lived their lives. Family-owned firms where working people often knew their owner-operators increasingly gave way to large, impersonal, bureaucratic, and hierarchical corporations. Production in the most modern factories took place on assembly lines, an unparalleled division of the labor process in which individual workers were trained in minute and repetitious tasks. They were the brainchild of the new field of scientific management or Taylorism (named after its founder F. W. Taylor). The second industrial revolution was not, however, simply economic. Taken together the advent of compulsory education, the extension of voting rights to the working class, and the revolution in mass communications transformed the nature of politics and culture. These changes were responsible for a vigorous mass culture aimed at ordinary working people. (In the late nineteenth century, daily newspapers first achieved circulations of more than a million copies per day.) And they brought about mass politics. On the one hand, existing political parties changed from being informal clubs of the moneyed and propertied classes to bureaucratic and hierarchical organizations that used mass communications to court its membership and appeal to the general public at elections. On the other hand, the working class emerged as an organized force in national politics—in labor and socialist parties and mass trade unions frequently comprising the unskilled workers of the second industrial revolution.

The intellectual and cultural response to this second transformation in the material life of European society is often referred to as 'modernism.' Its tone can be enthusiastic or disparaging, optimistic or gloomy. Some artists and writers viewed these changes as representing the intensification of the alienation of human beings from themselves and their environments. Others saw it as the triumph of a 'machine age'—a soulless society where individuals had become extensions of the machines that they had created. Two early modernist writers, who were influential voices in articulating this critical point of view, were the English poet Matthew Arnold and the German philosopher Friedrich Nietzsche (1844–

1900). Arnold (who already figured in the last section) and Nietzsche developed their ideas before the full development of the second industrial revolution took place: they are more properly described as precursors of modernism rather than examples of its full flowering. Arnold's poem "Dover Beach," often cited as one of the first modernist poems, explores the alienation of human beings from an indifferent nature and views the act of love as the only way of avoiding isolation. Nietzsche's parable "The Madman," from *The Gay Science, is* a deceptively simple story about the death of God. What does it mean to murder God? Does the fact that we have murdered God suggest that we have created a world in which the idea of God is no longer necessary? Is the act symbolic of our own spiritual impoverishment? In murdering God have we liberated or condemned ourselves? Why is it a madman who announces God's death?

Arnold and Nietzsche point to a crisis in meaning and values yet suggest that its resolution is potentially liberating. But there were others who had no such ambivalent feelings about the modern world. Just as there are computer junkies in our day who are wildly enthusiastic about cyberspace and the World Wide Web, there were those a hundred years ago who were equally rhapsodic about the machine age. For the poets and artists who comprised the Italian Futurists, the new world of machinery made everything obsolete, including all previous intellectual and artistic traditions that had come before. They viewed themselves as an *avant-garde*, a cutting-edge movement that was as revolutionary in its implications as the technological transformations that they worshipped. Taking their clues from the new mediums of time-lapse photography and the movies, they attempted to express in paintings and poetry a world of constant motion and speed. Filippo Tommaso Marinetti's (1876–1944) "Foundation and Manifesto of Futurism" is simultaneously a statement of Futurist principles and an appeal for others to join the crusade. In his manifesto, Marinetti pays tribute to the revolutionary power of speed as embodied in the automobile: "the love of danger, the habit of energy, and fearlessness" that it calls forth. Equally important, he uses language and imagery in a way that he believes is appropriate to a world which is constantly in flux.

One of the principles that Marinetti embraces in the "Futurist Manifesto" is the glorification of war, one of "the beautiful ideas worth dying for" and "the destructive gesture of freedom-bringers." Published in 1909, five years prior to the First World War (the Great War, as Europeans call it), Marinetti's praise of military combat reminds us of how eagerly many Europeans on both sides plunged into combat. Yet those who had hopes and dreams of performing heroic acts in the name of national honor were soon disappointed. They expected a short and limited war that would produce an early diplomatic settlement. What they got was one of the most devastating and far-reaching conflicts ever experienced: a "total war" that affected whole populations, was the first global conflict in human history, involved unparalleled technological sophistication, and was responsible for death and destruction on an unprecedented scale. Overall there were 37.5 million casualties, including 8.5 million dead. In Germany and France, the two nations that suffered the most, it seemed as if an entire generation of young men had been wiped out.

Two poets who reacted to the horrors of the war were the Englishman Wilfred Owen (1893–1918) and the Irishman William Butler Yeats (1865–1939). Owen served as an officer at the Battle of the Somme and, as a result of shell shock, was sent to an Edinburgh hospital to recover. He had already written poetry prior to the War, but his writing was transformed by his war experiences. His poetry gave expression to the continual nightmares that he endured during his recovery. The title, "Dulce Et Decorum Est," is a fragment from a sentence in Horace's *Odes:* "It is sweet and meet to die for one's country. Sweet! And decorous!" The poem itself explores the discrepancy between the language glorifying war and patriotism and the reality of what it is like to fight under modern conditions. Yeats, one of the most influential twentieth-century poets writing in English, views the war in broader terms than Owen. He is less concerned with the war as an event in itself than as a symbol of the collapse and fragmentation of European civilization. Yeats believes that the War represents the end of a historical cycle, but he is apprehensive about what will come next. He once wrote: "we may be about to accept the most implacable authority the world has known." In retrospect, such words seem like a prophesy of the authoritarian movements that came to dominate the politics of interwar Europe.

The final subject of this chapter is the position of women in European society. By the late nineteenth and early twentieth centuries, the idea that men should dominate the public world and women should confine themselves to the domestic sphere began to be challenged. Middle-class women began to enter the workplace as nurses, teachers, social workers, secretaries, and sales clerks. They were not only more visible in the world of business and the professions, but their status began to change also. Gradually, much sooner in some European nations than in others, they were able to own their own property, achieved the right to obtain a divorce, and began to enter higher education (the first women's colleges were established in the 1870s). At the beginning of the twentieth century, a women's suffrage movement challenged the political fabric of English society. Women, who had historically been portrayed as gentle, weak and passive creatures, embarked on a path of political militancy and violence to force an unyielding government to grant them the right to vote. Emmeline Pankhurst's Women's Social and Political Union led the fight for women's suffrage in England. The suffragette movement failed to budge the government, but it put the issue on the national agenda. It was the First World War, however, that dramatically altered women's status: women increasingly replaced men in the workplace, frequently in positions that conventional wisdom said women could never assume. The idea that women were incapable of exercising independent political judgment was dealt a serious blow. In England and Germany, women won the right to vote following the War; in other European nations they did not achieve that right until the Second World War, or later.

Though women's position in society began to change, and they attained rights that had been denied to them for centuries, women still faced numerous problems. They were paid significantly lower wages than men. They faced insurmountable barriers in gaining access to powerful and prestigious positions in society. Legal obstacles might have begun to disappear, but men still controlled the ideological landscape, thus ensuring that male dominance or 'patriarchy' remained secure. Rebecca West (1892–1983), Olive Schreiner (1855-1920), and Virginia Woolf (1882–1941) are three feminist writers who attacked the gender structures ensuring women's subservience. West, born Cicily Fairfield, took her pseudonym from a character that she played in an Ibsen play while she was still a teenager. Around the same time, she joined the militant suffragette group, the Social and Political Union. Though a supporter of Pankhurst, West was critical of her support of violent political action: not because West was a pacifist, but because she believed that it was not a useful political tool. West was a socialist-feminist who saw the women's liberation movement of her time as being engaged in the same struggle as the working class. In "Women and Wages," for instance, she views the exploitation of women and of workers as intrinsic to the capitalist mode of production. One reason, in her view, that the capitalist class pays women lower wages is that it keeps the exploited classes divided.

Where the selection from West's writing is mostly concerned with the economic and political exploitation of women, those drawn from Schreiner and Woolf have more to do with the more subtle forms of patriarchy. Schreiner lived for extended periods in both England and South Africa, the place of her birth, and became politically involved in both localities. She was a supporter of a multi-racial South Africa free of British imperial domination. Upon arriving in England in 1881, she became involved in the emerging feminist movement, and her book *Women and Labour* was referred to by suffragettes as their bible. "The Buddhist Priest's Wife" explores the invisible barriers that prevent women and men from having intimate and equal relations. It raises the question: do men who claim to want close relations with women who are their intellectual equals also want to marry them? The title itself underscores the dilemma: Buddhist priests do not have wives.

By the time that Virginia Woolf was writing the books that would make her one of the most important twentieth-century novelists, the majority of English women had won the right to vote. Many now thought that there was no longer a need for feminism. In *A Room of One's Own*, originally given as lectures at Newnham and Girton colleges, Cambridge University, Woolf reaffirms the continued importance of feminist thinking and suggests that there are more difficult fights for women ahead. At one level, the lectures are feminist explorations into why there have been so few important women writers. But they also offer a more general analysis of the inequality in gender relations. According to Woolf, men inflate their own self-image when they see women as being inferior: in their ascribed social role, women acted as distorting mirrors, reflecting the figure of men at twice their natural size. Woolf, Schreiner, and West expanded feminist thought by contributing to a general critique of gender roles in modern society.

MATTHEW ARNOLD
Dover Beach (1867)

The sea is calm to-night.
The tide is full, the moon lies fair
Upon the straits;—on the French coast the light
Gleams and is gone; the cliffs of England stand,
Glimmering and vast, out in the tranquil bay.
Come to the window, sweet is the night-air!
Only, from the long line of spray
Where the sea meets the moon-blanch'd land,
Listen! you hear the grating roar
Of pebbles which the waves draw back, and fling,
At their return, up the high strand,
Begin, and cease, and then again begin,
With tremulous cadence slow, and bring
The eternal note of sadness in.

Sophocles long ago
Heard it on the Ægæan, and it brought
Into his mind the turbid ebb and flow
Of human misery; we
Find also in the sound a thought,
Hearing it by this distant northern sea.

The Sea of Faith
Was once, too, at the full, and round earth's shore
Lay like the folds of a bright girdle furl'd.
But now I only hear
Its melancholy, long, withdrawing roar,
Retreating, to the breath
Of the night-wind, down the vast edges drear
And naked shingles of the world.

Ah, love, let us be true
To one another! for the world, which seems
To lie before us like a land of dreams,
So various, so beautiful, so new,
Hath really neither joy, nor love, nor light,
Nor certitude, nor peace, nor help for pain;
And we are here as on a darkling plain
Swept with confused alarms of struggle and flight,
Where ignorant armies clash by night.

FRIEDRICH NIETZSCHE

from The Gay Science (1882)

The Madman. Have you not heard of that madman who lit a lantern in the bright morning hours, ran to the market place, and cried incessantly, "I seek God! I seek God!" As many of those who do not believe in God were standing around just then, he provoked much laughter. Why, did he get lost? said one. Did he lose his way like a child? said another. Or is he hiding? Is he afraid of us? Has he gone on a voyage? or emigrated? Thus they yelled and laughed. The madman jumped into their midst and pierced them with his glances.

"Whither is God" he cried. "I shall tell you. *We have killed him*—you and I. All of us are his murderers. But how have we done this? How were we able to drink up the sea? Who gave us the sponge to wipe away the entire horizon? What did we do when we unchained this earth from its sun? Whither is it moving now? Whither are we moving now? Away from all suns? Are we not plunging continually? Backward, sideward, forward, in all directions? Is there any up or down left? Are we not straying as through an infinite nothing? Do we not feel the breath of empty space? Has it not become colder? Is not night and more night coming on all the while? Must not lanterns be lit in the morning? Do we not hear anything yet of the noise of the gravediggers who are burying God? Do we not smell anything yet of God's decomposition? Gods too decompose. God is dead. God remains dead. And we have killed him. How shall we, the murderers of all murderers, comfort ourselves? What was holiest and most powerful of all that the world has yet owned has bled to death under our knives. Who will wipe this blood off us? What water is there for us to clean ourselves? What festivals of atonement, what sacred games shall we have to invent? Is not the greatness of this deed too great for us? Must not we ourselves become gods simply to seem worthy of it? There has never been a greater deed; and whoever will be born after us—for the sake of this deed he will be part of a higher history than all history hitherto."

Here the madman fell silent and looked again at his listeners; and they too were silent and stared at him in astonishment. At last he threw his lantern on the ground, and it broke and went out. "I come too early," he said then; "my time has not come yet. This tremendous event is still on its way, still wandering—it has not yet reached the ears of man. Lightning and thunder require time, the light of the stars requires time, deeds require time even after they are done, before they can be seen and heard. This deed is still more distant from them than the most distant stars—*and yet they have done it themselves.*"

It has been related further that on that same day the madman entered divers churches and there sang his *requiem aeternam deo*. Led out and called to account, he is said to have replied each time, "What are these churches now if they are not the tombs and sepulchers of God?"

Filippo Tommaso Marinetti

The Foundation and Manifesto of Futurism (1909)

We had stayed up all night, my friends and I, under hanging mosque lamps with domes of filigreed brass, domes starred like our spirits, shining like them with the prisoned radiance of electric hearts. For hours we had trampled our atavistic ennui into rich oriental rugs, arguing up to the last confines of logic and blackening many reams of paper with our frenzied scribbling.

An immense pride was buoying us up, because we felt ourselves alone at that hour, alone, awake, and on our feet, like proud beacons or forward sentries against an army of hostile stars glaring down at us from their celestial encampments. Alone with stokers reeding the hellish fires of great ships, alone with the black spectres who grope in the red-hot bellies of locomotives launched down their crazy courses, alone with drunkards reeling like wounded birds along the city walls.

Suddenly we jumped, hearing the mighty noise of the huge double-decker trams that rumbled by outside, ablaze with coloured lights, like villages on holiday suddenly struck and uprooted by the flooding Po and dragged over falls and through gorges to the sea.

Then the silence deepened. But, as we listened to the old canal muttering its feeble prayers and the creaking bones of sickly palaces above their damp green beards, under the windows we suddenly heard the famished roar of automobiles.

'Let's go!' I said. 'Friends, away! Let's go! Mythology and the Mystic Ideal are defeated at last. We're about to see the Centaur's birth and, soon after, the first flight of Angels! . . . We must shake the gates of life, test the bolts and hinges. Let's go! Look there, on the earth, the very first dawn! There's nothing to match the splendour of the sun's red sword, slashing for the first time through our millennial gloom!'

We went up to the three snorting beasts, to lay amorous hands on their torrid breasts. I stretched out on my car like a corpse on its bier, but revived at once under the steering wheel, a guillotine blade that threatened my stomach.

The raging broom of madness swept us out of ourselves and drove us through streets as rough and deep as the beds of torrents. Here and there, sick lamplight through window glass taught us to distrust the deceitful mathematics of our perishing eyes.

I cried, 'The scent, the scent alone is enough for our beasts.'

And like young lions we ran after Death, its dark pelt blotched with pale crosses as it escaped down the vast violet living and throbbing sky.

But we had no ideal Mistress raising her divine form to the clouds, nor any cruel Queen to whom to offer our bodies, twisted like Byzantine rings! There was nothing to make us wish for death, unless the wish to be free at last from the weight of our courage!

And on we raced, hurling watchdogs against doorsteps, curling them under our burning tyres like collars under a flatiron. Death, domesticated, met me at every turn, gracefully holding out a paw, or once in a while hunkering down, making velvety caressing eyes at me from every puddle.

'Let's break out of the horrible shell of wisdom and throw ourselves like pride-ripened fruit into the wide, contorted mouth of the wind! Let's give ourselves utterly to the Unknown, not in desperation but only to replenish the deep wells of the Absurd!'

The words were scarcely out of my mouth when I spun my car around with the frenzy of a dog trying to bite its tail, and there, suddenly, were two cyclists coming towards me, shaking their fists, wobbling like two equally convincing but nevertheless contradictory arguments. Their stupid dilemma was blocking my way—Damn! Ouch! . . . I stopped short and to my disgust rolled over into a ditch with my wheels in the air. . . .

O maternal ditch, almost full of muddy water! Fair factory drain! I gulped down your nourishing sludge; and I remembered the blessed black breast of my Sudanese nurse. . . . When I came up—torn, filthy, and stinking—from under the capsized car, I felt the white-hot iron of joy deliciously pass through my heart!

A crowd of fishermen with handlines and gouty naturalists were already swarming around the prodigy. With patient, loving care those people rigged a tall derrick and iron grapnels to fish out my car, like a big beached shark. Up it came from the ditch, slowly, leaving in the bottom, like scales, its heavy framework of good sense and its soft upholstery of comfort.

They thought it was dead, my beautiful shark, but a caress from me was enough to revive it; and there it was, alive again, running on its powerful fins!

And so, faces smeared with good factory muck—plastered with metallic waste, with senseless sweat, with celestial soot—we, bruised, our arms in slings, but unafraid, declared our high intentions to all the *living* of the earth:

Manifesto of Futurism

1. We intend to sing the love of danger, the habit of energy and fearlessness.
2. Courage, audacity, and revolt will be essential elements of our poetry.
3. Up to now literature has exalted a pensive immobility, ecstasy, and sleep. We intend to exalt aggressive action, a feverish insomnia, the racer's stride, the mortal leap, the punch and the slap.
4. We affirm that the world's magnificence has been enriched by a new beauty: the beauty of speed. A racing car whose hood is adorned with great pipes, like serpents of explosive breath—a roaring car that seems to ride on grapeshot is more beautiful than the *Victory of Samothrace*.
5. We want to hymn the man at the wheel, who hurls the lance of his spirit across the Earth, along the circle of its orbit.
6. The poet must spend himself with ardour, splendour, and generosity, to swell the enthusiastic fervour of the primordial elements.

7. Except in struggle, there is no more beauty. No work without an aggressive character can be a masterpiece. Poetry must be conceived as a violent attack on unknown forces, to reduce and prostrate them before man.

8. We stand on the last promontory of the centuries! . . . Why should we look back, when what we want is to break down the mysterious doors of the Impossible? Time and Space died yesterday. We already live in the absolute, because we have created eternal, omnipresent speed.

9. We will glorify war—the world's only hygiene—militarism, patriotism, the destructive gesture of freedom-bringers, beautiful ideas worth dying for, and scorn for woman.

10. We will destroy the museums, libraries, academies of every kind, will fight moralism, feminism, every opportunistic or utilitarian cowardice.

11. We will sing of great crowds excited by work, by pleasure, and by riot; we will sing of the multicoloured, polyphonic tides of revolution in the modern capitals; we will sing of the vibrant nightly fervour of arsenals and shipyards blazing with violent electric moons; greedy railway stations that devour smoke-plumed serpents; factories hung on clouds by the crooked lines of their smoke; bridges that stride the rivers like giant gymnasts, flashing in the sun with a glitter of knives; adventurous steamers that sniff the horizon; deep-chested locomotives whose wheels paw the tracks like the hooves of enormous steel horses bridled by tubing; and the sleek flight of planes whose propellers chatter in the wind like banners and seem to cheer like an enthusiastic crowd.

It is from Italy that we launch through the world this violently upsetting incendiary manifesto of ours. With it, today, we establish *Futurism*, because we want to free this land from its smelly gangrene of professors, archaeologists, *ciceroni* and antiquarians. For too long has Italy been a dealer in second-hand clothes. We mean to free her from the numberless museums that cover her like so many graveyards.

Museums: cemeteries! . . . Identical, surely, in the sinister promiscuity of so many bodies unknown to one another. Museums: public dormitories where one lies forever beside hated or unknown beings. Museums: absurd abattoirs of painters and sculptors ferociously slaughtering each other with colour-blows and line-blows, the length of the fought-over walls!

That one should make an annual pilgrimage, just as one goes to the graveyard on All Souls' Day—that I grant. That once a year one should leave a floral tribute beneath the *Gioconda*, I grant you that. . . . But I don't admit that our sorrows, our fragile courage, our morbid restlessness should be given a daily conducted tour through the museums. Why poison ourselves? Why rot?

And what is there to see in an old picture except the laborious contortions of an artist throwing himself against the barriers that thwart his desire to express his dream completely? . . . Admiring an old picture is the same as pouring our sensibility into a funerary urn instead of hurling it far off, in violent spasms of action and creation.

Do you, then, wish to waste all your best powers in this eternal and futile worship of the past, from which you emerge fatally exhausted, shrunken, beaten down?

In truth I tell you that daily visits to museums, libraries, and academies (cemeteries of empty exertion, Calvaries of crucified dreams, registries of aborted beginnings!) are, for artists, as damaging as the prolonged supervision by parents of certain young people drunk with their talent and their ambitious wills. When the future is barred to them, the admirable past may be a solace for the ills of the moribund, the sickly, the prisoner. . . . But we want no part of it, the past, we the young and strong *Futurists*!

So let them come, the gay incendiaries with charred fingers! Here they are! Here they are! . . . Come on! set fire to the library shelves! Turn aside the canals to flood the museums! . . . Oh, the joy of seeing the glorious old canvases bobbing adrift on those waters, discoloured and shredded! . . . Take up your pickaxes, your axes and hammers and wreck, wreck the venerable cities, pitilessly.

The oldest of us is thirty: so we have at least a decade for finishing our work. When we are forty, other younger and stronger men will probably throw us in the wastebasket like useless manuscripts—we want it to happen!

They will come against us, our successors, will come from far away, from every quarter, dancing to the winged cadence of their first songs, flexing the hooked claws of predators, sniffing doglike at the academy doors the strong odour of our decaying minds, which will already have been promised to the literary catacombs.

But we won't be there. . . . At last they'll find us—one winter's night—in open country, beneath a sad roof drummed by a monotonous rain. They'll see us crouched beside our trembling aeroplanes in the act of warming our hands at the poor little blaze that our books of today will give out when they take fire from the flight of our images.

They'll storm around us, panting with scorn and anguish, and all of them, exasperated by our proud daring, will hurtle to kill us, driven by a hatred the more implacable the more their hearts will be drunk with love and admiration for us.

Injustice, strong and sane, will break out radiantly in their eyes.

Art, in fact, can be nothing but violence, cruelty, and injustice.

The oldest of us is thirty: even so we have already scattered treasures, a thousand treasures of force, love, courage, astuteness, and raw will-power; have thrown them impatiently away, with fury, carelessly, unhesitatingly, breathless, and unresting. . . . Look at us! We are still untired! Our hearts know no weariness because they are fed with fire, hatred, and speed! . . . Does that amaze you? It should, because you can never remember having lived! Erect on the summit of the world, once again we hurl our defiance at the stars!

You have objections?—Enough! Enough! We know them. . . . We've understood! . . . Our fine deceitful intelligence tells us that we are the revival and extension of our ancestors—Perhaps! . . . If only it were so!—But who cares? We don't want to understand! . . . Woe to anyone who says those infamous words to us again!

Lift up your heads!

Erect on the summit of the world, once again we hurl defiance to the stars!

WILFRED OWEN

Dulce Et Decorum Est (1920)

[handwritten note: soldiers in bad condition marching]

Bent double, like old beggars under sacks,
Knock-kneed, coughing like hags, we cursed through sludge,
Till on the haunting flares we turned our backs
And towards our distant rest began to trudge.
Men marched asleep. Many had lost their boots
But limped on, blood-shod. All went lame; all blind;
Drunk with fatigue; deaf even to the hoots
Of tired, outstripped Five-Nines that dropped behind.

[handwritten note: Gas War]

Gas! GAS! Quick, boys!—An ecstasy of fumbling,
Fitting the clumsy helmets just in time;
But someone still was yelling out and stumbling,
And flound'ring like a man in fire or lime. . .
Dim through the misty panes and thick green light,
As under a green sea, I saw him drowning.

[handwritten note: not in time w/ mask]

In all my dreams, before my helpless sight,
He plunges at me, guttering, choking, drowning.

If in some smothering dreams you too could pace
Behind the wagon that we flung him in,
And watch the white eyes writhing in his face,
His hanging face, like a devil's sick of sin;
If you could hear, at every jolt, the blood
Come gargling from the froth-corrupted lungs,
Obscene as cancer, bitter as the cud
Of vile, incurable sores on innocent tongues,—
My friend, you would not tell with such high zest
To children ardent for some desperate glory,
The old Lie: Dulce et decorum est
Pro patria mori.

October 1917–March 1918

WILLIAM BUTLER YEATS

The Second Coming (1920)

Turning and turning in the widening gyre
The falcon cannot hear the falconer;
Things fall apart; the centre cannot hold;
Mere anarchy is loosed upon the world,
The blood-dimmed tide is loosed, and everywhere
The ceremony of innocence is drowned;
The best lack all conviction, while the worst
Are full of passionate intensity.

Surely some revelation is at hand;
Surely the Second Coming is at hand.
The Second Coming! Hardly are those words out
When a vast image out of *Spiritus Mundi*
Troubles my sight: somewhere in the sands of the desert
A shape with lion body and the head of a man,
A gaze blank and pitiless as the sun,
Is moving its slow thighs, while all about it
Reel shadows of the indignant desert birds.
The darkness drops again; but now I know
That twenty centuries of stony sleep
Were vexed to nightmare by a rocking cradle,
And what rough beast, its hour come round at last,
Slouches towards Bethlehem to be born?

REBECCA WEST

Women and Wages (1912)
The Sin of Self-Sacrifice (1913)

Women and Wages

Blacklegging and Timidity

In the *Daily Citizen* of 9 October there was a sentimental quotation, seemingly of feminist import, from *The Shipping World*. A new Act in the States has decreed that every vessel navigating on the American coast or the great lakes must carry a wireless operator; and it furthermore provides that women are eligible to qualify as operators.

And why not? [asks *The Shipping World*]. The invention opens out a new career for women, in which their special abilities can be used to the best advantage. If acuteness of hearing, rapidity of decision and suppleness of wrist and fingers count for anything, then, surely, the Marconi house on the bridge deck seems to be the natural goal for a self-reliant woman with cool nerves and efficient brain.

It is an alluring picture, and one flattering to women. In the mind's eye one sees the Marconi operator sitting gracefully at her work, with a rose in her hair, surrounded by votive offerings from passengers, operating much, much better than any mere man ever did. And, apart from *The Shipping World*'s idealisation of the prospects, it does seem an interesting new occupation for women. Women have had to settle down to occupations which were too tame for men and in which there are few opportunities for the adventurous-minded. The young woman who wants to see over the edge of the world would probably love the life of a wireless operator.

Yet, 'I fear the Greeks even when they bring gifts,' said the one wise Trojan, when he saw his fellow-Trojans dragging the wooden horse into Troy. I fear the Marconi Company even when they bring gifts.

Ah! Here we have it. Here is the powder in the jam, the snake in the grass, the wolf in feminist's clothing. I thought there must be some reason for this sudden lyric outburst of feminist enthusiasm. 'Probably she will be less expensive to the shipowner than the male operator, and quite as reliable.' One might have remembered that the capitalist respects woman in only one capacity; not as the worker or the wife or the mother, but as the black-leg. That takes the pride out of the working woman. If she becomes a Marconi operator on these terms, no matter how efficient and plucky she may be, she is living on the wages of dishonour. She has bought her job with the flesh and blood of her fellow man.

Though it is galling for the woman worker to know that she is not loved for herself alone, she may get a good deal of satisfaction out of the encouraging words that are let fall by the capitalist on the make. For instance, there was that remarkable wave of feminism that passed over local authorities four years ago, when they became obliged to appoint school medical officers. All over the country councillors enthusiastically declared to one another that it was imperative that children should be attended to by women; that men were far too coarse and tactless to deal with them; that every woman (even though she be a doctor) is a mother at heart . . . and that while men doctors were asking £250 a year they could probably get women for £150. The wiles of the municipal seducers were in vain. Women doctors, being in the main middle-class women, had savings and homes to fall back on; so they stood loyally by their male colleagues and refused to blackleg. Not one woman doctor in Great Britain applied for a £150 post. And there was an abrupt subsidence in the wave of feminism among local authorities.

What reason is there that women should play the part of blacklegs? The underpayment of women is one of those 'ninepence for fourpence' tricks that capitalists have ever loved to play on the people whenever they had the chance. Capitalists have said to women: 'We deduct fourpence from your wages so that we can pay men larger wages, and then they can support you as their wives. So in the end you will make at least ninepence out of it.' It is only an excuse for sweating more money out of the people. It pretends that women have no dependants. A woman, according to the capitalist, is an air-bubble blown between earth and sky, with no human ties of any sort. True it is that man recognises that first imperative necessity which is plain to the lowest savage, the duty to provide for the next generation. But there is another duty which is patent only to the more civilised (if one was a really bitter feminist, one might say that that was why it fell to the women), and that is the duty to provide for the old. Miss Grace Neal, of the Domestic Workers' Union, states that it is the rule and not the exception of the members of her Union to send money home to support their parents. And sometimes widowhood lays the burden of both generations on a woman.

Women ought to understand that in submitting themselves to this swindle of underpayment, they are not only insulting themselves, but doing a deadly injury to the community. The capitalist sucks strength out of an exploited class which enables him to exploit other classes. An example of the infectiousness of poverty and the persistence of disease is the terrible economic condition of Edinburgh, which is directly due to the Battle of Flodden Field in 1513. Most of the able-bodied men were killed off and their widows had to set about earning a living for their fatherless children. They got 'woman's wages'. That meant that wages all round were depressed, and capitalism in Edinburgh got a good hold over labour by planting its feet on a solid substratum of the blackest and most helpless poverty. Labour has never shaken itself free.

How can women bear to be willing instruments of this crime against themselves and the community? The industrial women seem to consent to the indignity without resentment. Every woman who has risen from the floral stage of political activity (that is, the Primrose League), or the vegetable stage (that is, the Women's Liberal Association), must admire the suffragettes. Yet we may wish that they had spared a little of their dear irreverence and blessed pluck to stir up the industrial women to revolt. We have clever Miss Pankhurst trying to get the vote and earnest Miss Macarthur trying to organise trade unions; but seemingly we have no women who have read the signs of the times, who have discovered that political power and trade unionism are pin-pricks in the hide of the capitalist monster. Where are our women syndicalists?

Ladies of Great Britain, we are clever, we are efficient, we are trustworthy, we are twice the women that our grandmothers were, but we have not enough devil in us. We are afraid of going back to first causes. We want to earn good wages. But we try to do it by being amenable and competent wage-slaves, and thus pleasing the capitalist. We never try to do it by fighting the capitalist and turning him out of the workshop. The other day Mr. Ramsay MacDonald complained that women do not make good enough socialists for him. The whole trouble is that women make socialists which are just good enough for Mr. Ramsay MacDonald. They accept as doles from the capitalist class what they should take as rights. Wherever one gets a gathering of women socialists, one gets a programme of such charity gifts from the State as free meals and school clinics for children: excellent things, but dangerous unless taken discontentedly as niggardly instalments of a long-due debt. They should watch such things critically lest their children grow up in servitude. A slave is more of a slave when he is well fed than when he is hungry.

It is strange that women who are independent and fearless in private life should not introduce their independence and fearlessness into their public life. This occurs to me especially in connection with elementary-schoolteachers. The cheerfulness with which they have shouldered the responsibilities thrown on them by the free meals and medical examination of schoolchildren explains why the children love their school and their teachers. Yet they submit to being paid salaries of from one-half to two-thirds the amount paid to men for similar work. They submit in spite of the fact that they could end the injustice in a week by a strike. What could the Government do if women teachers struck? There are no hungry teachers walking the streets, so degraded by poverty that—God forgive them and punish the capitalists—they will help to drag their fellows down to poverty, too, by blacklegging. The women teachers of England have their remedy in their own hands.

Yet not only do they not use it, but they consent to remain members of a quaint body called the National Union of Teachers, which, although it exacts an equal subscription from men and women alike, maintains this principle of unequal payment. The scale which it suggests for certificated class-teachers is quite a humorous little effort. Apparently the male class-teacher is intended to get married at once, as his minimum salary is higher than the female's. True the difference is but £10, but the maintenance of a family can be the only excuse for any difference at all. His maximum salary is £200 against the female's £160. Puzzle: If the NUT thinks a class-teacher can keep a wife on the £10 surplus, how many children does it expect him to rear on the £40 surplus? Surely the birth-rate can't be going down!

I am no teacher, but I don't think much of that Union. I like to get value for my money, and a union that takes my money and does not give me equal benefits with my fellow-unionist is no use to me. Decidedly the women members of the NUT ought to withdraw their support from their ungracious colleagues and form a union of their own.

But what is the explanation of the meekness which makes such impositions on women possible? It is perhaps nothing disgraceful to ourselves, nothing that need make us doubt our worthiness as citizens of the ideal State. Nietzsche says that a man who is aiming at Supermanhood passes through three phases: the camel, the lion and the child. At first the soul becomes mastered by the idea of duty and self-sacrifice. It desires to be a preserver of life. Thus far have women gone. They have no time to travel further, having left the home so recently. 'But when the camel is loaded, it goeth to the desert, and there it is transformed into a lion.' The soul finds that the life for which it has sacrificed itself is in its present state hardly worthy of preserving. It turns to rend and destroy life, that out of its wreck it may make a new and more beautiful life. To this stage have men come.

Let women make haste to become lions, and fearlessly attack the social system. So that together men and women may be transformed for the last time into the child, who, untroubled with the consciousness of material things, is concerned only with love and happiness.

The Clarion, 18 October 1912

The Sin of Self-Sacrifice

The basis of the anti-feminist position is the idea that women ought to sacrifice the development of their own personalities for the sake of men and children: that even if they are fit to vote and to fulfil other activities of men they should not do so, because all their energies should be spent in the service of their families. Such is the view of the governing classes in this country today, and its passionate advocacy by Ellen Key has changed the continental woman's movement from a march towards freedom to a romp towards voluptuous servitude. According to these folk a woman should from her childhood be guarded from the disturbance of intellectual effort and should pass automatically through a serenely sentimental adolescence to a home. There the tranquil flame of her unspoiled soul should radiate purity and nobility upon an indefinitely extended family, exposed to the world's winds only when she goes wisely marketing. Inconceivably incandescent, inconceivably economical, like the advertisement of a motor-lamp come true.

This amounts to a claim to halos for women: for a halo is the only thing I have ever heard of that gives out light yet needs no fuel. Unless a human being is being inspired with wisdom by some supernatural power he can only gain wisdom by an experience compounded of his sensations: that is, the vibration caused by collision between his nerves and external things. We are dependent for the value of this basis of wisdom on the extent to which we lean out of ourselves and adventure among alien things. The only times when a woman's physical feelings are concentrated within herself are when she has indigestion and appendicitis; when she is well she is thinking how warmly the sunlight lies on her face or how sweet the wet loaves smell. Similarly, when a woman's mental feelings are concentrated within herself she must have inflammation of the brain. Only the mad wonder continually whether they are men or poached eggs, and discuss whether the world uses them well or ill. The sane look round on their fellow-men and delight to see who will help them in their work of making the world less madly governed: they walk the earth to choose their battlefields, and touch all it contains to find the substance most fit for the forging of weapons. Then they glow with the exhilaration of wisdom and radiate glory. So might many women were they given freedom; but they must remain tinged with no clearer light than the reflection of the kitchen range so long as they are made to ape the self-sufficiency of the maniac. As they are ignorant how can they hope to inspire those who are not ignorant? What influence can a wife who has passed from playing with dolls in her father's house to playing with saucepans and babies in her husband's house hope to have over a man who has been disciplined by years of responsible enterprise among all sorts of men? Her courage has been tried by childbirth, but her character has stood no other test.

It may be said that this is underestimating the value of homekeeping as an occupation. Of course it is. But it is a wild generalisation to say that the majority of wives in Great Britain are homekeepers in the sense of being essential to the existence of the home as was the wife in medieval agricultural England. If she were there would be no need to discuss feminism, for where a woman pays her way by performing labour she usually forces the community (if it be not too corrupt with capitalism) into recognising her equality. While the silk industry made the Burmese women economically independent, they were not submissive to men; but now that this is taken out of their hands they are threatened with that humiliation. And I was recently told by 'A. E.' that there is no need for the preaching of feminism in modern agricultural Ireland, for the farmer and the farmer's wife depend so much on each other's labour that it never occurs to them to imagine that they are different and unequal sorts. The rough home-keeping of the past, and the present in remote districts, presented difficulties which had to be met by skill and determination. Where the cow had to be milked and the churn persuaded, one simply waits for the coming of a milkman who, perhaps, has rarely seen a cow; where jelly had to be forced to jell one buys small packets from some unknown controller of jellies; where one sheared the sheep and spun its wool and wove the cloth and cut out the dress one goes to a shop and buys the finished thing easily, though probably at three times its real cost. It is all very simple and quite artificial. The woman who does these things may fill up her day with them, but the practice of them is hardly a craft. For they are tricks that a performing dog who could count his change might pull off just as well. That there is no interest in the occupation to counterbalance the solitude it entails, in these days of small homes unconnected by any local corporate life, is shown by the numbers of domestic servants who fly from its monotony to the life of the streets. And evidently their mistresses found the home no more educative, for they have not prevented their husbands and sons from preying on these women till, in their misery, they have revenged themselves on society by their disease and drunkenness. Here, in a rather important matter, the home-keeping woman has failed to radiate purity and nobility.

It may be said that the failure of women to create or influence morality does not matter: that their business lies simply with the physical nurture of the race. This is like saying that a doctor has no right to concern himself with the study of poisons because his business is with the preservation of the human body. When the body evolved the mind it evolved a queer, treacherous governor, who never knows what he does with his subject. Just as the African mind, by turning to commerce, has betrayed the African body, because sleeping-sickness travelled along the trade routes as safely as the goods, so the Western mind has betrayed the Western body by inventing the ingenious and in many ways convenient system of capitalism. So long as it persists no wealthy mother can look at her child without remembering that:

The strongest poison ever known
Came from Caesar's laurel crown.

No poor mother can hold her healthy child (life is such an indestructible and generous thing that nearly every baby is born healthy) without seeing him the bent extension of a machine. Men have not been able to fight the forces we have in an honest quest for civilisation called up from hell: all the energy of the world is needed to battle with them. The woman who cares merely for the physical nurture of her children is by her softness encouraging the famine that may some day starve them.

The fact is that this idea of sacrificing the individual to the race never works. It hints at a philosophical heresy, such as the belief disproved by Berkeley that matter has a substance apart from its attributes. 'There is nothing behind the facts,' said Chauncey Depew, when offered an idealist system that would 'harmonise' and 'explain' the facts of life. There is nothing behind the race but the individuals. If half the individuals agree to remain weak and undeveloped half the race is weak and undeveloped. And if every alternate link of a chain is weak it matters not how strong the others are: the chain will beak all the same. Every nation that has contained a slave class has fallen to dust and ashes in spite of all its military glories and its pride of brains. And I cannot remember that any individual has ever benefited the race by self-sacrifice. I can well believe that St. Simon Stylites did not like perching and the Savonarola's heart bled at his own denunciation of beauty and jollity; but these men saved no race. The people who draw down salvation to earth are the people who insist on self-realisation whether it leads to death or gaiety. Florence Nightingale saved war from its worse disgrace and helped the sick because she hated disorder, not because she thought she ought to do something toilsome. Marx set humanity on its feet because he was interested in economics. Darwin uncovered the significant eyes of truth because he enjoyed zoology.

And truly these are among the saviours of men.

And the recognition of this is the real virtue of the militant suffrage movement. Its later manifestations have seemed to some of us not immoral but pointless and extravagant. Desirable residences are more common than desirable Cabinet Ministers, yet they are sufficiently rare to be preserved. No house is wholly built with hands: it has taken many mental triumphs of the organisation of civilisation to secure that bricklayers shall unmolested lay their bricks and quarrymen convey their stone unrobbed. A house is an achievement not to be burned in a night. And these sporadic attacks on the voter are ineffective, for they create no widespread terror that would cry out to the Government for immediate pacification of the terrorists. They merely make England into a patchwork of irritations. But how admirable is the spirit of the militants! How splendidly selfish they are! There is no doubt that now Mrs. Pankhurst is out of gaol again they will keep her out. All over the country we can help her. There is nothing like sympathetic reference to a lawbreaker for turning the heart of the law to water. We got Jim Larkin out of Mountjoy because we said we liked him. We can keep Mrs. Pankhurst out of Holloway if, remembering what her movement really means, and how it has brought the supreme virtue of selfishness to thousands of English women, we speak well of her.

The Clarion, 12 December 1913

OLIVE SCHREINER
The Buddhist Priest's Wife (1923)

Cover her up! How still it lies! You can see the outline under the white. You would think she was asleep. Let the sunshine come in; it loved it so. She that had travelled so far, in so many lands, and done so much and seen so much, how she must like rest now! Did she ever love anything absolutely, this woman whom so many men loved, and so many women; who gave so much sympathy and never asked for anything in return! did she ever need a love she could not have? Was she never obliged to unclasp her fingers from anything to which they clung? Was she really so strong as she looked? Did she never wake up in the night crying for that which she could not have? Were thought and travel enough for her? Did she go about for long days with a weight that crushed her to earth? Cover her up! I do not think she would have liked us to look at her. In one way she was alone all her life; she would have liked to be alone now! . . . . Life must have been very beautiful to her, or she would not look so young now. Cover her up! Let us go!

Many years ago in a London room, up long flights of stairs, a fire burnt up in a grate. It showed the marks on the walls where pictures had been taken down, and the little blue flowers in the wall-paper and the blue felt carpet on the floor, and a woman sat by the fire in a chair at one side.

Presently the door opened, and the old woman came in who took care of the entrance hall downstairs.

'Do you not want anything to-night?' she said.

'No, I am only waiting for a visitor; when they have been, I shall go.'

'Have you got all your things taken away already?'

'Yes, only these I am leaving.'

The old woman went down again, but presently came up with a cup of tea in her hand.

'You must drink that; it's good for one. Nothing helps one like tea when one's been packing all day.'

The young woman at the fire did not thank her, but she ran her hand over the old woman's from the wrist to the fingers.

'I'll say good-bye to you when I go out.'

The woman poked the fire, put the last coals on, and went.

When she had gone the young one did not drink the tea, but drew her little silver cigarette case from her pocket and lighted a cigarette. For a while she sat smoking by the fire; then she stood up and walked the room.

When she had paced for a while she sat down again beside the fire. She threw the end of her cigarette away into the fire, and then began to walk again with her hands behind her. Then she went back to her seat and lit another cigarette, and paced again. Presently she sat down, and looked into the fire; she pressed the palms of her hands together, and then sat quietly staring into it.

Then there was a sound of feet on the stairs and someone knocked at the door.

She rose and threw the end into the fire and said without moving, 'Come in.'

The door opened and a man stood there in evening dress. He had a great-coat on, open in front.

'May I come in? I couldn't get rid of this downstairs; I didn't see where to leave it!' He took his coat off. 'How are you? This is a real bird's nest!'

She motioned to a chair.

'I hope you did not mind my asking you to come?'

'Oh no, I am delighted. I only found your note at my club twenty minutes ago.'

'So you really are going to India? How delightful! But what are you to do there? I think it was Grey told me six weeks ago you were going, but regarded it as one of those mythical stories which don't deserve credence. Yet I am sure I don't know! Why, nothing would surprise me.'

He looked at her in a half-amused, half-interested way.

'What a long time it is since we met! Six months, eight?'

'Seven,' she said.

'I really thought you were trying to avoid me. What have you been doing with yourself all this time?'

'Oh, been busy. Won't you have a cigarette?'

She held out the little case to him.

'Won't you take one yourself? I know you object to smoking with men, but you can make an exception in my case!'

'Thank you.' She lit her own and passed him the matches.

'But really what have you been doing with yourself all this time? You've entirely disappeared from civilised life. When I was down at the Grahams' in the spring, they said you were coming down there, and then at the last moment cried off. We were all quite disappointed. What is taking you to India now? Going to preach the doctrine of social and intellectual equality to the Hindu women and incite them to revolt? Marry some old Buddhist Priest, build a little cottage on the top of the Himalayas and live there, discuss philosophy and meditate? I believe that's what you'd like. I really shouldn't wonder if I heard you'd done it!'

She laughed and took out her cigarette case.

She smoked slowly.

'I've been here a long time, four years, and I want change. I was glad to see how well you succeeded in that election,' she said. 'You were much interested in it, were you not?'

'Oh, yes. We had a stiff fight. It tells in my favour, you know, though it was not exactly a personal matter. But it was a great worry.'

'Don't you think,' she said, 'you were wrong in sending that letter to the papers? It would have strengthened your position to have remained silent.'

'Yes, perhaps so; I think so now, but I did it under advice. However, we've won, so it's all right.' He leaned back in the chair.

'Are you pretty fit?'

'Oh, yes; pretty well; bored, you know. One doesn't know what all this working and striving is for sometimes.'

'Where are you going for your holiday this year?'

'Oh, Scotland, I suppose; I always do; the old quarters.'

'Why don't you go to Norway? It would be more change for you and rest you more. Did you get a book on sport in Norway?'

'Did you send it me? How kind of you! I read it with much interest. I was almost inclined to start off there and then. I suppose it is the kind of *vis inertiae* that creeps over one as one grows older that sends one back to the old place. A change would be much better.'

'There's a list at the end of the book,' she said, 'of exactly the things one needs to take. I thought it would save trouble; you could just give it to your man, and let him get them all. Have you still got him?'

'Oh, yes. He's as faithful to me as a dog. I think nothing would induce him to leave me. He won't allow me to go out hunting since I sprained my foot last autumn. I have to do it surreptitiously. He thinks I can't keep my seat with a sprained ankle; but he's a very good fellow; takes care of me like a mother.' He smoked quietly with the firelight glowing on his black coat. 'But what are you going to India for? Do you know anyone there?'

'No,' she said. 'I think it will be so splendid. I've always been a great deal interested in the East. It's a complex, interesting life.'

He turned and looked at her.

'Going to seek for more experience, you'll say, I suppose. I never knew a woman throw herself away as you do; a woman with your brilliant parts and attractions, to let the whole of life slip through your hands, and make nothing of it. You ought to be the most successful woman in London. Oh, yes; I know what you're going to say: "You don't care." That's just it; you don't. You are always going to get experience, going to get everything, and you never do. You are always going to write when you know enough, and you are never satisfied that you do. You ought to be making your two thousand a year, but you don't care. That's just it! Living, burying yourself here with a lot of old frumps. You will never do anything. You could have everything and you let it slip.'

'Oh, my life is very full,' she said. 'There are only two things that are absolute realities, love and knowledge, and you can't escape them.'

She had thrown her cigarette end away and was looking into the fire, smiling.

'I've let these rooms to a woman friend of mine.' She glanced round the room, smiling. 'She doesn't know I'm going to leave these things here for her. She'll like them because they were mine. The world's very beautiful, I think—delicious.'

'Oh, yes. But what do you do with it? What do you make of it? You ought to settle down and marry like other women, not go wandering about the world to India and China and Italy, and God knows where. You are simply making a mess of your life. You're always surrounding yourself with all sorts of extraordinary people. If I hear any man or woman is a great friend of yours, I always say: "What the matter? Lost his money? Lost his character? Got an incurable disease?" I believe the only way in which anyone becomes interesting to you is by having some complaint of mind or body. I believe you worship rags. To come and shut yourself up in a place like this away from everybody and everything! It's a mistake; it's idiotic, you know.'

'I'm very happy,' she said. 'You see,' she said, leaning forwards towards the fire with hands on her knees, 'what matters is that something should need you. It isn't a question of love. What's the use of being near a thing if other people could serve it as well as you can. If they could serve it better, it's pure selfishness. It's the need of one thing for another that makes the organic bond of union. You love mountains and horses, but they don't need you; so what's the use of saying anything about it! I suppose the most absolutely delicious thing in life is to feel a thing needs you, and to give at the moment it needs. Things that don't need you, you must love from a distance.'

'Oh, but a woman like you ought to marry, ought to have children. You go squandering yourself on every old beggar or forlorn female or escaped criminal you meet; it may be very nice for them, but it's a mistake from your point of view.'

He touched the ash gently with the tip of his little finger and let it fall.

'I intend to marry. It's a curious thing,' he said, resuming his pose with an elbow on one knee and his head bent forward on one side, so that she saw the brown hair with its close curls and little tinged with grey at the sides, 'that when a man reaches a certain age he wants to marry. He doesn't fall in love; it's not that he definitely plans anything; but he has a feeling that he ought to have a home and a wife and children. I suppose it is the same kind of feeling that makes a bird build nests at certain times of the year. It's not love; it's something else. When I was a young man I used to despise men for getting married; wondered what they did it for; they had everything to lose and nothing to gain. But when a man gets to be six-and-thirty his feeling changes. It's not love, passion, he wants; it's a home; it's a wife and children. He may have a house and servants; it isn't the same thing. I should have thought a woman would have felt it too.'

She was quiet for a minute, holding a cigarette between her fingers; then she said slowly:

'Yes, at times a woman has a curious longing to have a child, especially when she gets near to thirty or over it. It's something distinct from love for any definite person. But it's a thing one has to get over. For a woman, marriage is much more serious than for a man. She might pass her life without meeting a man whom she could possibly love, and, if she met him, it might not be right or possible. Marriage has become very complex now it has become so largely intellectual. Won't you have another?'

She held out the case to him. 'You can light it from mine.' She bent forward for him to light it.

'You are a man who ought to marry. You've no absorbing mental work with which the woman would interfere; it would complete you.' She sat back, smoking serenely.

'Yes,' he said, 'but life is too busy; I never find time to look for one, and I haven't a fancy for the pink-and-white prettiness so common and that some men like so. I need something else. If I am to have a wife I shall have to go to America to look for one.'

'Yes, an American would suit you best.'

'Yes,' he said, 'I don't want a woman to look after; she must be self-sustaining and she mustn't bore you. You know what I mean. Life is too full of cares to have a helpless child added to them.'

'Yes,' she said, standing up and leaning with her elbow against the fireplace. 'The kind of woman you want would be young and strong; she need not be excessively beautiful, but she must be attractive; she must have energy, but not too strongly marked an individuality; she must be largely neutral; she need not give you too passionate or too deep a devotion, but she must second you in a thoroughly rational manner. She must have the same aims and tastes that you have. No woman has the right to marry a man if she has to bend herself out of shape for him. She might wish to, but she could never be to him with all her passionate endeavour what the other woman could be to him without trying. Character will dominate over all and will come out at last.'

She looked down into the fire.

'When you marry you mustn't marry a woman who flatters you too much. It is always a sign of falseness somewhere. If a woman absolutely loves you as herself, she will criticise and understand you as herself. Two people who are to live through life together must be able to look into each other's eyes and speak the truth. That helps one through life. You would find many such women in America,' she said: 'women who would help you to succeed, who would not drag you down.'

'Yes, that's my idea. But how am I to obtain the ideal woman?'

'Go and look for her. Go to America instead of Scotland this year. It is perfectly right. A man has a right to look for what he needs. With a woman it is different. That's one of the radical differences between men and women.

She looked downwards into the fire.

'It's a law of her nature and of sex relationship. There's nothing arbitrary or conventional about it any more than there is in her having to bear her child while the male does not. Intellectually we may both be alike. I suppose if fifty men and fifty women had to solve a mathematical problem, they would all do it in the same way; the more abstract and intellectual, the more alike we are. The nearer you approach to the personal and sexual, the more different we are. If I were to represent men's and women's natures,' she said, 'by a diagram, I would take two circular discs; the right side of each I should paint bright red; then I would shade the red away till in a spot on the left edge it became blue in the one and green in the other. That spot represents sex, and the nearer you come to it, the more the two discs differ in colour. Well then, if you turn them so that the red sides touch, they seem to be exactly alike, but if you turn them so that green and blue paint form their point of contact, they will seem to be entirely unlike. That's why you notice the brutal, sensual men invariably believe women are entirely different from men, another species of creature; and very cultured, intellectual men sometimes believe we are exactly alike. You see, sex love in its substance may be the same in both of us; in the form of its expression it must differ. It is not man's fault; it is nature's. If a man loves a woman, he has a right to try to make her love him because he can do it openly, directly, without bending. There need be no subtlety, no indirectness. With a woman it's not so; she can take no love that is not laid openly, simply, at her feet. Nature ordains that she should never show what she feels; the woman who had told a man she loved him would have put between them a barrier once and for ever that could not be crossed; and if she subtly drew him towards her, using the woman's means— silence, finesse, the dropped handkerchief, the surprise visit, the gentle assertion she had not thought to see him when she had come a long way to meet him, then she would be damned; she would hold the love, but she would have desecrated it by subtlety; it would have no value. Therefore she must always go with her arms folded sexually; only the love which lays itself down at her feet and implores of her to accept it is love she can ever rightly take up. That is the true difference between a man and a woman. You may seek for love because you can do it openly; we cannot because we must do it subtly. A woman should always walk with her arms folded. Of course friendship is different. You are on a perfect equality with man then; you can ask him to come and see you as I asked you. That's the beauty of the intellect and intellectual life to a woman, that she drops her shackles a little; and that is why she shrinks from sex so. If she were dying perhaps, or doing something equal to death, she might. . . . Death means so much more to a woman than a man; when you knew you were dying, to look round on the world and feel the bond of sex that has broken and crushed you all your life gone, nothing but the human left, no woman any more, to meet everything on perfectly even ground. There's no reason why you shouldn't go to America and look for a wife perfectly deliberately. You will have to tell no lies. Look till you find a woman that you absolutely love, that you have not the smallest doubt suits you apart from love, and then ask her to marry you. You must have children; the life of an old childless man is very sad.'

'Yes, I should like to have children. I often feel now, what is it all for, this work, this striving, and no one to leave it to? It's a blank, suppose I succeed. . .?'

'Suppose you get your title?'

'Yes; what is it all worth to me if I've no one to leave it to? That's my feeling. It's really very strange to be sitting and talking like this to you. But you are so different from other women. If all women were like you, all your theories of the equality of men and women would work. You're the only woman with whom I never realise that she is a woman.'

'Yes,' she said.

She stood looking down into the fire.

'How long will you stay in India?'

'Oh, I'm not coming back.'

'Not coming back! That's impossible. You will be breaking the hearts of half the people here if you don't. I never knew a woman who had such power of entrapping men's hearts as you have in spite of that philosophy of yours. I don't know,' he smiled, 'that I should not have fallen into the snare myself—three years ago I almost thought I should—if you hadn't always attacked me so incontinently and persistently on all and every point and on each and every occasion. A man doesn't like pain. A succession of slaps damps him. But it doesn't seem to have that effect on other men. . . . There was that fellow down in the country when I was there last year, perfectly ridiculous. You know his name. . . .' He moved his fingers to try and remember it—'big, yellow moustache, a major, gone to the east coast of Africa now; the ladies unearthed it that he was always carrying about a photograph of yours in his pocket; and he used to take out little scraps of things you printed and show them to people mysteriously. He almost had a duel with a man one night after dinner because he mentioned you; he seemed to think there was something incongruous between your name and—'

'I do not like to talk of any man who has loved me,' she said. 'However small and poor his nature may be, he has given me his best. There is nothing ridiculous in love. I think a woman should feel that all the love men have given her which she has not been able to return is a kind of crown set up above her which she is always trying to grow tall enough to wear. I can't bear to think that all the love that has been given me has been wasted on something unworthy of it. Men have been very beautiful and greatly honoured me. I am grateful to them. If a man tells you he loves you,' she said, looking into the fire, 'with his breast uncovered before you for you to strike him if you will, the least you can do is to put out your hand and cover it up from other people's eyes. If I were a deer,' she said, 'and a stag got hurt following me, even though I could not have him for a companion, I would stand still and scrape the sand with my foot over the place where his blood had fallen; the rest of the herd should never know he had been hurt there following me. I would cover the blood up, if I were a deer,' she said, and then she was silent.

Presently she sat down in her chair and said, with her hand before her: 'Yet, you know, I have not the ordinary feeling about love. I think the one who is loved confers the benefit on the one who loves, it's been so great and beautiful that it should be loved. I think the man should be grateful to the woman or the woman to the man whom they have been able to love, whether they have been loved back or whether circumstances have divided them or not.' She stroked her knee softly with her hand.

'Well, really, I must go now.' He pulled out his watch. 'It's so fascinating sitting here talking that I could stay all night, but I've still two engagements.' He rose; she rose also and stood before him looking up at him for a moment.

'How well you look! I think you have found the secret of perpetual youth. You don't look a day older than when I first saw you just four years ago. You always look as if you were on fire and being burnt up, but you never are, you know.'

He looked down at her with a kind of amused face as one does at an interesting child or a big Newfoundland dog.

'When shall we see you back?'

'Oh, not at all!'

'Not at all! Oh, we must have you back; you belong here, you know. You'll get tired of your Buddhist and come back to us.'

'You didn't mind my asking you to come and say good-bye?' she said in a childish manner unlike her determinateness when she discussed anything impersonal. 'I wanted to say good-bye to everyone. If one hasn't said good-bye one feels restless and feels one would have to come back. If one has said good-bye to all one's friends, then one knows it is all ended.'

'Oh, this isn't a final farewell! You must come in ten years' time and we'll compare notes—you about your Buddhist Priest, I about my fair ideal American; and we'll see who succeeded best.'

She laughed.

'I shall always see your movements chronicled in the newspapers, so we shall not be quite sundered; and you will hear of me perhaps.'

'Yes, I hope you will be very successful.'

She was looking at him, with her eyes wide open, from head to foot. He turned to the chair where his coat hung.

'Can't I help you put it on?'

'Oh, no, thank you.'

He put it on.

'Button the throat,' she said, 'the room is warm.'

He turned to her in his great-coat and with his gloves. They were standing near the door.

'Well, good-bye. I hope you will have a very pleasant time.'

He stood looking down upon her, wrapped in his great-coat.

She put up one hand a little in the air. 'I want to ask you something,' she said quickly.

'Well, what is it?'

'Will you please kiss me?'

For a moment he looked down at her, then he bent over her.

In after years he could never tell certainly, but he always thought she put up her hand and rested it on the crown of his head, with a curious soft caress, something like a mother's touch when her child is asleep and she does not want to wake it. Then he looked round, and she was gone. The door had closed noiselessly. For a moment he stood motionless, then he walked to the fireplace and looked down into the fender at a little cigarette end lying there, then he walked quickly back to the door and opened it. The stairs were in darkness and silence. He rang the bell violently. The old woman came up. He asked her where the lady was. She said she had gone out, she had a cab waiting. He asked when she would be back. The old woman said, 'Not at all'; she had left. He asked where she had gone. The woman said she did not know; she had left orders that all her letters should be kept for six or eight months till she wrote and sent her address. He asked whether she had no idea where he might find her. The woman said no. He walked up to a space in the wall where a picture had hung and stood staring at it as though the picture were still hanging there. He drew his mouth as though he were emitting a long whistle, but no sound came. He gave the old woman ten shillings and went downstairs.

That was eight years ago.

How beautiful life must have been to it that it looks so young still!

VIRGINIA WOOLF
from A Room of One's Own (1929)

. . . Life for both sexes—and I looked at them, shouldering their way along the pavement—is arduous, difficult, a perpetual struggle. It calls for gigantic courage and strength. More than anything, perhaps, creatures of illusion as we are, it calls for confidence in oneself. Without self-confidence we are as babes in the cradle. And how can we generate this imponderable quality, which is yet so invaluable, most quickly? By thinking that other people are inferior to oneself. By feeling that one has some innate superiority—it may be wealth, or rank, a straight nose, or the portrait of a grandfather by Romney—for there is no end to the pathetic devices of the human imagination—over other people. Hence the enormous importance to a patriarch who has to conquer, who has to rule, of feeling that great numbers of people, half the human race indeed, are by nature inferior to himself. It must indeed be one of the chief sources of his power. But let me turn the light of this observation on to real life, I thought. Does it help to explain some of those psychological puzzles that one notes in the margin of daily life? Does it explain my astonishment the other day when Z, most humane, most modest of men, taking up some book by Rebecca West and reading a passage in it, exclaimed, "The arrant feminist! She says that men are snobs!" The exclamation, to me so surprising—for why was Miss West an arrant feminist for making a possibly true if uncomplimentary statement about the other sex?—was not merely the cry of wounded vanity; it was a protest against some infringement of his power to believe in himself. Women have served all these centuries as looking-glasses possessing the magic and delicious power of reflecting the figure of man at twice its natural size. Without that power probably the earth would still be swamp and jungle. The glories of all our wars would be unknown. We should still be scratching the outlines of deer on the remains of mutton bones and bartering flints for sheep-skins or whatever simple ornament took our unsophisticated taste. Supermen and Fingers of Destiny would never have existed. The Czar and the Kaiser would never have worn their crowns or lost them. Whatever may be their use in civilised societies, mirrors are essential to all violent and heroic action. That is why Napoleon and Mussolini both insist so emphatically upon the inferiority of women, for if they were not inferior, they would cease to enlarge. That serves to explain in part the necessity that women so often are to men. And it serves to explain how restless they are under her criticism; how impossible it is for her to say to them this book is bad, this picture is feeble, or whatever it may be, without giving far more pain and rousing far more anger than a man would do who gave the same criticism. For if she begins to tell the truth, the figure in the looking-glass shrinks; his fitness for life is diminished. How is he to go on giving judgement, civilising natives, making laws, writing books, dressing up and speechifying at banquets, unless he can see himself at breakfast and at dinner at least twice the size he really is? So I reflected, crumbling my bread and stirring my coffee and now and again looking at the people in the street. The looking-glass vision is of supreme importance because it charges the vitality; it stimulates the nervous system. Take it away and man may die, like the drug fiend deprived of his cocaine. Under the spell of that illusion, I thought, looking out of the window, half the people on the pavement are striding to work. They put on their hats and coats in the morning under its agreeable rays. They start the day confident, braced, believing themselves desired at Miss Smith's tea party; they say to themselves as they go into the room, I am the superior of half the people here, and it is thus that they speak with that self-confidence, that self-assurance, which have had such profound consequences in public life and lead to such curious notes in the margin of the private mind. . . .

. . . women have burnt like beacons in all the works of all the poets from the beginning of time—Clytemnestra, Antigone, Cleopatra, Lady Macbeth, Phèdre, Cressida, Rosalind, Desdemona, the Duchess of Malfi, among the dramatists; then among the prose writers: Millamant, Clarissa, Becky Sharp, Anna Karenina, Emma Bovary, Madame de Guermantes—the names flock to mind, nor do they recall women "lacking in personality and character." Indeed, if woman had no existence save in the fiction written by men, one would imagine her a person of the utmost importance; very various; heroic and mean; splendid and sordid; infinitely beautiful and hideous in the extreme; as great as a man, some think even greater.[1] But this is woman in fiction. In fact, as Professor Trevelyan points out, she was locked up, beaten and flung about the room.

A very queer, composite being thus emerges. Imaginatively she is of the highest importance; practically she is completely insignificant. She pervades poetry from cover to cover; she is all but absent from history. She dominates the lives of kings and conquerors in fiction; in fact she was the slave of any boy whose parents forced a ring upon her finger. Some of the most inspired words, some of the most profound thoughts in literature fall from her lips; in real life she could hardly read, could scarcely spell, and was the property of her husband.

It was certainly an odd monster that one made up by reading the historians first and the poets afterwards—a worm winged like an eagle; the spirit of life and beauty in a kitchen chopping up suet. But these monsters, however amusing to the imagination, have no existence in fact. What one must do to bring her to life was to think poetically and prosaically at one and the same moment, thus keeping in touch with fact—that she is Mrs. Martin, aged thirty-six, dressed in blue, wearing a black hat and brown shoes; but not losing sight of fiction either—that she is a vessel in which all sorts of spirits and forces are coursing and flashing perpetually. The moment, however, that one tries this method with the Elizabethan woman, one branch of illumination fails; one is held up by the scarcity of facts. One knows nothing detailed, nothing perfectly true and substantial about her. History scarcely mentions her. . . .

. . . Let me imagine, since facts are so hard to come by, what would have happened had Shakespeare had a wonderfully gifted sister, called Judith, let us say. Shakespeare himself went, very probably—his mother was an heiress—to the grammar school, where he may have learnt Latin—Ovid, Virgil and Horace—and the elements of grammar and logic. He was, it is well known, a wild boy who poached rabbits, perhaps shot a deer, and had, rather sooner than he should have done, to marry a woman in the neighbourhood, who bore him a child rather quicker than was right. That escapade sent him to seek his fortune in London. He had, it seemed, a taste for the theatre; he began by holding horses at the stage door. Very soon he got work in the theatre, became a successful actor, and lived at the hub of the universe, meeting everybody, knowing everybody, practising his art on the boards, exercising his wits in the streets, and even getting access to the palace of the queen. Meanwhile his extraordinarily gifted sister, let us suppose, remained at home. She was as adventurous, as imaginative, as agog to see the world as he was. But she was not sent to school. She had no chance of learning grammar and logic, let alone of reading Horace and Virgil. She picked up a book now and then, one of her brother's perhaps, and read a few pages. But then her parents came in and told her to mend the stockings or mind the stew and not moon about with books and papers. They would have spoken sharply but kindly, for they were substantial people who knew the conditions of life for a woman and loved their daughter—indeed, more likely than not she was the apple of her father's eye. Perhaps she scribbled some pages up in an apple loft on the sly, but was careful to hide them or set fire to them. Soon, however, before she was out of her teens, she was to be betrothed to the son of a neighbouring wool-stapler. She cried out that marriage was hateful to her, and for that she was severely beaten by her father. Then he ceased to scold her. He begged her instead not to hurt him, not to shame him in this matter of her marriage. He would give her a chain of beads or a fine petticoat, he said; and there were tears in his eyes. How could she disobey him? How could she break his heart? The force of her own gift alone drove her to it. She made up a small parcel of her belongings, let herself down by a rope one summer's night and took the road to London. She was not seventeen. The birds that sat in the hedge were not more musical than she was. She had the quickest fancy, a gift like her brother's, for the tune of words. Like him, she had a taste for the theatre. She stood at the stage door; she wanted to act, she said. Men laughed in her face. The manager—a fat, loose-lipped man—guffawed. He bellowed something about poodles dancing and women acting—no woman, he said, could possibly be an actress. He hinted—you can imagine what. She could get no training in her craft. Could she even seek her dinner in a tavern or roam the streets at midnight? Yet her genius was for fiction and lusted to feed abundantly upon the lives of men and women and the study of their ways. At last—for she was very young, oddly like Shakespeare the poet in her face, with the same grey eyes and rounded brows—at last Nick Greene the actor-manager took pity on her; she found herself with child by the gentleman and so—who shall measure the heat and violence of the poet's heart when caught and tangled in a woman's body?—killed herself one winter's night and lies buried at some cross-roads where the omnibuses now stop outside the Elephant and Castle.

That, more or less, is how the story would run, I think, if a woman in Shakespeare's day had had Shakespeare's genius. But for my part, I agree with the deceased bishop, if such he was—it is unthinkable that any woman in Shakespeare's day should have had Shakespeare's genius. For genius like Shakespeare's is not born among labouring, uneducated, servile people. It was not born in England among the Saxons and the Britons. It is not born today among the working classes. How, then, could it have been born among women whose work began, according to Professor Trevelyan, almost before they were out of the nursery, who were forced to it by their parents and held to it by all the power of law and custom? Yet genius of a sort must have existed among women as it must have existed among the working classes. Now and again an Emily Brontë or a Robert Burns blazes out and proves its presence. But certainly it never got itself on to paper. When, however, one reads of a witch being ducked, of a woman possessed by devils, of a wise woman selling herbs, or even of a very remarkable man who had a mother, then I think we are on the track of a lost novelist, a suppressed poet, of some mute and inglorious Jane Austen, some Emily Brontë who dashed her brains out on the moor or mopped and mowed about the high- ways crazed with the torture that her gift had put her to. Indeed, I would venture to guess that Anon, who wrote so many poems without signing them, was often a woman. It was a woman Edward Fitzgerald, I think, suggested who made the ballads and the folk-songs, crooning them to her children, beguiling her spinning with them, or the length of the winter's night.

This may be true or it may be false—who can say?—but what is true in it, so it seemed to me, reviewing the story of Shakespeare's sister as I had made it, is that any woman born with a great gift in the sixteenth century would certainly have gone crazed, shot herself, or ended her days in some lonely cottage outside the village, half witch, half wizard, feared and mocked at. For it needs little skill in psychology to be sure that a highly gifted girl who had tried to use her gift for poetry would have been so thwarted and hindered by other people, so tortured and pulled asunder by her own contrary instincts, that she must have lost her health and sanity to a certainty. . . .

. . . But it is obvious that the values of women differ very often from the values which have been made by the other sex; naturally, this is so. Yet it is the masculine values that prevail. Speaking crudely, football and sport are "important"; the worship of fashion, the buying of clothes "trivial." And these values are inevitably transferred from life to fiction. This is an important book, the critic assumes, because it deals with war. This is an insignifi- cant book because it deals with the feelings of women in a drawing-room. A scene in a battlefield is more important than a scene in a shop—everywhere and much more subtly the difference of value persists. The whole structure, therefore, of the early nineteenth- century novel was raised, if one was a woman, by a mind which was slightly pulled from the straight, and made to alter its clear vision in deference to external authority. One has only to skim those old forgotten novels and listen to the tone of voice in which they are written to divine that the writer was meeting criticism; she was saying this by way of aggression, or that by way of conciliation. She was admitting that she was "only a woman," or protesting that she was "as good as a man." She met that criticism as her temperament dictated, with docility and diffidence, or with anger and emphasis. It does not matter which it was; she was thinking of something other than the thing itself. Down comes her book upon our heads. There was a flaw in the centre of it. And I thought of all the women's novels that lie scattered, like small pock-marked apples in an orchard, about the second- hand book shops of London. It was the flaw in the center that had rotted them. She had altered her values in deference to the opinion of others.

But how impossible it must have been for them not to budge either to the right or to the left. What genius, what integrity it must have required in face of all that criticism, in the midst of that purely patriarchal society, to hold fast to the thing as they saw it without shrinking. Only Jane Austen did it and Emily Brontë. It is another feather, perhaps the finest, in their caps. They wrote as women write, not as men write. Of all the thousand women who wrote novels then, they alone entirely ignored the perpetual admonitions of the eternal pedagogue—write this, think that. They alone were deaf to that persistent voice, now grumbling, now patronising, now domineering, now grieved, now shocked, now angry, now avuncular, that voice which cannot let women alone, but must be at them, like some too conscientious governess, adjuring them, like Sir Egerton Brydges, to be refined; dragging even into the criticism of poetry criticism of sex;[2] admonishing them, if they would be good and win, as I suppose, some shiny prize, to keep within certain limits which the gentleman in question thinks suitable: ". . . female novelists should only aspire to excellence by courageously acknowledging the limitations of their sex."[3] That puts the matter in a nutshell, and when I tell you, rather to your surprise, that this sentence was written not in August 1828 but in August 1928, you will agree, I think, that however delightful it is to us now, it represents a vast body of opinion—I am not going to stir those old pools, I take only what chance has floated to my feet—that was far more vigorous and far more vocal a century ago. It would have needed a very stalwart young woman in 1828 to disregard all those snubs and chidings and promises of prizes. One must have been something of a firebrand to say to oneself, Oh, but they can't buy literature too. Literature is open to everybody. . . .

How can I further encourage you to go about the business of life? Young women, I would say, and please attend, for the peroration is beginning, you are, in my opinion, disgracefully ignorant. You have never made a discovery of any sort of importance. You have never shaken an empire or led an army into battle. The plays of Shakespeare are not by you, and you have never introduced a barbarous race to the blessings of civilisation. What is your excuse? It is all very well for you to say, pointing to the streets and squares and forests of the globe swarming with black and white and coffee-coloured inhabitants, all busily engaged in traffic and enterprise and love-making, we have had other work on our hands. Without our doing, those seas would be unsailed and those fertile lands a desert. We have borne and bred and washed and taught, perhaps to the age of six or seven years, the one thousand six hundred and twenty-three million human beings who are, according to statistics, at present in existence, and that, allowing that some had help, takes time.

There is truth in what you say—I will not deny it. But at the same time may I remind you that there have been at least two colleges for women in existence in England since the year 1866; that after the year 1880 a married woman was allowed by law to possess her own property; and that in 1919—which is a whole nine years ago—she was given a vote? May I also remind you that the most of the professions have been open to you for close on ten years now? When you reflect upon these immense privileges and the length of time during which they have been enjoyed, and the fact that there must be at this moment some two thousand women capable of earning over five hundred a year in one way or another, you will agree that the excuse of lack of opportunity, training, encouragement, leisure and money no longer holds good. Moreover, the economists are telling us that Mrs. Seton has had too many children. You must, of course, go on bearing children, but, so they say, in twos and threes, not in tens and twelves.

Thus, with some time on your hands and with some book learning in your brains—you have had enough of the other kind, and are sent to college partly, I suspect, to be uneducated—surely you should embark upon another stage of your very long, very laborious and highly obscure career. A thousand pens are ready to suggest what you should do and what effect you will have. My own suggestion is a little fantastic, I admit; I prefer, therefore, to put it in the form of fiction.

I told you in the course of this paper that Shakespeare had a sister; but do not look for her in Sir Sidney Lee's life of the poet. She died young—alas, she never wrote a word. She lies buried where the omnibuses now stop, opposite the Elephant and Castle. Now my belief is that this poet who never wrote a word and was buried at the crossroads still lives. She lives in you and in me, and in many other women who are not here tonight, for they are washing up the dishes and putting the children to bed. But she lives; for great poets do not die; they are continuing presences; they need only the opportunity to walk among us in the flesh. This opportunity, as I think, it is now coming within your power to give her. For my belief is that if we live another century or so—I am talking of the common life which is the real life and not of the little separate lives which we live as individuals—and have five hundred a year each of us and rooms of our own; if we have the habit of freedom and the courage to write exactly what we think; if we escape a little from the common sitting-room and see human beings not always in their relation to each other but in relation to reality; and the sky, too, and the trees or whatever it may be in themselves; if we look past Milton's bogey, for no human being should shut out the view; if we face the fact, for it is a fact, that there is no arm to cling to, but that we go alone and that our relation is to the world of reality and not only to the world of men and women, then the opportunity will come and the dead poet who was Shakespeare's sister will put on the body which she has so often laid down. Drawing her life from the lives of the unknown who were her forerunners, as her brother did before her, she will be born. As for her coming without that preparation, without that effort on our part, without that determination that when she is born again she shall find it possible to live and write her poetry, that we cannot expect, for that would be impossible. But I maintain that she would come if we worked for her, and that so to work, even in poverty and obscurity, is worth while.

Notes

1. "It remains a strange and almost inexplicable fact that in Athena's city, where women were kept in almost Oriental suppression as odalisques or drudges, the stage should yet have produced figures like Clytemnestra and Cassandra, Attosa and Antigone, Phèdre and Medea, and all the other heroines who dominate play after play of the 'misogynist' Euripides. But the paradox of this world where in real life a respectable woman could hardly show her face alone in the street, and yet on the stage woman equals or surpasses man, has never been satisfactorily explained. In modern tragedy the same predominance exists. At all events, a very cursory survey of Shakespeare's work (similarly with Webster, though not with Marlowe or Jonson) suffices to reveal how this dominance, this initiative of women, persists from Rosalind to Lady Macbeth. So too in Racine; six of his tragedies bear their heroines' names; and what male

characters of his shall we set against Hermione and Andromaque, Bérénice and Roxane, Phèdre and Athalie? So again with Ibsen: what men shall we match with Solveig and Nora, Hedda and Hilda Wangel and Rebecca West?"—F. L. Lucas, *Tragedy*, pp. 114–15.

2. "[She] has a metaphysical purpose, and that is a dangerous obsession, especially with a woman, for women rarely possess men's healthy love of rhetoric. It is a strange lack in the sex which is in other things more primitive and more materialistic."—*New Criterion*, June 1928.

3. "If, like the reporter, you believe that female novelists should only aspire to excellence by courageously acknowledging the limitations of their sex (Jane Austen [has] demonstrated how gracefully this gesture can be accomplished) . . . . "—*Life and Letters*, August 1928.

VII. The Third Reich, the Second World War, and the Holocaust

Many intellectuals, poets, and artists were pessimistic about the human condition following the First World War. But there were others who hoped that lessons learned from the War would make it possible to produce a lasting peace. Moreover, with the return of economic prosperity in the later part of the 1920s, there was renewed optimism about the European future. But just as it appeared that there was a return to peace, growth, and normalcy, the greatest economic downturn of the twentieth century—the Great Depression—swept through the capitalist world with unprecedented speed and intensity, placing unbearable strains on already fragile societies.

The most famous casualty was the German Weimar Republic. Germany's first experiment in liberal democracy, shaped in the power vacuum created by a defeated and discredited regime in 1918, would have found it difficult to succeed under the best of circumstances. But from the onset, it faced conditions that seriously undermined its authority. In the public imagination—exploited by the Nazis—it was responsible for the humiliation of Germany at the postwar peace talks. The Weimar Republic was blamed for the crushing reparations that Germany had to pay the victorious Allies; and it was never forgiven for its recognition (forced upon it) of German responsibility for the War. It managed to survive the out-of-control inflation of the early 1920s, when an egg cost 150 billion marks, only to be destroyed by the economic devastation of the 1930s, when unemployment hovered at 25%.

One of the first signs of decay was the disintegration of the political center. As conditions in Germany worsened, the forces that stood for compromise and moderation gave way to those preaching confrontation and radical change. Among those who benefited, though it proved to be short-lived, was the German Communist party. A group of dedicated revolutionaries composed of intellectuals and workers, it saw the Great Depression as the final crisis of capitalism predicted by Marx in *The Communist Manifesto.* The Soviet Regime—which proved immune to the Depression—appeared to them as the wave of the future. Of course, the real story of the thirties was the rapid growth of the radical right— particularly the National Socialist or Nazi Party—which used the economic collapse as an avenue to move from the periphery to the mainstream of German politics.

National Socialism was a tributary of a broader 'fascist' stream. The word *fascism* comes from the Latin *fasces,* a word signifying the bundle of rods with ax head carried by Roman magistrates. The fascist parties of the interwar years were simultaneously anticapitalist and anticommunist, seeing the "total state" as an alternative to the chaos of liberalism and the internationalism preached by the Bolsheviks. Fascists embraced a nationalist rhetoric which they delivered in a highly-charged emotional form. Central to their success was their skill at exploiting the new means of mass communications—such as radio and film—for propaganda purposes and their ability to create tightly-knit party organizations. The fascist parties saw themselves as being engaged in a war over the culture of Europe: the maintenance of 'traditional' values was as important as industrial growth and development.

The importance that Adolf Hitler (1889–1945) attached to the struggle over culture is evident in his speech dedicating the House of German Art in July 1937. The museum was the first public building project of the Third Reich. It was designed by Hitler's favorite architect at the time, Paul Ludwig Troost, in a style of monumental classicism, a visual proclamation that the Reich represented the culmination of Western Civilization. In the present context, what interests us about Hitler's speech are not only the 'traditional' and 'nationalist value' in art that he embraces, but the 'modernist' ones that he condemns. Hitler uses the occasion to denounce modernism in painting and architecture, movements to which German artists and architects were major contributors. He lumps together modernism, the Jews, and the Bolsheviks, seeing them all as different expressions of the same 'decadence.' And he wonders whether artists who have such twisted, distorted visions should be allowed to produce offspring. As farfetched as this might sound, Hitler was reiterating what was already established Nazi policy. In 1933, one of the first legislative acts of the Third Reich declared that compulsory sterilization of 'undesirables' was necessary to ensure the elimination of inferior genes. In all, four hundred thousand undesirables—both men and women—became the victims of forced sterilization.

There are of course only a few steps between forced sterilization and the "final solution" of the Holocaust. So much as been written about this darkest of all European episodes that it is virtually impossible to say anything about it that hasn't been said before. Yet in a book which is about the "trials of modernity" it is perhaps worth pointing out how 'modern' the death camps were—how 'rational,' 'scientific,' and 'efficient' the methods of extermination. Indeed, the Holocaust is as much a part of the modern experience as is a scientific breakthrough in fighting a disease or a revolutionary technological development such as the automobile or the computer. In addition, while the Jews suffered more than any other group—six million of them perished in the camps—they were not the only victims. As many as five million others—including Slavs, Soviet prisoners of war, communists, gypsies, and homosexuals—were victims as well. Both the extent of Jewish suffering and the fact that others suffered also is suggested in the stirring account by Leon Ginsburg (b. 1932) of his effort to escape capture and certain death during the Nazi occupation of the Ukraine. Ginsburg's story is so extraordinary that a fictionalized version could hardly be more dramatic. He is one of countless survivors who endured because of a remarkable will to live and an extraordinary degree of luck at crucial moments. Many survivors went on to live fruitful and productive lives, but they are permanently marked by their experiences, and have told their stories so that we will never forget.

Fascism was effective because it was able to prey on the worst side of human beings. But its success was not universal, and no picture of the period is complete without reference to those men and women who refused to accept it, either by covert resistance or by helping those who were potentially its victims. The European Resistance has been romanticized; its numbers have been inflated; and its impact has been exaggerated. But this does mean it is not important. Two intellectuals who were important voices in the struggle against fascism were Jean-Paul Sartre (1905–1980) and Bertolt Brecht (1898–1956). Perhaps the most important French thinker of the twentieth century, Sartre was a philosopher, novelist, playwright, essayist, and political activist. He joined the French army in 1939 and was taken prisoner in Alsace during the German invasion. After nine months in a prisoner-of-war camp—an experience which made him optimistic about human solidarity—he went to Paris and took part in the Resistance movement, writing for clandestine publications such as *Combat*. Sartre is arguably the most famous proponent of the philosophy of existentialism, and in his essay "Existentialism is a Humanism" he provides a famous definition of it: "existence precedes essence." Equally important, the essay demonstrates his Resistance experience. Writing in the aftermath of the War, Sartre denies that existentialism is a pessimistic philosophy. He stresses individual moral responsibility.

While Sartre spent the war years in Nazi-occupied France, the German playwright Bertolt Brecht was forced to leave his homeland because of his anti-fascist views. He migrated to Denmark, Finland, and Sweden before he settled in the United States in 1941. He returned to East Germany after the War where he lived until his death. As a playwright, Brecht attempted to create an "epic theater"—one in which the audience was forced to think about and take sides, rather than simply identify, with what was taking place on stage. In "Writing the Truth: Five Difficulties," the first version of which was published in 1934 (only one year after Hitler came to power), he confronts how an author can speak the truth when the world that he lives in is founded on lies. Unlike Sartre, Brecht's perspective is founded on a highly personal interpretation of Marxism. Yet both men are alike in that they reiterate the most basic human truths at a time when the world in which they inhabit seems to have forgotten them.

Adolf Hitler

from Speech Dedicating the House of German Art (1937)

Four years ago, when the festive cornerstone-laying ceremonies for this structure took place, we were all aware that not only was a stone being laid in place for a building, but that the ground had to be prepared for a new and truly German art. It was imperative to bring about a turning point in the development of all German cultural activity. . . .

The collapse and general decline of Germany was, as we know, not only economic and political but, possibly to a greater extent, cultural. Moreover, these proceedings were not to be explained solely through the fact of a lost war. Such catastrophes have often affected states and peoples, and it has been those which have not infrequently been the stimulus for purification and, thereby, inner uplifting. That flood of slime and filth which the year 1918 vomited to the surface was not created by the loss of the war, but was instead only released by it. A body tainted inherently, through and through, discovered only through defeat the total extent of its own decomposition. . . .

Certainly the economic decline had naturally been felt the most because its effect alone was emphatically able to reach the awareness of the great masses. The political decline, on the other hand, was either flatly denied by countless Germans or at the least not recognized, while the cultural decline was neither seen nor understood by the majority of the people. It is noteworthy that during this time of general decline and collapse catchwords and phrases simultaneously began to make their triumphant appearance. . . . But the general distress, especially the misery of the millions of unemployed, could not be denied, and neither could the consequences for those affected be excused. It was therefore more difficult to hide the economic than the political collapse of the nation with catchwords or phrases.

In the political sphere for a time the democratic and Marxist phraseology of the November [i.e., Weimar] Republic, as well as continual references to various aspects of international solidarity and the effectiveness of international institutions, and so on, was able to veil from the German people the unparalleled decline and collapse. . . . Far more successful and, above all, far more enduring was the effect of these phrases and catchwords in the cultural field, where they created complete confusion concerning the essential character of culture in general and about German cultural life in particular. . . . In this sphere, more than in others, the Jews employed all means and devices that shape and guide public opinion. The Jews were especially clever in utilizing their control of the press and with the aid of so-called art critics were able not only to create confusion about the character and purpose of art but were also able to destroy generally sound perceptions. . . .

Art was said to be an experience of the international community, and thus all understanding of its essential association with a people was destroyed. Art was said to be associated with a particular age, so that there was no actual art of a people or of a race, but only an art form of a certain period. According to this theory the Greeks did not create Greek art, but instead it was the expression of a certain age. The same was said to be true of Rome. . . . So today there is no German, French, Japanese, or Chinese art, but there is only simply "modern" art. . . . According to such a theory art and artistry is put on the same level as the craftsmanship of our modern tailor shops and fashion studios, according to the principle of something different every year. One time Impressionism, then Futurism, Cubism, perhaps even Dadaism . . . If it were not so tragic, it would be almost comical to find out how many catchwords and phrases these so-called students of art used during recent years to describe and interpret their wretched creations.

It was sad to experience how these catchwords and this verbal nonsense created not only a general feeling of uncertainty in the appraisal of artistic achievement or endeavor but contributed to the intimidation of those who might otherwise have protested against this cultural Bolshevism. . . . And so, just as today clothes are judged not by their beauty but only according to whether or not they are modern, so are the old masters simply rejected because they are not modern and it is not fashionable to admire them or to acquire their works.

But true art is and remains eternal, it does not follow the law of seasonal fashion assessment of works created in dress design studios. It merits appreciation because it is an eternal revelation arising from the depths of the essential character of a people. . . .

. . . But those whose works do not have eternal value do not like to speak of eternities. They prefer to dim the radiance of these giants who reach from out of the past into the future, in order that contemporaries might discover their own tiny flames. These lightweight smear artists are at best only the products of a day. Yesterday they did not exist, today they are modern, and the day after tomorrow they will be forgotten. These littlest producers of art were overjoyed by the Jewish discovery that art was connected to a certain period. Lacking all qualifications for eternal value, their art could now at least be the art of the present time. . . .

It is these artistic dwarfs who themselves demand the greatest tolerance in the judgment of their own works, but who in turn are extremely intolerant in their valuation of the works of others, be they artists from the past or the present. Just as in politics, there was here, too, a conspiracy of incapacity and mediocrity against better works of the past, present, and the anticipated future. . . . These miserable art-critiquing windbags were always able to take advantage of the cowardice and insecurity of our so-called wealthy citizens because these nouveau-riche types were too uncultivated to pass their own judgment on art. . . . These types of art creators and art dealers loved nothing better than to play into each other's hands, and to characterize all those who saw through their scheme as "uncultivated philistines." But where the parvenu was concerned, the favored and surest method to counteract any latent doubts and resistance was to emphasize right from the beginning that the artwork in question was not easy for just anyone to understand and that because of that its price was set correspondingly high. These so-called art connoisseurs have grown rich by these methods, but no one understandably wants to be told by one of these types that he lacks appreciation for art, or does not have the money to pay for it. This type of buyer often judged the quality of a work simply by the amount of the price being asked for it. And when this nonsense was then also praised in obscure phrases, it became all the easier to come up with the money. In the end, one could still secretly hope that the thing that one did not understand oneself, one's neighbor most certainly would not understand either. . . .

Here today I want to make the following declaration: until the seizure of power by National Socialism, there existed in Germany a so-called modern art; that is, as the word implies—almost every year there was a new one. National Socialist Germany, however, desires to have again a "German art," which, like all creative works of a people, should and will be an eternal one. When the cornerstone was laid for this building it signaled the beginning of the construction of a temple for art; not for a so-called modern art, but for an eternal German art; better yet: a House of Art for the German people, and not for an international art for the year 1937, '40, '50, or '60. Art is not dependent on an age but on a people. . . . Time changes, the years come and go . . . but the people are a constant point within the entire range of phenomena. . . . There can therefore be no standard of yesterday and today, of modern and unmodern, but only of "valueless" or "valuable," or of "eternal" or "transitory." . . . And therefore when I speak of German art—for which this House was built—what I want to see is the standard for that art in the German people, in their character and their life, in their feeling, their emotions, and in their development.

From the history of the development of our race we know that it is composed of a number of more or less distinct races that in the course of thousands of years, thanks to the formative influence of a certain outstanding racial kernel, produced that mixture we see before us in our people today. This force, which formed the people in time past and which still today continues to shape it, stems from the same Aryan branch of mankind we recognize not only as the carrier of our own civilization but of the earlier civilizations of the ancient world.

The way in which our race was composed has produced the manysidedness of our own cultural development. . . . But nonetheless, we the German people, as the end result of this historical development, wish to have an art that corresponds to the ever-increasing homogeneity of our racial composition, and that would then in itself present the characteristics of unity and homogeneity. The question has often been posed, to define just what it means "to be German." Among all the many definitions that have been put forth, it appears to me that the most praiseworthy are those that have not attempted to arrive at a definition but have instead chosen to state a law. The most fitting law I would propose has already been expressed by a great German: "To be German is to be clear." What this means is that to be German is to be logical and above all, to be true. . . . The deepest inner desire to have such a truly German art is reflected in this law of clarity, and has always been present in our people. It has inspired our great painters, our sculptors, our architects, our thinkers and poets, and above all our musicians. . . .

During the long years of planning the formation of a new Reich, I thought much about the tasks that would confront us in the cultural cleansing of the people's life, because Germany was to have not only a political and economic rebirth, but above all else, Germany was to undergo a cultural renaissance. . . .

. . . I was convinced, after our collapse, that a people that have stumbled and from then on have been trampled on by the whole world have all the greater duty consciously to assert their own value toward their oppressors. There can be no greater proof of the highest rights of a people to their own life than immortal cultural achievements. I was therefore always determined that if fate should one day give us power I would debate these issues with no one, but would make my own decisions. Because an understanding for such great tasks has not been granted to everyone. . . .

Among the countless plans that floated through my mind both during the war and in the period following the collapse was the thought of building in Munich, the city with the greatest tradition of cultural exhibits, a great new exhibition palace. This was needed in view of the totally undignified condition of the old building. Years ago I also thought about the location where this building now stands. . . . In 1931, the seizure of power by National Socialism still appeared to be in the distant future, and there was little prospect of reserving for the Third Reich the building of a new exhibition palace. For a time it actually did look as though the men of November wanted to create an art exhibit building in Munich which had very little in common with art, but which would have corresponded to the Bolshevik tenor of the times. Possibly some of you remember the plans that were drawn up during those days. . . . The intended building was difficult to define, and could easily have served as a Saxon yarn factory, a market hall of a town, or possibly even a train station or [an indoor] swimming pool . . . but the lack of resolve of my former political enemies [to carry out this project] gave me joy and provided the only hope that in the end the erection of the new building . . . might still fall to the Third Reich, and that it would become its first task. . . .

This new building we have conceived is, you will no doubt agree, of a truly bold and artistic design. It is so unique and so individual that it cannot be compared with anything else. . . . It is, I daresay, a true monument for this city and, beyond that, for German art. . . . This House that has arisen here possesses proper dignity and will enable the highest artistic achievements to present themselves to the German people. This House represents a turning point; it brings to an end the era of chaotic, incompetent architecture. This, the first of the new buildings, will take its place among the immortal achievements of our German artistic life.

But you understand now that it is not enough merely to provide the House . . . the exhibit itself must also bring about a turning point. . . . If I presume to make a judgment, speak my opinion, and act accordingly. I do this not just because of my outlook on German art, but I claim this right because of the contribution I myself have made to the restoration of German art. Because our present state, which I and my comrades in the struggle have created, has alone provided German art with the conditions for a new, vigorous flowering.

It was not Bolshevik art collectors or their literary henchmen who laid the foundation for a new art or even secured the continued existence of art in Germany. No, we were the ones who created this state and have since then provided vast sums for the encouragement of art. We have given art great new tasks. . . . I declare here and now that it is my irrevocable resolve that just as in the sphere of political bewilderment, I am going to make a clean sweep of phrases in the artistic life of Germany. "Worth of art" which cannot be comprehended and are validated only through bombastic instructions for use . . . from now on will no longer be foisted upon the German people!

We are more interested in ability than in so-called intent. An artist who is counting on having his works displayed, in this House or anywhere else in Germany, must possess ability. Intent is something that is self-evident. These windbags have tried to make their works more palatable by representing them as expressions of a new age; but they need to be told that art does not create a new age, that it is the general life of peoples which fashions itself anew and therefore often seeks to express itself anew. . . . Men of letters are not the creators of new epochs; it is the fighters, those who truly shape and lead peoples, who make history. . . . Aside from that, it is either impudent effrontery or an inscrutable stupidity to exhibit to our own age works that might have been made ten or twenty thousand years ago by a man of the Stone Age. They talk of primitive art, but they forget that it is not the function of art to retreat backward from the level of development a people has already reached. The function of art can only be to symbolize the vitality of this development.

The new age of today is at work on a new human type. Tremendous efforts are being made in countless spheres of life in order to elevate our people, to make our men, boys, lads, girls, and women more healthy and thereby stronger and more beautiful. From this strength and beauty streams forth a new feeling of life, and a new joy in life. Never before was humanity in its external appearance and perceptions closer to the ancient world than it is today.

This type of human, which we saw last year during the Olympic games . . . exuding proud physical strength—this my good prehistoric art-stutterers—this is the "type" of the new age. But what do you manufacture? Deformed cripples and cretins, women who inspire only disgust, men who are more like wild beasts, children who, if they were alive, would be regarded as God's curse! . . . Let no one say that that is how these artists see things. From the pictures submitted for exhibition, I must assume that the eye of some men shows them things different from the way they really are. There really are men who can see in the shapes of our people only decayed cretins; who feel that meadows are blue, the heavens green, clouds sulphur-yellow. They like to say that they experience these things in this way.

I do not want to argue about whether or not they really experience this. But in the name of the German people I only want to prevent these pitiable unfortunates, who clearly suffer from defective vision, from attempting with their chatter to force on their contemporaries the results of their faulty observations, and indeed from presenting them as "art." Here there are only two possibilities open: either these so-called artists really do see things this way and believe in that which they create—and if so, one has to investigate how this defective vision arose—if it is a mechanical problem or if it came about through heredity. The first case would be pitiable, while the second would be a matter for the Ministry of the Interior, which would then deal with the problem of preventing the perpetuation of such horrid disorders. Or they themselves do not believe in the reality of such impressions, but are for different reasons attempting to annoy the nation with this humbug. If this is the case, then it is a matter for a criminal court.

This House, in any case, was not planned or built for the works of art incompetents or for maltreaters of art. A thousand workmen did not labor for four and a half years on this building only to have creations exhibited here by people who are lazy to excess and who spend but five hours bespattering a canvas, while hoping confidently that the boldness of the pricing would produce the desired effect and result in the hailing of the work as the most brilliant lightning-birth of a genius. No, the hard work of the builders of this House demands equally hard work from those who want to exhibit here. I do not care in the least if these pseudo-artists then are left to cackle over each other's eggs!

The artist does not create for the artist, but for the people! We will see to it that from here no the people will be called on to judge their own art. No one must say that the people have no appreciation for a truly valuable enrichment of its cultural life. Long before the critics did justice to the genius of a Richard Wagner he had the people on his side. For their part, however, during the last few years the people have had no affinity for the so-called modern art that was placed before them. The mass of the people moved through our art exhibits in a completely uninterested fashion or stayed away altogether. The people's healthy perceptions recognized that all these smearings of canvas were really the outcome of an impudent and unashamed arrogance or of a simply shocking lack of skill. Millions of people felt instinctively that these art-stammerings of the last few decades were more like the achievements that might have been produced by untalented children of from eight to ten years old and could under no circumstances be regarded as the expression of our own time or of the German future.

Since we know today that the development of millions of years repeats itself in every individual but is compressed into a few decades, we have the proof that an artistic creation that does not surpass the achievement of eight-year-old children is not "modern" or even "futuristic" but is, on the contrary, highly archaic. It probably is not as developed as the art of the Stone Age period, when the people scratched pictures of their environment on the walls of caves. . . .

I know, therefore, that when the *Volk* passes through these galleries it will recognize in me its own spokesman and counselor . . . it will draw a sigh of relief and joyously express its agreement with this purification of art. And this is decisive, for an art that cannot count on the ready inner agreement of the broad, healthy mass of the people, but which must instead rely on the support of small, partially indifferent cliques, is intolerable. . . . We are convinced that the German people will again fully support and joyously appreciate the future truly great artists from within their ranks. . . .

This exhibition then is but a beginning. . . . But the opening of this exhibit is also the beginning of the end of the stultification of German art and the end of the cultural destruction of our people. . . . Many of our young artists will recognize the path they will have to take; they will draw inspiration from the greatness of the time in which we all live, and they will draw the courage to work hard and will in the end complete the task. And when a sacred conscientiousness at last comes into its own, then, I have no doubt, the Almighty will lift from this mass of decent creators of art, several individuals who will rise to the eternal star-covered heaven of immortal, God-favored artists of great ages. . . . We believe that especially today, when in so many spheres the highest individual achievements are standing the test, so also in the sphere of art will the highest value of personality again emerge to assert itself.

LEON GINSBURG

The Ordeal (1993)

Leon Ginsburg, sixty, is slim and wiry in a neat, dark-gray suit, striped shirt, and flowered tie. An electrical engineer, Leon owns a company that manufactures high-tech dental equipment for which he holds several patents. The home he shares with his wife in Rockland County, New York, is impeccably neat—except for Leon's study, a small room crammed to the gills with stacks of Holocaust-related material, including pictures, maps, books, and his own personal notes. "This is where I go to steal away from everything," he explains. "Sometimes we think of forgetting. Some people want to forget, but I feel more than ever now that we need to remember."

"I was born in 1932 in Maciejow, a small town at the border where Poland ends and Russia begins. Our community was basically Hasidic. We all kept our heads covered, and the older men wore beards. The Ukrainians who ruled that part of Poland were viciously anti-Semitic, but we were unprepared for the Germans and their absolute policy of getting rid of the Jews. I was on the street the day the Germans marched into town. As a gesture of friendship the rabbi was sitting at a little table on the street with bread and salt, the traditional way of saying welcome. Suddenly one of the Germans pushed the table over and told the rabbi to get out of there. I didn't understand what was happening.

"Shortly after that an SS group settled in the town. The first thing they did was to order all the men between sixteen and sixty to report. The SS made it clear that anyone who didn't go could be killed. So most of the people reported. But once they lined up, they couldn't get out; they were covered by machine guns. I was just a little boy, but I saw what was happening, and I got out of that area quickly. Later I heard the shots. All those people had been marched inside the headquarters and killed. After that the killing was at random, but for us Jews normal life was over. We had a six P.M. curfew. If you were caught outside after that, you were shot. I would hear the German patrols marching on the cobblestone streets a block away.

"One night we were all at my grandparents' house on the outskirts of town when they began rounding up Jews. I woke up and saw a light from outside on the ceiling. Yelling in German, the soldiers pounded on the door. My grandfather's name was Yakov, and they were calling his name. 'Yakov, open up!' My brother was afraid to go, but I opened the door, and they came in with flashlights. Right away they asked me where the women were. Almost in a crying way, I said, 'I don't know, they took them away! Maybe *you* can tell *me*!

"Ignoring me, the soldiers began to search. One of them ran down to the basement. Then he came up and asked me where the attic was. I pointed. He said, 'Anybody up there?' My mother, sister, grandmother, and aunts were all up there, but I said no. Then the soldier took out his gun and put it to my head and cocked it. He said, "If we find somebody there, you're caput.' He asked me again, 'Anybody there?' I said, 'No.' And you know what? When I think of it now, I feel sorry for that young child I was with my little round red cheeks that all the relatives loved to pinch. Either I didn't understand fear or maybe I didn't think that they would really do anything to me. Luckily the attic was big, and everyone up there was hiding in a corner, blocked off from view so that the Germans never saw them.

"That roundup was over in a week. After that things were quiet until 1942, when Hitler became so maddened and poisoned with his wish to get rid of Jews that he ordered complete annihilation. Our town was one of three in a row. They concentrated first on killing twenty-four thousand Jews in Kovel, one of the other towns. They dug big ditches or graves. They would just take the people there, shoot them on the spot, and push them in. We weren't allowed to move from our town, but a Polish woman who came from Kovel talked about corpses in the street.

"Our turn came in August. There was a feeling in the air that something was going to happen, so my mother arranged for a hiding place in a basement we entered through a tunnel under an outside toilet. We slept there that night. There must have been fifty people in that place. Early the next morning we heard voices. It seemed that the Ukrainians and the Germans were going through all the houses looking for Jews.

"We stayed quiet and were safe that day, but there was one woman with us who had five children, including a little girl who wouldn't stop crying. When that little girl finally fell asleep, her mother carried her up to the house above our hiding place. That was a tremendous decision to make; it was certain death for that little girl. Of course, if she'd stayed below with us, then we'd all have been caught.

"However, the plan backfired. When the little girl woke up, the Ukrainians were in the house and asked where her mother was. The little girl ran to the area where the toilet was, but the soldiers couldn't understand her. They searched inside the house for hours. Finally they realized that this girl was pointing to the toilet, so they touched it and realized it moved. Then they found our place—and that was basically it. We were trapped! People started filing out.

"There was a space boarded up where there had once been a window. As most of the people were going out, my mother suddenly ripped off one piece of board. She whispered for me to get in there and put the board back. When I got in, I had to hold the nail in place with my hand. Then my mother hid under some bedding. By then it was dark, and the police were lighting matches. One had a rifle with a bayonet on it. He was right next to me. Suddenly he took that bayonet and stabbed my mother, who was still hiding under the bedding. She screamed. I didn't know how badly she was hurt, but they took her away. I sat there frozen! They were only inches away from me—so close I had to stop breathing.

"I don't know how long I sat like that. Probably for hours. Then I heard someone speaking Yiddish. I peeked out and I recognized one of the Jews from the town. He said he was looking for a pair of galoshes. He was going into the woods and he was worried about mud! I followed him up to the attic of his house. Then we heard a noise. The man peered down—right into the face of a Ukrainian militiaman with a gun. The militiaman saw the Jew and grabbed him. I stayed hidden as the Jewish man was taken away.

"I sat there stunned, not knowing what to do. I felt like a tiny fish swimming in a sea of danger. Everybody was ready to grab me. Where was I supposed to go? What was I supposed to do? As I sat there, I heard a wagon pull up. Then I realized that soldiers were looting the house, which was the practice. I had to get out. Fortunately I remembered my mother mentioning another hiding place a few houses away, so I went to it, and there I found a little opening, just big enough to crawl through. Suddenly I was dizzy and I almost fainted. Someone hiding in there pulled me in and poured a little whiskey on my lips, which revived me. At last I felt safe! I stayed there for the next few days. These people had a barrel of water, but when we needed more, we had to sneak out to the well, which was the chain type that you crank, and it made a lot of noise squeaking. One of us had to do it very carefully, while someone else watched.

"Soon, however, food became a problem. I volunteered to go get some fruit from the orchard right next to the German headquarters. I chose a Sunday when I knew that most people would be in church. Then I sneaked over there. When the old woman at the orchard saw me, she crossed herself; she couldn't believe any Jewish kid was still alive. She was afraid the Ukrainian workers would see me, so she gave me some fruit and hid me in her attic. She told me to wait until dark, when it would be safe. However, I was scared to wait, so I put the fruit inside my shirt, crept out the window and down to the ground below.

"In order to get back to the hiding place where I had been staying, I had to go through town. Before I knew it, there was somebody in a wagon yelling, 'Jew!' It was a fifteen-year-old boy who lived next door to my grandfather, so I acted casual, not running. Then this teenager jumped off the wagon and started chasing me. As I ran, he grabbed me. He yelled, 'I got you.' A second later I put my hand in my pocket as if I had a gun. I said, 'Are you going to let me go or not?'

"Amazingly he fell for the trick! This kid, who was five years older and so much bigger than I, said in a cringing tone, 'You know I didn't mean anything.' All he had to do was hold me for another thirty seconds, because the other guys were coming around the corner. But I just said, 'I gotta go.' I ran as fast as I could. When I came close to the hiding place, nobody was chasing me anymore, so I dashed back in. A minute later I heard my pursuers running by. They didn't know where I went! We managed to stay in that hiding place another week. Meanwhile the Ukrainians were going around boarding up the houses, convinced that the Jews were gone. They had hatchets and they were hitting the walls.

"When I realized they were about to break into our hiding place, I crawled out a little window. I heard people yelling, 'Jews!' and at first I thought they meant me. I looked down and saw that nobody was paying attention to me, so with a carefully contrived show of nonchalance I walked away. I kept walking, right out of town and all the way to the next village.

"I knew a farmer in that village who had been friendly with my grandfather. I greeted him, but he told me to stay in the bushes because it was dangerous. It seemed that his whole village was collaborating with the Germans. He couldn't take me in, but he advised me to go twenty miles farther, to a town called Luboml, where there was still a Jewish ghetto and where I had some relatives. My uncle, who lived in Luboml, had a big house filled with people who had fled from surrounding areas, including two aunts who had left our town earlier. When I reached his place, I went to sleep exhausted. In the morning, the day when I tried to get up, my legs were so swollen from all the walking I had done the day before, I couldn't move them.

"A few days later my brother showed up, telling a horrible story. He had been caught and taken to the synagogue in our town, and they were about to shoot him, when he and another boy managed to crawl into a big stove. The police shot into the oven and killed the other boy. My brother was wounded in the leg, but the police didn't see him. When it was dark and the coast was clear, my brother sneaked out and made his way to my uncle's place. That night my brother and I slept, holding each other, and he said, 'I will never leave you again.'

"We had been there for about a week when I woke up at four A.M. to the sound of gunfire. I knew what was going on: They were rounding up Jews, just as they had done in our town. I looked out, and sure enough I saw the Germans and Ukrainians with guns, bayonets, and dogs. Quickly we all went to hide in a room that was boarded up except for the entrance, through a fireplace that moved. I was packed in there with my father's first cousin, his wife and two children, and other people as well. We stayed there all night.

"It must have been on the second day that one of the cousins wanted some water. He opened up the secret door. That alerted two Ukrainian militiamen, who shot into the wall, right next to me. I realized that this was about to be a repetition of what had happened in the other basement when my mother was taken. But I had gone through it already, so I knew what to do.

"The other people were all saying, 'Close it up!' But my logic said, 'Close up what? They've got us.' I said, 'No,' and started to crawl out. The militiaman pushed me back. He wanted gold. I crawled in again with a hat, to collect everybody's jewelry. Then I crawled out again and I gave the militiaman the hat with everything in it. The soldier's eyes bugged out! He was so excited by the gold, he wasn't pushing me back anymore . . . and I was able to get out of the hole! I pulled my brother behind me. He was petrified; he couldn't move. I actually had to pull him by the hair, and then we were both out. I looked at the soldier, who was still busy with the gold. I inched over to a window. Now I was sitting on the window ledge. I motioned to my brother to get up there with me. Suddenly the militiaman saw us, pointed his rifle, and ordered us down.

"At that moment someone from the hiding place handed them more valuables, and the Ukrainian militiaman got distracted. We ran up some steps to the next floor and dashed into a bedroom and hid under a bed. One of the militiamen ran after us and searched the rooms, but he didn't find us.

"When it seemed safe at last, we headed out the window. My brother went first, to help me down, but we were spotted. We had to run back up a ladder into the attic of the house next door. A militiaman was already in that house! He tried to push open the attic door, but my brother and I were sitting on it, holding on and pushing. The soldier saw it wasn't opening, so he left. We stayed in the attic. Within an hour I heard them leading out the people from our former hiding place at my uncle's. My father's cousin's little girl, who was eight, asked, 'Mommy are they going to shoot us?' I couldn't hear what her mother answered because so many people were crying.

"That evening my brother and I were hungry. I said I'd go down and get something, but my brother very firmly said, 'You're not going anywhere.' Later I looked around the attic and I didn't see him. Assuming that he had gone to look for food, I decided to go too. I went back to the old hiding place. I couldn't find anything, but while I was looking, I heard voices yelling in German. The Nazis had found the attic—and my brother *was* still in there! I never saw him again.

"That night I met Esther, a cousin of mine who was nineteen and kind of a leader, heading off to the woods with six others, so I followed. It was so dark that I had to hold on to somebody. We had to pass the main railroad area, which was brightly lit up to make sure no Jews got out. When there was a minute between flares, we crossed the tracks. We walked and walked and finally we sat down to rest near a Ukrainian cemetery. The moment I sat down, I fell asleep. When I woke up, everyone was gone.

"Right away my mind started working: What do you do next? I was scared of cemeteries! Kids were always talking about ghosts, and I believed in them. I didn't want to go into the cemetery to look for my companions. I calculated the real risk, and I said to myself, You're afraid, but don't be afraid. Nobody kills people in a cemetery. I climbed the stone wall and dropped down into the cemetery. I was shaking as I searched among the graves. I softly called, 'Isaac,' who was one of the boys with us.

"There was no answer. It was pitch-dark. Then I saw something a little darker, and I went in that direction. When I got a little closer, I saw it was a farm. I looked for the barn and made my way to the stall where a cow slept. I thought, A cow is a nice, friendly animal. So I lay down and slept next to the cow's head. I felt its warm, comforting breath. Just before dawn I woke up and saw a hayloft. It was high up, but I managed to jump up and grab one of the boards and pull myself up—quite an amazing feat for a little boy! Later the farmer's wife came to milk the cow. I coughed to get her attention. She was scared. I said, 'Don't be afraid.' I told her I was lost and I promised I would leave soon.

"She said, 'Don't leave now. Wait until the shepherd comes and takes the cows out.' She brought me a glass of milk and piece of bread. But while I hid, I heard talk about 'Jews hiding in the graveyard with gold.' I figured those must be my relatives and I'd better warn them. Without a sound I sneaked out to the cemetery, which wasn't far. Sure enough I found my cousins hiding under bushes. Now it seemed our lives were balanced on a hair.

"Our plan was to go to the next town, where there were Jews still in the ghetto. It was a long walk. One night we slept in the woods, and it was so cold, my clothes were frozen stiff. Amazingly I didn't catch cold. Now when I walk without shoes on cold tile, I get sick. But then? Being cold was the least of my problems!

"At one point I volunteered to go into the woods to find one of my cousins. I got lost and walked most of the day. Finally I got back, but I was tired and lagging behind the others. All of a sudden I heard a noise behind me, and when it got closer, I could see it was a guy on a bicycle with a rifle. He passed me and stopped. Then he took off his rifle, shot it in the air, and yelled. I lay down and started crawling away. Elated, I realized that he hadn't even seen me. Then I heard more Nazis coming. I started running, and they started shooting at me. A bullet went through my legs, grazed my shoe, and burned my foot a little bit.

"Wondering what to do, I spotted a drainage pipe that went under the road. I crawled in there. Luckily it didn't go straight, so the Nazis couldn't see me when they looked in. Then I heard them taking my cousins away. I was sitting there in water, afraid to get out. After a while I lifted my head and peeked. There was nobody around. Soaking wet, I climbed out and started walking. By the time I reached a farm, I was so tired, I made a hole in the nearest haystack, burrowed in, and immediately dropped off to sleep.

"I awoke with a start: The woman of the farm was jabbing me with a pitchfork. She was cursing me. Evidently she thought I was some kind of animal! Afraid she'd kill me, I put out my hand. The woman ran screaming for her husband. He was there in a moment, yanking me out and demanding to know who I was. Truthfully I told him, 'Ginsburg from Luboml is my uncle.' The farmer nodded. My uncle, who had owned a bar, had gotten along well with the farmers, who came to town on market day. Now this farmer gave me milk and break and directions to the home of another farmer named Sliva, who had also known my uncle.

"As I started out, I passed a wagon full of drunk militia with guns. They were rowdy, but I had to play 'You guys don't bother me.' While they were passing, I was paying attention to the other side of the road. It took two days to reach the Sliva farm. When I arrived, the woman there said I couldn't stay. The Slivas had been helping Jews, so they were suspect. They let me stay one night, but advised me to join some other Jews hiding in the woods.

"The next day I found the place they told me to go, but the people were eaten up with all kinds of vermin. It was horrible! As it happened, the Ukrainians found them and killed them with hand grenades. So it was good I didn't stay! Sliva told me that farmers don't always lock the barns. He said, 'Like, for instance, I have a little door that I never lock.' Now I knew there was a place I could sneak in at night and sleep in the hay. When I heard the roosters, that was my alarm clock!

"In this particular farm colony most of the people were not Catholics, but Seventh-Day Adventists. Their philosophy, their mentality, was different. In other words they may still have had anti-Semitism ingrained in them, but they would not betray a Jew. So I was safer. Finally I found a family who said they would keep me if I gave them something. I decided to go to the ghetto of Vlodzimiez Volinsk and see what I could find.

"Mr. Sliva was going in that direction by horse and wagon. Together we left at four A.M. with plans to meet a week later for the trip back. Mr. Sliva dropped me off near the ghetto. He showed me the gate, where they let me walk right in. I saw a Ukrainian militiaman with a gun, and I realized I was in a ghetto surrounded by barbed wire and soldiers. I understood with surprise and dismay that I was trapped, with no way to get out.

"I went to the empty, cleaned-out part of the ghetto in search of clothes. All I could find was a ripped sheepskin. A woman sewed it up for me. I found two shoes—both left feet—lost or abandoned by a Russian soldier. They were too big, but I took them anyway . . . and started planning. How would I get out? There seemed to be no way. Finally I had an idea: I put that sheepskin and those big shoes on to make myself look bigger. I waited until the line of people going out to work in the morning all got counted. Then I got in line, and somehow, once outside, I got away.

"That was Tuesday morning. When I got to the meeting place, Sliva wasn't there. I waited a while but knew it would be dangerous to hang around too long. The important thing was not to draw attention to myself, as they were still killing Jews all over the place. Finally I started walking, and eventually I did meet up with Sliva, who took me to the folks who had agreed to keep me. To my surprise those people already had another six Jews hiding in their barn and under the kitchen.

"I spent the whole next winter there. It was the first time since I lost my mother that I felt safe enough to cry. I felt so sorry that I hadn't gotten out to help her. Theoretically there was nothing I could have done, and if I'd tried, I would have just died too. At least I took some comfort from the fact that when my mother went to her death, she knew that they hadn't gotten me. That was a victory for her!

"When spring came, I felt I ought to earn my keep, so I took a job as a shepherd and worked until summer. At this time the Ukrainians decided that the Jews were all gone, and they started attacking Polish villages. Some of these Seventh-Day Adventists believed, as many Jews did, that God would intercede and smite the Germans. Just like the Jews, those Protestants and Catholic Poles were taken to their death—forty thousand of them! Some of them didn't want to run away. I knew of one family that was killed except for one boy who ran away. He saw the Ukrainians kill everyone in his family, bayoneting children to the walls, just like they'd done with the Jews before.

"Where was I to run now? The family I was staying with knew the attack was to come, and they sent me out on the road to watch, like a spy. When I heard shots, they almost left me there, but we ended up hiding on church property. After that there were many close calls. One day that teenager who'd chased me in the city when I got away by pretending that I had a gun appeared. He stared at me and said, 'I know you.' It had only been about a year. I tried to get away, but he followed me. Desperate, I played the game, acting cool. Finally he went away.

"On another occasion two German officers had taken over half the farmhouse where I was working. They took a liking to me. They thought I was Christian. Every time they got their rations, they would give me the candy. When they saw what a hard worker I was, they said that their mother had a farm in Germany and they wanted to send me to her. I got scared because that was all I needed! I knew if I got to Germany, they would give me an inspection and I'd be finished. I had to tell them, 'No, I'm waiting here. My parents may be alive.' Somehow I got out of that.

"Finally the war and my hiding ordeal were over. I was brought to the United States in a group of orphans. I went to live with an aunt. I spoke no English, but always resourceful, I managed to excel in school, earning grades of ninety-five and higher. Later I put myself through college, first with a job selling ice cream and candy in the subways and then with a part-time job in a factory. Now, four decades later, I have beautiful wife who was also hidden as a child, three successful children, and even a grandchild.

"I'm certainly grateful to the United States, my adopted country, for the freedom and opportunity I've had to contribute and belong. For example, I'm an electrical engineer. A long while ago I came up with a new and much better way of making a furnace that processes dental porcelain. It was something I figured out . A manufacturer who was the king of the industry at that time looked at my plans and smiled. He said, 'It'll never work.' However, he was wrong: I had virtually revolutionized the process, and I got the patent.

"Fortunately I never lost my wartime ability to size up a situation and know what to do. Not long ago I was at my factory in the Bronx, having just come back from the bank with the payroll. When I walked in the door, there was a big guy ready to hit me with a lead pipe. Bang! He brought the pipe down on my head, but I moved so fast, the blow was cushioned. I fought with him. He must have thought I was crazy. Maybe I *was* at that point! Moments later I had his hat in my hand, and I was chasing him down the street. I ended up with some bruises, but thanks to my very, very fast reaction, I was—once again—the clever little boy outsmarting the bully who wanted me dead.

"When I look back at what happened to me during the war, it all seems so crazy. I've read a great deal about the Holocaust, and I've made a lot of notes. But up until now I've kept my own story to myself. In fact I haven't even shared it fully with my three children, even though my daughter is a psychiatrist. It's still such a soft and vulnerable part of me. When I think about all my relatives who died, I'm afraid I might cry, and that is something I don't allow myself to do.

"However, lately I'm feeling that I can't stay quiet any longer. I was just reading about an organization that's been putting ads in college newspapers, claiming that the Holocaust never happened. In response I wrote an article, giving a little of my background. I sent it to the editor of the Rutgers University newspaper. I felt I had to go on record. I realize that the older survivors are passing away, and I'm getting older myself. When I'm gone, there will be very few people left with any firsthand experience. So what can I do but tell the truth?"

JEAN-PAUL SARTRE

from Existentialism Is a Humanism (1946)

. . . what can be said from the very beginning is that by existentialism we mean a doctrine which makes human life possible and, in addition, declares that every truth and every action implies a human setting and a human subjectivity.

As is generally known, the basic charge against us is that we put the emphasis on the dark side of human life. . . . we are said to be naturalists; and if we are, it is rather surprising that in this day and age we cause so much more alarm and scandal than does naturalism, properly so called. The kind of person who can take in his stride such a novel as Zola's *The Earth* is disgusted as soon as he starts reading an existentialist novel. . . .

. . . There are still . . . the people who say, "It's only human!" whenever a more or less repugnant act is pointed out to them . . . these are the people who accuse existentialism of being too gloomy, and to such an extent that I wonder whether they are complaining about it, not for its pessimism, but much rather its optimism. Can it be that what really scares them in the doctrine I shall try to present here is that it leaves to man a possibility of choice? To answer this question, we must re-examine it on a strictly philosophical plane. What is meant by the term *existentialism*? . . .

. . . What complicates matters is that there are two kinds of existentialists; first, those who are Christian, among whom I would include Jaspers and Gabriel Marcel, both Catholic; and on the other hand the atheistic existentialists among whom I class Heidegger, and then the French existentialists and myself. What they have in common is that they think that existence precedes essence, or, if you prefer, that subjectivity must be the starting point.

. . . Atheistic existentialism, which I represent . . . states that if God does not exist, there is at least one being in whom existence precedes essence, a being who exists before he can be defined by any concept, and that this being is man. . . . What is meant here by saying that existence precedes essence? It means that, first of all, man exists, turns up, appears on the scene, and, only afterwards, defines himself. If man, as the existentialist conceives him, is indefinable, it is because at first he is nothing. Only afterward will he be something, and he himself will have made what he will be. Thus, there is no human nature, since there is no God to conceive it. Not only is man what he conceives himself to be, but he is also only what he wills himself to be after this thrust toward existence.

Man is nothing else but what he makes of himself. Such is the first principle of existentialism. . . . if existence really does precede essence, man is responsible for what he is. Thus, existentialism's first move is to make every man aware of what he is and to make the full responsibility of his existence rest on him. And when we say that a man is responsible for himself, we do not only mean that he is responsible for his own individuality, but that he is responsible for all men. . . .

. . . When we say that man chooses his own self, we mean that every one of us does likewise; but we also mean by that that in making this choice he also chooses all men. In fact, in creating the man that we want to be, there is not a single one of our acts which does not at the same create an image of man as we think he ought to be. To choose to be this or that is to affirm at the same time the value of what we choose, because we can never choose evil. We always choose the good, and nothing can be good for us without being good for all.

If . . . existence precedes essence, and if we grant that we exist and fashion our image at one and the same time, the image is valid for everybody and for our whole age. Thus, our responsibility is much greater than we might have supposed, because it involves all mankind. If I am a workingman and choose to join a Christian trade-union rather than be a communist, and if by being a member I want to show that the best thing for man is resignation, that the kingdom of man is not of this world, I am not only involving my own case—I want to be resigned for everyone. As a result, my action has involved all humanity. To take a more individual matter, if I want to marry, to have children; even if this marriage depends solely on my own circumstances or passion or wish, I am involving all humanity in monogamy and not merely myself. Therefore, I am responsible for myself and for everyone else. I am creating a certain image of man of my own choosing. In choosing myself, I choose man.

This helps us understand what the actual content is of such rather grandiloquent words as anguish, forlornness, despair. As you will see, it's all quite simple.

First, what is meant by anguish? The existentialists say at once that man is anguish. What that means is this: the man who involves himself and who realizes that he is not only the person he chooses to be, but also a lawmaker who is, at the same time, choosing all mankind as well as himself, can not help escape the feeling of his total and deep responsibility. Of course, there are many people who are not anxious; but we claim that they are hiding their anxiety, that they are fleeing from it. Certainly, many people believe that when they do something, they themselves are the only ones involved, and when someone says to them, "What if everyone acted that way?" they shrug their shoulders and answer, "Everyone doesn't act that way." But really, one should always ask himself, "What would happen if everybody looked at things that way?" There is no escaping this disturbing thought except by a kind of double-dealing. A man who lies and makes excuses for himself by saying "Not everybody does that," is someone with an uneasy conscience, because the act of lying implies that a universal value is conferred upon the lie.

Anguish is evident even when it conceals itself. . . .

When we speak of forlornness . . . we mean only that God does not exist and that we have to face all the consequences of this. . . .

. . . all possibility of finding values in a heaven of ideas disappears along with Him; there can no longer be an *a priori* Good, since there is no infinite and perfect consciousness to think it. Nowhere is it written that the Good exists, that we must be honest, that we must not lie; because the fact is we are on a plane where there are only men. Dostoievsky said,

"If God didn't exist, everything would be possible." That is the very starting point of existentialism. Indeed, everything is permissible if God does not exist, and as a result man is forlorn, because neither within him nor without does he find anything to cling to. He can't start making excuses for himself.

If existence really does precede essence, there is no explaining things away by reference to a fixed and given human nature. In other words, there is no determinism, man is free, man is freedom. On the other hand, if God does not exist, we find no values or commands to turn to which legitimize our conduct. So, in the bright realm of values, we have no excuse behind us, nor justification before us. We are alone, with no excuses.

That is the idea I shall try to convey when I say that man is condemned to be free. Condemned, because he did not create himself, yet, in other respects is free; because, once thrown into the world, he is responsible for everything he does. . . .

As for despair. . . . It means that we shall confine ourselves to reckoning only with what depends upon our will, or on the ensemble of probabilities which make our action possible. . . . The moment the possibilities I am considering are not rigorously involved by my action, I ought to disengage myself from them, because no God, no scheme, can adapt the world and its possibilities to my will. When Descartes said, "Conquer yourself rather than the world," he meant essentially the same thing. . . .

. . . Quietism is the attitude of people who say, "Let others do what I can't do." The doctrine I am presenting is the very opposite of quietism, since it declares, "There is no reality except in action." Moreover, it goes further, since it adds, "Man is nothing else than his plan; he exists only to the extent that he fulfills himself; he is therefore nothing else than the ensemble of his acts, nothing else than his life."

According to this, we can understand why our doctrine horrifies certain people. Because often the only way they can bear their wretchedness is to think, "Circumstances have been against me. What I've been and done doesn't show my true worth. . . ."

. . . A man is involved in life, leaves his impress on it, and outside of that there is nothing. To be sure, this may seem a harsh thought to someone whose life hasn't been a success. But, on the other hand, it prompts people to understand that reality alone is what counts, that dreams, expectations, and hopes warrant no more than to define a man as a disappointed dream, as miscarried hopes, as vain expectations. In other words, to define him negatively and not positively. . . . What we mean is that a man is nothing else than a series of undertakings, that he is the sum, the organization, the ensemble of the relationships which make up these undertakings.

When all is said and done, what we are accused of, at bottom, is not our pessimism, but an optimistic toughness. If people throw up to us our works of fiction in which we write about people who are soft, weak, cowardly, and sometimes even downright bad, it's not because these people are soft, weak, cowardly, or bad; because if we were to say, as Zola did, that they are that way because of heredity, the workings of environment, society, because of biological or psychological determinism, people would be reassured. They would say, "Well, that's what we're like, no one can do anything about it." But when the existentialist writes about a coward, he says that this coward is responsible for his cowardice. He's not like that because he has a cowardly heart or lung or brain; he's not like that on account of his physiological make-up; but he's like that because he has made himself a coward by his acts. . . . what makes cowardice is the act of renouncing or yielding. . . .

What the existentialist says is that the coward makes himself cowardly, that the hero makes himself heroic. There's always a possibility for the coward not to be cowardly any more and for the hero to stop being heroic. What counts is total involvement; some one particular action or set of circumstances is not total involvement. . . .

. . . if it is impossible to find in every man some universal essence which would be human nature, yet there does exist a universal human condition. It's not by chance that today's thinkers speak more readily of man's condition than of his nature. By condition they mean, more or less definitely, the *a priori* limits which outline man's fundamental situation in the universe. Historical situations vary; a man may be born a slave in a pagan society or a feudal lord or a proletarian. What does not vary is the necessity for him to exist in the world, to be at work there, to be there in the midst of other people, and to be mortal there. . . . And though the configurations may differ, at least none of them are completely strange to me, because they all appear as attempts either to pass beyond these limits or recede from them or deny them or adapt to them. Consequently, every configuration, however individual it may be, has a universal value.

Every configuration, even the Chinese, the Indian, or the Negro, can be understood by a Westerner. "Can be understood" means that by virtue of a situation that he can imagine, a European of 1945 can, in like manner, push himself to his limits and reconstitute within himself the configuration of the Chinese, the Indian, or the African. Every configuration has universality in the sense that every configuration can be understood by every man. This does not at all mean that this configuration defines man forever, but that it can be met with again. There is always a way to understand the idiot, the child, the savage, the foreigner, provided one has the necessary information.

In this sense we may say that there is a universality of man; but it is not given, it is perpetually being made. I build the universal in choosing myself; I build it in understanding the configuration of every other man, whatever age he might have lived in. . . .

. . . Existentialism isn't so atheistic that it wears itself out showing that God doesn't exist. Rather, it declares that even if God did exist, that would change nothing. There you've got our point of view. Not that we believe that God exists, but we think that the problem of His existence is not the issue. In this sense existentialism is optimistic, a doctrine of action, and it is plain dishonesty for Christians to make no distinction between their own despair and ours and then to call us despairing.

BERTOLT BRECHT

from Writing the Truth: Five Difficulties (1935)

Nowadays, anyone who wishes to combat lies and ignorance and to write the truth must overcome at least five difficulties. He must have the *courage* to write the truth when truth is everywhere opposed; the *keenness* to recognize it, although it is everywhere concealed; the *skill* to manipulate it as a weapon; the *judgment* to select those in whose hands it will be effective; and the *cunning* to spread the truth among such persons. These are formidable problems for writers living under Fascism, but they exist also for those writers who have fled or been exiled; they exist even for writers working in countries where civil liberty prevails.

1. The Courage to Write the Truth

It seems obvious that whoever writes should write the truth in the sense that he ought not to suppress or conceal truth or write anything deliberately untrue. He ought not to cringe before the powerful, nor betray the weak. It is, of course, very hard not to cringe before the powerful, and it is highly advantageous to betray the weak. To displease the possessors means to become one of the dispossessed. To renounce payment for work may be the equivalent of giving up the work, and to decline fame when it is offered by the mighty may mean to decline it forever. This takes courage.

Times of extreme oppression are usually times when there is much talk about high and lofty matters. At such times it takes courage to write of low and ignoble matters such as food and shelter for workers; it takes courage when everyone else is ranting about the vital importance of sacrifice. When all sorts of honors are showered upon the peasants it takes courage to speak of machines and good stock feeds which would lighten their honorable labor. When every radio station is blaring that a man without knowledge or education is better than one who has studied, it takes courage to ask: better for whom? When all the talk is of perfect and imperfect races, it takes courage to ask whether it is not hunger and ignorance and war that produce deformities.

And it also takes courage to tell the truth about oneself, about one's own defeat. Many of the persecuted lose their capacity for seeing their own mistakes. It seems to them that the persecution itself is the greatest injustice. The persecutors are wicked simply because they persecute; the persecuted suffer because of their goodness. But this goodness has been beaten, defeated, suppressed; it was therefore a weak goodness, a bad, indefensible, unreliable goodness. For it will not do to grant that goodness must be weak as rain must be wet. *It takes courage to say that the good were defeated not because they were good, but because they were weak.*

Naturally, in the struggle with falsehood we must write the truth, and this truth must not be a lofty and ambiguous generality. When it is said of someone, "He spoke the truth," this implies that some people or many people or at least one person said something unlike the truth—a lie or a generality—but *he* spoke the truth, he said something practical, factual, undeniable, something to the point.

It takes little courage to mutter a general complaint, in a part of the world where complaining is still permitted, about the wickedness of the world and the triumph of barbarism, or to cry boldly that the victory of the human spirit is assured. There are many who pretend that cannon are aimed at them when in reality they are the target merely of opera glasses. They shout their generalized demands to a world of friends and harmless persons. They insist upon a generalized justice for which they have never done anything; they ask for a generalized freedom and demand a share of the booty which they have long since enjoyed. They think that truth is only what sounds nice. If truth should prove to be something statistical, dry, or factual, something difficult to find and requiring study, they do not recognize it as truth; it does not intoxicate them. They possess only the external demeanor of truth-tellers. The trouble with them is: *they do not know the truth*.

2. The Keenness to Recognize the Truth

Since it is hard to write the truth because truth is everywhere suppressed, it seems to most people to be a question of character whether the truth is written or not written. They believe that courage alone suffices. They forget the second obstacle: the difficulty of *finding* the truth. It is impossible to assert that the truth is easily ascertained.

First of all we strike trouble in determining *what* truth is worth the telling. For example, before the eyes of the whole world one great civilized nation after the other falls into barbarism. Moreover, everyone knows that the domestic war which is being waged by the most ghastly methods can at any moment be converted into a foreign war which may well leave our continent a heap of ruins. This, undoubtedly, is one truth, but there are others. Thus, for example, it is not untrue that chairs have seats and that rain falls downward. Many poets write truths of this sort. They are like a painter adorning the walls of a sinking ship with a still life. Our first difficulty does not trouble them and their consciences are clear. Those in power cannot corrupt them, but neither are they disturbed by the cries of the oppressed; they go on painting. The senselessness of their behavior engenders in them a "profound" pessimism which they sell at good prices; yet such pessimism would be more fitting in one who observes these masters and their sales. At the same time it is not easy to realize that their truths are truths about chairs or rain; they usually sound like truths about important things. For it is the nature of artistic creation to confer importance. But upon closer examination it is possible to see that they say merely: a chair is a chair; and: no one can prevent the rain from falling down.

They do not discover the truths that are worth writing about. On the other hand, there are some who deal only with the most urgent tasks, who embrace poverty and do not fear rulers, and who nevertheless cannot find the truth. These lack knowledge. They are full of ancient superstitions, with notorious prejudices that in bygone days were often put into beautiful words. The world is too complicated for them; they do not know the facts; they do not perceive relationships. In addition to temperament, knowledge, which can be acquired, and methods, which can be learned, are needed. What is necessary for all writers in this age of perplexity and lightning change is a knowledge of the materialistic dialectic of economy and history. This knowledge can be acquired from books and from practical instruction, if the necessary diligence is applied. Many truths can be discovered in simpler fashion, or at least portions of truths, or facts that lead to the discovery of truths. Method is good in all inquiry, but it is possible to make discoveries without using any method— indeed, even without inquiry. But by such a casual procedure one does not come to the kind of presentation of truth which will enable men to act on the basis of that presentation. People who merely record little facts are not able to arrange the things of this world so that they can be easily controlled. Yet truth has this function alone and no other. Such people cannot cope with the requirement that they write the truth.

If a person is ready to write the truth and able to recognize it, there remain three more difficulties.

3. The Skill to Manipulate the Truth as a Weapon

The truth must be spoken with a view to the results it will produce in the sphere of action. As a specimen of a truth from which no results, or the wrong ones, follow, we can cite the widespread view that bad conditions prevail in a number of countries as a result of barbarism. In this view, Fascism is a wave of barbarism which has descended upon some countries with the elemental force of a natural phenomenon.

According to this view, Fascism is a new, third power beside (and above) capitalism and socialism; not only the socialist movement but capitalism as well might have survived without the intervention of Fascism. And so on. This is, of course, a Fascist claim; to accede to it is a capitulation to Fascism. Fascism is a historic phase of capitalism; in this sense it is something new and at the same time old. In Fascist countries capitalism continues to exist, but only in the form of Fascism; and *Fascism can be combatted as capitalism alone, as the nakedest, most shameless, most oppressive, and most treacherous form of capitalism.*

But how can anyone tell the truth about Fascism, unless he is willing to speak out against capitalism, which brings it forth? What will be the practical results of such truth?

Those who are against Fascism without being against capitalism, who lament over the barbarism that comes out of barbarism, are like people who wish to eat their veal without slaughtering the calf. They are willing to eat the calf, but they dislike the sight of blood. They are easily satisfied if the butcher washes his hands before weighing the meat. They are not against the property relations which engender barbarism; they are only against barbarism itself. They raise their voices against barbarism; and they do so in countries where precisely the same property relations prevail, but where the butchers wash their hands before weighing the meat.

Outcries against barbarous measures may be effective as long as the listeners believe that such measures are out of the question in their own countries. Certain countries are still able to maintain their property relations by methods that appear less violent than those used in other countries. Democracy still serves in these countries to achieve the results for which violence is needed in others, namely, to guarantee private ownership of the means of production. The private monopoly of factories, mines, and land creates barbarous conditions everywhere, but in some places these conditions do not so forcibly strike the eye. Barbarism strikes the eye only when it happens that monopoly can be protected only by open violence.

Some countries, which do not yet find it necessary to defend their barbarous monopolies by dispensing with the formal guarantees of a constitutional state, as well as with such amenities as art, philosophy, and literature, are particularly eager to listen to visitors who abuse their native lands because those amenities are denied there. They gladly listen because they hope to derive from what they hear advantages in future wars. Shall we say that they have recognized the truth who, for example, loudly demand an unrelenting struggle against Germany "because that country is now the true home of Evil in our day, the partner of hell, the abode of the Antichrist"? We should rather say that these are foolish and dangerous people. For the conclusion to be drawn from this nonsense is that since poison gas and bombs do not pick out the guilty, Germany must be exterminated—the whole country and all its people.

The man who does not know the truth expresses himself in lofty, general, and imprecise terms. He shouts about "the" German, he complains about Evil in general, and whoever hears him cannot make out what to do. Shall he decide not to be a German? Will hell vanish if he himself is good? The silly talk about the barbarism that comes out of barbarism is also of this kind. The source of barbarism is barbarism, and it is combatted by culture, which comes from education. All this is put in general terms; it is not meant to be a guide to action and is in reality addressed to no one.

Such vague descriptions point to only a few links in the chain of causes. Their obscurantism conceals the real forces making for disaster. If light be thrown on the matter it promptly appears that disasters are caused by certain men. For we live in a time when the fate of man is determined by men.

Fascism is not a natural disaster which can be understood simply in terms of "human nature." But even when we are dealing with natural catastrophes, there are ways to portray them which are worthy of human beings because they appeal to man's fighting spirit.

After a great earthquake that destroyed Yokohama, many American magazines published photographs showing heaps of ruins. The captions read: STEEL STOOD. And, to be sure, though one might see only ruins at first glance, the eye swiftly discerned, after noting the caption, that a few tall buildings had remained standing. Among the multitudinous descriptions that can be given of an earthquake, those drawn up by construction engineers concerning the shifts in the ground, the force of stresses, the heat developed, etc., are of the greatest importance, for they lead to future construction which will withstand earthquakes. If anyone wishes to describe Fascism and war, great disasters which are not natural catastrophes, he must do so in terms of a practical truth. He must show that these disasters are launched by the possessing classes to control the vast numbers of workers who do not own the means of production.

If one wishes successfully to write the truth about evil conditions, one must write it so that its avertible causes can be identified. If the preventable causes can be identified, the evil conditions can be fought.

4. The Judgment to Select Those in Whose Hands the Truth Will Be Effective

The century-old custom of trade in critical and descriptive writing and the fact that the writer has been relieved of concern for the destination of what he has written have caused him to labor under a false impression. He believes that his customer or employer, the middle-man, passes on what he has written to everyone. The writer thinks: I have spoken and those who wish to hear will hear me. In reality he has spoken and those who are able to *pay* hear him. A great deal, though still too little, has been said about this; I merely want to emphasize that "writing for someone" has been transformed into merely "writing." But the truth cannot merely be written; it must be written *for someone,* someone who can do something with it. The process of recognizing truth is the same for writers and readers. In order to say good things, one's hearing must be good and one must hear good things. The truth must be spoken deliberately and listened to deliberately. And for us writers it is important to whom we tell the truth and who tells it to us.

We must tell the truth about evil conditions to those for whom the conditions are worst, and we must also learn the truth from them. We must address not only people who hold certain views, but people who, because of their situation, should hold these views. And the audience is continually changing. Even the hangmen can be addressed when the payment for hanging stops, or when the work becomes too dangerous. The Bavarian peasants were against every kind of revolution, but when the war went on too long and the sons who came home found no room on their farms, it was possible to win them over to revolution.

It is important for the writer to strike the true note of truth. Ordinarily, what we hear is a very gentle, melancholy tone, the tone of people who would not hurt a fly. Hearing this one, the wretched become more wretched. Those who use it may not be foes, but they are certainly not allies. The truth is belligerent; it strikes out not only against falsehood, but against particular people who spread falsehood.

5. The Cunning to Spread the Truth Among the Many

Many people, proud that they possess the courage necessary for the truth, happy that they have succeeded in finding it, perhaps fatigued by the labor necessary to put it into workable form and impatient that it should be grasped by those whose interests they are espousing, consider it superfluous to apply any special cunning in spreading the truth. For this reason they often sacrifice the whole effectiveness of their work. At all times cunning has been employed to spread the truth, whenever truth was suppressed or concealed. Confucius falsified an old, patriotic historical calendar. He changed certain words. Where the calendar read, "The ruler of Hun had the philosopher Wan killed because he said so and so," Confucius replaced *killed* by *murdered.* If the calendar said that tyrant so and so *died by assassination,* he substituted *was executed.* In this manner Confucius opened the way for a fresh interpretation of history.

In our times anyone who says *population* in place of *people* or *race*, and *privately owned land* in place of *soil*, is by that simple act withdrawing his support from a great many lies. He is taking away from these words their rotten, mystical implications. The word *people* (*Volk*) implies a certain unity and certain common interests; it should therefore be used only when we are speaking of a number of peoples, for then alone is anything like community of interest conceivable. The population of a given territory may have a good many different and even opposed interests—and this is a truth that is being suppressed. In like manner, whoever speaks of soil and describes vividly the effect of plowed fields upon nose and eyes, stressing the smell and color of earth, is supporting the rulers' lies. For the fertility of the soil is not the question, nor men's love for the soil, nor their industry in working it; what is of prime importance is the price of grain and the price of labor. Those who extract profits from the soil are not the same people who extract grain from it, and the earthy smell of a turned furrow is unknown on the produce exchanges. The latter have another smell entirely. *Privately owned land* is the right expression; it affords less opportunity for deception.

Where oppression exists, the word *obedience* should be employed instead of *discipline*, for discipline can be self-imposed and therefore has something noble in its character that obedience lacks. And a better word than *honor* is *human dignity*; the latter tends to keep the individual in mind. We all know very well what sort of scoundrels thrust themselves forward, clamoring to defend the honor of a people. And how generously they distribute honors to the starvelings who feed them. Confucius' sort of cunning is still valid today. Thomas More in his *Utopia* described a country in which just conditions prevailed. It was a country very different from the England in which he lived, but it resembled that England very closely, except for the conditions of life.

Lenin wished to describe exploitation and oppression on Sakhalin Island, but it was necessary for him to beware of the Czarist police. In place of Russia he put Japan, and in place of Sakhalin, Korea. The methods of the Japanese bourgeoisie reminded all his readers of the Russian bourgeoisie and Sakhalin, but the pamphlet was not blamed because Russia was hostile to Japan. Many things that cannot be said in Germany about Germany can be said about Austria.

There are many cunning devices by which a suspicious State can be hoodwinked.

Voltaire combatted the Church doctrine of miracles by writing a gallant poem about the Maid of Orleans. He described the miracles that undoubtedly must have taken place in order that Joan of Arc should remain a virgin in the midst of an army of men, a court of aristocrats, and a host of monks. By the elegance of his style, and by describing erotic adventures such as characterized the luxurious life of the ruling class, he threw discredit upon a religion which provided them with the means to pursue a loose life. . . .

Propaganda that stimulates thinking, in no matter what field, is useful to the cause of the oppressed. Such propaganda is very much needed. Under governments which serve to promote exploitation, thought is considered base.

Anything that serves those who are oppressed is considered base. It is base to be constantly concerned about getting enough to eat; it is base to reject honors offered to the defenders of a country in which those defenders go hungry; base to doubt the Leader when his leadership leads to misfortunes; base to be reluctant to do work that does not feed the worker; base to revolt against the compulsion to commit senseless acts; base to be indifferent to a family which can no longer be helped by any amount of concern.

The starving are reviled as voracious wolves who have nothing to defend; those who doubt their oppressors are accused of doubting their own strength; those who demand pay for their labor are denounced as idlers. Under such governments thinking in general is considered base and falls into disrepute. Thinking is no longer taught anywhere, and wherever it does emerge, it is persecuted. . . .

What counts is that the right sort of thinking be taught, a kind of thinking that investigates the transitory and changeable aspect of all things and processes. Rulers have an intense dislike for significant changes. They would like to see everything remain the same—for a thousand years, if possible. They would love it if sun and moon stood still. Then no one would grow hungry any more, no one would want his supper. When the rulers have fired a shot, they do not want the enemy to be able to shoot; theirs must be the last shot. A way of thinking that stresses change is a good way to encourage the oppressed. . . .

Cunning is necessary to spread the truth.

Summary

The great truth of our time is that our continent is giving way to barbarism because private ownership of the means of production is being maintained by violence. Merely to recognize this truth is not sufficient, but should it not be recognized, no other truth of importance can be discovered. Of what use is it to write something courageous which shows that the condition into which we are falling is barbarous (which is true) if it is not clear why we are falling into this condition? We must say that torture is used in order to preserve property relations. To be sure, when we say this we lose a great many friends who are against torture only because they think property relations can be upheld without torture, which is untrue.

We must tell the truth about the barbarous conditions in our country in order that the thing should be done which will put an end to them—the thing, namely, which will change property relations.

Furthermore, we must tell this truth to those who suffer most from existing property relations and who have the greatest interest in their being changed—the workers and those whom we can induce to be their allies because they too have really no control of the means of production even if they do share in the profits.

And we must proceed cunningly.

All these five difficulties must be overcome at one and the same time, for we cannot discover the truth about barbarous conditions without thinking of those who suffer from them; cannot proceed unless we shake off every trace of cowardice; and when we seek to discern the true state of affairs in regard to those who are ready to use the knowledge we give them, we must also consider the necessity of offering them the truth in such a manner that it will be a weapon in their hands, and at the same time we must do it so cunningly that the enemy will not discover and hinder our offer of the truth.

That is what is required of a writer when he is asked to write the truth.

VIII. Since 1945

In some ways it is difficult to generalize about the last fifty years because they are still so much a part of the present. Only recently have most European nations selected political leaders from the postwar generation; only in the last decade has the postwar division of Europe into East and West begun to be dismantled; only as they have become elderly have many children of the Holocaust told their stories. In the half-century since the Second World War, Europeans have continued to revisit issues that have concerned Europe for centuries; they have also addressed new issues that were virtually unimaginable in the past.

To understand late twentieth-century Europe it is necessary to think globally. For five hundred years, Europe understood itself as the center of the world—culturally, intellectually, politically, economically. The literalness with which we have taken that metaphor is embodied in the words commonly used in English (until very recently) to name different areas on the globe. Geographical designations such as 'West Indies' and 'East Indies,' 'Near East,' 'Middle East,' and 'Far East' sound reasonable if you are standing in London, but quite illogical if you stand in Delhi, Tokyo, or Los Angeles. Traditional notions of center and periphery have had to give way as nations once considered by Europeans to be peripheral to European culture and politics—particularly the United States and the Soviet Union—have acted as major participants in recent European history. This de-centering of Europe has been compounded by the process of de-colonization; since 1945 over 50 independent nations have been established where representatives of a few European empires once governed.

From our vantage point, Munch's *The Scream* seems a prescient response to the cataclysmic events of the twentieth century—the Great War, the Second World War, the Holocaust, the atom bomb. These events shattered irrevocably nineteenth-century optimism that the world was progressing and becoming increasingly civilized, and that science could provide the answers to all human questions. It is not surprising that Sartrean existentialism, born in part out of the war experience, rejected the assumption that human beings are inherently good for an emphasis on responsibility and action. In the decades since the Second World War, people in many parts of the globe have reconsidered their European cultural legacies and faced unavoidable questions. What is the legacy of the scientific revolution—the atom bomb? What remains of enlightenment after the final solution? How can cultures, and cultural differences, best be understood after the discrediting of social Darwinism and the end of empires? As women and men question a legacy of differentiation based on gender, race, and class, what new forms of social order and new philosophies may, or should, develop? In a postmodern world in which everything has always already been tried, done, or said, how can one create something new, or be authentic?

Simone de Beauvoir (1908–1986), born into a conservative Catholic family in Paris, studied philosophy at the Sorbonne and became a leading figure among French intellectuals. In her novels and memoirs, she explores the experiences of women and men and the formation of the self in a modern, existential world. Beauvoir is best known, however, for her monumental treatise *The Second Sex*, which examines women's subordination to men throughout European history, particularly the ways women are socialized and the contradictions between myths about women and the realities of women's lives. "One is not born, but rather becomes, a woman," Beauvoir argues, for what we have understood the term 'woman' to stand for is something artificial, man-made, rather than natural. 'Woman' is the *second* sex because she has been "defined and differentiated with reference to man and not he with reference to her; she is the incidental, the inessential as opposed to the essential. He is the Subject, he is the Absolute—she is the Other." A landmark work in both feminist and existentialist thought, *The Second Sex* has been one of the most influential books published in the last half-century.

It is impossible to separate the personal stories of twentieth-century Europeans from the larger history to which they are, in the words of English novelist Penelope Lively, "shackled . . . like it or not." Years after the Second World War, the past continues to shape the present, perhaps nowhere more pointedly than in lives affected directly by Nazi Germany. German novelist Christa Wolf (b. 1929) opens an autobiographical novel about growing up under Nazism with these words: "What is past is not dead; it is not even past. We cut ourselves off from it; we pretend to be strangers." In the two short essays included in this reader, written during the 1960s in the German Democratic Republic (East Germany), Wolf reflects on the ways individual stories, national histories, and politics are inextricably intertwined.

Social changes in the last fifty years have helped to call into question the conventional definition of 'culture' as something elite and distinct from ordinary existence. As Raymond Williams (1921–1988) explains, such definitions serve artificially to separate high cultural products—art and literature—from the circumstances that produced them, to make them inaccessible, and to overvalue them at the expense of attending to real-life circumstances. Williams's argument comes both from his personal experience and Marxist theory: son of a railway signalman in Wales, he became a highly influential cultural critic and one of the first members of the working class to be named Professor at Cambridge University.

Establishing European cultural institutions in colonies was part of the process of imperialism; rethinking, and in many cases dismantling, those institutions has been part of the program of decolonization. The stakes here are high, and complex. Modernization has its origins in Europe, but has substantially affected every part of the world; figuring out which modern institutions and European practices serve the needs of a particular culture, and which do not, is a difficult and controversial process. In his powerful polemic *Decolonising the Mind*, Ngũgĩ wa Thiong'o (b. 1938) describes the process of colonial education, a process which teaches respect for the colonizer's culture at the price of alienation from one's own. Ngũgĩ, a writer and activist, grew up in colonial Kenya and studied at the University of Leeds in Britain. His first published works were originally written in English, but in the

1980s he began writing in his own language, Gĩkũyũ. Ngũgĩ, who was detained in prison in 1980 after one of his works was performed by peasants and workers, emphasizes the idea that culture and politics cannot be separated.

And, lastly, postmodernism. As the introduction to this reader notes, contemporary thinkers have begun to question whether the cultural condition or epoch called 'modernity' continues to exist today. One form this questioning takes is the characterization of the present historical moment as 'postmodern.' Whether 'postmodern' means 'beyond modernism,' 'beyond modernity,' 'the last wave of modernism,' or something else has been the topic of much debate. A common thread in each way postmodernism is defined is the sense that the modern has played out all its variations, that it is exhausted or bankrupt, that it is in need of critique. For some, then, postmodernism is both a political and cultural stance. For others, including Italian theorist and novelist Umberto Eco (b. 1929), it is more a frame of mind. The moderns tried to destroy the past, but failed, Eco writes; the postmodern reply, he suggests, is to recognize that since the past cannot be destroyed it must be revisited, from another standpoint, with irony rather than innocence.

SIMONE DE BEAUVOIR

from The Second Sex (1949)

from Chapter XI

Myth and Reality

The myth of woman plays a considerable part in literature; but what is its importance in daily life? To what extent does it affect the customs and conduct of individuals? In replying to this question it will be necessary to state precisely the relations this myth bears to reality.

There are different kinds of myths. This one, the myth of woman, sublimating an immutable aspect of the human condition—namely, the "division" of humanity into two classes of individuals—is a static myth. It projects into the realm of Platonic ideas a reality that is directly experienced or is conceptualized on a basis of experience; in place of fact, value, significance, knowledge, empirical law, it substitutes a transcendental Idea, timeless, unchangeable, necessary. This idea is indisputable because it is beyond the given: it is endowed with absolute truth. Thus, as against the dispersed, contingent, and multiple existences of actual women, mythical thought opposes the Eternal Feminine, unique and changeless. If the definition provided for this concept is contradicted by the behavior of flesh-and-blood women, it is the latter who are wrong: we are told not that Femininity is a false entity, but that women concerned are not feminine. The contrary facts of experience are impotent against the myth. In a way, however, its source is in experience. Thus it is quite true that woman is other than man, and this alterity is directly felt in desire, the embrace, love; but the real relation is one of reciprocity; as such it gives rise to authentic drama. Through eroticism, love, friendship, and their alternatives, deception, hate, rivalry, the relation is a struggle between conscious beings each of whom wishes to be essential, it is the mutual recognition of free beings who confirm one another's freedom, it is the vague transition from aversion to participation. To pose Woman is to pose the absolute Other, without reciprocity, denying against all experience that she is a subject, a fellow human being.

In actuality, of course, women appear under various aspects; but each of the myths built up around the subject of woman is intended to sum her up *in toto*; each aspires to be unique. In consequence, a number of incompatible myths exist, and men tarry musing before the strange incoherencies manifested by the idea of Femininity. As every woman has a share in a majority of these archetypes—each of which lays claim to containing the sole Truth of woman—men of today also are moved again in the presence of their female companions to an astonishment like that of the old sophists who failed to understand how man could be blond and dark at the same time! Transition toward the absolute was indicated long ago in social phenomena: relations are easily congealed in classes, functions in types, just as relations, to the childish mentality, are fixed in things. Patriarchal society, for example, being centered upon the conservation of the patrimony, implies necessarily, along with those who own and transmit wealth, the existence of men and women who take property away from its owners and put it into circulation. The men—adventurers, swindlers, thieves, speculators—are generally repudiated by the group; the women, employing their erotic attraction, can induce young men and even fathers of families to scatter their patrimonies, without ceasing to be within the law. Some of these women appropriate their victims' fortunes or obtain legacies by using undue influence; this role being regarded as evil, those who play it are called "bad women." But the fact is that quite to the contrary they are able to appear in some other setting—at home with their fathers, brothers, husbands, or lovers—as guardian angels; and the courtesan who "plucks" rich financiers is, for painters and writers, a generous patroness. It is easy to understand in actual experience the ambiguous personality of Aspasia or Mme de Pompadour. But if woman is depicted as the Praying Mantis, the Mandrake, the Demon, then it is most confusing to find in woman also the Muse, the Goddess Mother, Beatrice.

As group symbols and social types are generally defined by means of antonyms in pairs, ambivalence will seem to be an intrinsic quality of the Eternal Feminine. The saintly mother has for correlative the cruel stepmother, the angelic young girl has the perverse virgin: thus it will be said sometimes that Mother equals Life, sometimes that Mother equals Death, that every virgin is pure spirit or flesh dedicated to the devil.

Evidently it is not reality that dictates to society or to individuals their choice between the two opposed basic categories; in every period, in each case, society and the individual decide in accordance with their needs. Very often they project into the myth adopted the institutions and values to which they adhere. Thus the paternalism that claims woman for hearth and home defines her as sentiment, inwardness, immanence. In fact every existent is at once immanence and transcendence; when one offers the existent no aim, or prevents him from attaining any, or robs him of his victory, then his transcendence falls vainly into the past—that is to say, falls back into immanence. This is the lot assigned to woman in the patriarchate; but it is in no way a vocation, any more than slavery is the vocation of the slave. The development of this mythology is to be clearly seen in Auguste Comte. To identify Woman with Altruism is to guarantee to man absolute rights in her devotion, it is to impose on women a categorical imperative. . . .

Few myths have been more advantageous to the ruling caste than the myth of woman: it justifies all privileges and even authorizes their abuse. Men need not bother themselves with alleviating the pains and the burdens that physiologically are women's lot, since these are "intended by Nature"; men use them as a pretext for increasing the misery of the feminine lot still further, for instance by refusing to grant woman any right to sexual pleasure, by making her work like a beast of burden.

Of all these myths, none is more firmly anchored in masculine hearts than that of the feminine "mystery." It has numerous advantages. And first of all it permits an easy explanation of all that appears inexplicable; the man who "does not understand" a woman is happy to substitute an objective resistance for a subjective deficiency of mind; instead of admitting his ignorance, he perceives the presence of a "mystery" outside himself: an alibi, indeed, that flatters laziness and vanity at once. A heart smitten with love thus avoids many disappointments: if the loved one's behavior is capricious, her remarks stupid, then the mystery serves to excuse it all. And finally, thanks again to the mystery, that negative relation is perpetuated which seemed to Kierkegaard infinitely preferable to positive possession; in the company of a living enigma man remains alone—alone with his dreams, his hopes, his fears, his love, his vanity. This subjective game, which can go all the way from vice to mystical ecstasy, is for many a more attractive experience than an authentic relation with a human being. What foundations exist for such a profitable illusion? . . .

. . . Mystery is never more than a mirage that vanishes as we draw near to look at it.

We can see now that the myth is in large part explained by its usefulness to man. The myth of woman is a luxury. It can appear only if man escapes from the urgent demands of his needs; the more relationships are concretely lived, the less they are idealized. The fellah of ancient Egypt, the Bedouin peasant, the artisan of the Middle Ages, the worker of today has in the requirements of work and poverty relations with his particular woman companion which are too definite for her to be embellished with an aura either auspicious or inauspicious. The epochs and the social classes that have been marked by the leisure to dream have been the ones to set up the images, black and white, of femininity. But along with luxury there was utility; these dreams were irresistibly guided by interests. Surely most of the myths had roots in the spontaneous attitude of man toward his own existence and toward the world around him. But going beyond experience toward the transcendent Idea was deliberately used by patriarchal society for purposes of self-justification; through the myths this society imposed its laws and customs upon individuals in a picturesque, effective manner; it is under a mythical form that the group-imperative is indoctrinated into each conscience. Through such intermediaries as religion, traditions, language, tales, songs, movies, the myths penetrate even into such existences as are most harshly enslaved to material realities. Here everyone can find sublimation of his drab experiences: deceived by the woman he loves, one declares that she is a Crazy Womb; another, obsessed by his impotence, calls her a Praying Mantis; still another enjoys his wife's company: behold, she is Harmony, Rest, the Good Earth! The taste for eternity at a bargain, for a pocket-sized absolute, which is shared by a majority of men, is satisfied by myths. The smallest emotion, a slight annoyance, becomes the reflection of a timeless Idea—an illusion agreeably flattering to the vanity.

The myth is one of those snares of false objectivity into which the man who depends on ready-made valuations rushes headlong. Here again we have to do with the substitution of a set idol for actual experience and the free judgments it requires. For an authentic relation with an autonomous existent, the myth of Woman substitutes the fixed contemplation of a mirage. . . .

from Chapter XII

Childhood

One is not born, but rather becomes, a woman. No biological, psychological, or economic fate determines the figure that the human female presents in society; it is civilization as a whole that produces this creature, intermediate between male and eunuch, which is described as feminine. Only the intervention of someone else can establish an individual as an *Other*.

from Chapter XIII

The Young Girl

Beyond the lack of initiative that is due to women's education, custom makes independence difficult for them. If they roam the streets, they are stared at and accosted. I know young girls who, without being at all timid, find no enjoyment in taking walks alone in Paris because, importuned incessantly, they must be always on the alert, which spoils their pleasure. If girl students run in gay groups through the streets, as boys do, they make a spectacle of themselves; to walk with long strides, sing, talk, or laugh loudly, or eat an apple, is to give provocation; those who do will be insulted or followed or spoken to. Careless gaiety is in itself bad deportment; the self-control that is imposed on women and becomes second nature in "the well-bred young girl" kills spontaneity; her lively exuberance is beaten down. The result is tension and ennui.

This ennui is catching: young girls quickly tire of one another; they do not band together in their prison for mutual benefit; and this is one of the reasons why the company of boys is necessary to them. This incapacity to be self-sufficient engenders a timidity that extends over their entire lives and is marked even in their work. They believe that outstanding success is reserved for men; they are afraid to aim too high. We have seen that little girls of fourteen, comparing themselves with boys, declared that "the boys are better." This is a debilitating conviction. It leads to laziness and mediocrity. A young girl, who had no special deference for the stronger sex, was reproaching a man for his cowardice; it was remarked that she herself was a coward. "Oh, a woman, that's different!" declared she, complacently.

The fundamental reason for such defeatism is that the adolescent girl does not think herself responsible for her future; she sees no use in demanding much of herself since her lot in the end will not depend on her own efforts. Far from consigning herself to man because she recognizes her inferiority, it is because she is thus consigned to him that, accepting the idea of her inferiority, she establishes its truth.

And, actually, it is not by increasing her worth as a human being that she will gain value in men's eyes; it is rather by modeling herself upon their dreams. When still inexperienced, she is not always aware of this fact. She may be as aggressive as the boys; she may try to make their conquest with a rough authority, a proud frankness; but this attitude almost surely dooms her to failure. All girls, from the most servile to the haughtiest, learn in time that to please they must abdicate. Their mothers enjoin upon them to treat the boys no longer as comrades, not to make advances, to take a passive role. If they wish to start a friendship or a flirtation, they must carefully avoid seeming to take the initiative in it; men do not like *garçons manqués*, or bluestockings, or brainy women; too much daring, culture, or intelligence, too much character, will frighten them. In most novels, as George Eliot remarks, it is the blonde and silly heroine who is in the end victorious over the more mannish brunette; and in *The Mill on the Floss* Maggie tries in vain to reverse the roles; but she finally dies and the blonde Lucy marries Stephen. In *The Last of the Mohicans* the vapid Alice gains the hero's heart, not the valiant Clara; in *Little Women* the likable Jo is only a childhood playmate for Laurie: his love is reserved for the insipid Amy and her curls.

To be feminine is to appear weak, futile, docile. The young girl is supposed not only to deck herself out, to make herself ready, but also to repress her spontaneity and replace it with the studied grace and charm taught to her by her elders. Any self-assertion will diminish her femininity and her attractiveness. The young man's journey into existence is made relatively easy by the fact that there is no contradiction between his vocation as human being and as male; and this advantage is indicated even in childhood. Through self-assertion in independence and liberty, he acquires his social value and concurrently his prestige as male: the ambitious man, like Balzac's Rastignac, aims at wealth, celebrity, and women in one and the same enterprise; one of the stereotypes which stimulate his effort is that of the powerful and famous man whom women adore.

But for the young woman, on the contrary, there is a contradiction between her status as a real human being and her vocation as a female. And just here is to be found the reason why adolescence is for a woman so difficult and decisive a moment. Up to this time she has been an autonomous individual: now she must renounce her sovereignty. Not only is she torn, like her brothers, though more painfully, between the past and the future, but in addition a conflict breaks out between her original claim to be subject, active, free, and, on the other hand, her erotic urges and the social pressure to accept herself as passive object. Her spontaneous tendency is to regard herself as the essential: how can she make up her mind to become the inessential? But if I can accomplish my destiny only as the *Other*, how shall I give up my Ego? Such is the painful dilemma with which the woman-to-be must struggle. Oscillating between desire and disgust, between hope and fear, declining what she calls for, she lingers in suspense between the time of childish independence and that of womanly submission. It is this uncertainly that, as she emerges from the awkward age, gives her the sharp savor of a fruit still green.

CHRISTA WOLF
A Speech (1964)
Twenty-five Years (1966)

A Speech

It has happened to all of you often enough, that someone has suddenly started to tell you about his past life. You have all talked about yourselves to someone or even to several people. Many of my generation or an older one feel that their past lives have been pretty exciting and improbable. How often you hear a person say: If only someone would write that down, it would make a real novel! And have you ever noticed how many so-called true stories begin something like this: What a pity! Things like that just can't be put down in writing . . .

I do not intend to carry on the old argument here as to whether everything that happens in a person's life can or must find a place in art; I simply want to try and tell you a couple of life stories. The lives of two men now in their mid-thirties who told me about themselves. I sat facing one of them recently in the office of a big factory. No one can ever write about that, he kept saying, himself surprised.

He was born in a shabby workers' district in an old town, one of a big working class family. He was as poor as he was intelligent and thirsty for knowledge and ambitious. His mother accepted a high school stipend for him from the Nazi government. The boy donned a brown shirt and "Führer" badge and thought he was a member of the master race, his path led from the workers' district to Poland and Russia, countries inhabited by inferior races. Until he was sixteen years old he had never heard the word "class" spoken without hatred and contempt. Decked out in a steel helmet too large for him, with a gun too heavy over his shoulder, he had clung fanatically to a desperate troop trying to defend their home town in 1945. Then sent off into the depths of Russia with one of the first transports of incorrigible war criminals—for three years. "There from the working class was I, polishing officers' boots again," he said. "It's impossible to describe what was going on inside me."

He came home again. Those who had sent him away, Communists, were willing to hold out a helping hand now. He refused to take it. He began as an unskilled laborer in a factory.

Now thirty-five years old, this same man is a doctor of economy and manager of a big plant. What has happened to him in the past fifteen or twenty years probably ought to be called the birth of a man. Wherever he turns up he is always involved in heated arguments: "Man, what's going on here is indescribable!"

Early this year I sat together with a young man in West Germany—a contemporary of that young factory manager. His story had another refrain that I heard then for the first time: "I sometimes wonder what would have become of me if I had lived over there with you in the G.D.R."

This young man had a better start than our plant manager. His father, a Social Democratic journalist, did not let the Nazis take his son away from him. When the war was over he introduced the boy to politics. He became an enthusiastic young Social Democratic functionary, arguing bitterly with Communists at meetings. Everyone said he had a great career before him.

And he is now a minor official in a small government office. One day he was faced with the choice between following the anti-revolutionary path taken by his party or sticking to his own new-found political convictions. He was expelled from the SPD because of his too evident left-wing leanings. His former party now warns people against him as a dangerous Communist infiltrator. People who know him, say that he has ruined his own career. He lives his life in the evenings and at weekends, when he can visit young people, talk to them, win them over and organize them. Most of his talent and ability lies fallow. "What would I be doing now if I had lived in the G.D.R.?" he asks.

The bourgeois novels and plays of the past two hundred years are full of tragedies, of young men who long to make their great, noble dreams come true but break down, physically or morally, in face of the limitations, the uselessness, the apathy of their society. Werther, Julien Sorel, Anna Karenina must all perish. The sacrifices resulting from wars have been recorded in analyses and statistics for hundreds of years. There are no statistics of the drama of people whose talents, perhaps even genius, have been misused or stifled. No one will ever count the number of people who died the slow death of bitterness, resignation, self-abandonment.

We are just beginning to write the first sentences of other stories, certainly not fairy stories of eternally smiling people reclining on rosy clouds, but stories of people working hard, often to the limits of their endurance, of people who have made up their minds to think of "happiness" as being productive, not as a chance to be indolent and of "unhappiness" as the loss of opportunity to be creative, not as the loss of possessions. For the first time, life presents us with subject matter that does not drive us to cause our characters to end in physical or moral ruin. The conflicts are no less powerful, on the contrary they are sharper, more moral, that is to say, more human. There are thousands of different, often complicated and genuinely thrilling answers to the same old question of whether a man can form himself, without being pushed, working voluntarily and consciously together with his own kind.

Everyone faces the danger of underestimating or overestimating specific personal experiences and events of the time. It may take a long period to understand the importance of a decision, a friendship, the scope of the consequences of a mistake or something left undone. The history books are full of the most curious false estimates arrived at by clever people about their own times. We, who are thinking more profoundly about our history than was formerly done in Germany, do not claim to have achieved our aim after these fifteen years. Experience has taught us that beyond each aim new needs emerge. What we can say is that in this part of Germany, dominated by the Nazis twenty years ago and inhabited by embittered, confused and hate-filled people, the foundations have been laid for human beings to live reasonably together. Reason, we call it socialism, has penetrated into everyday life. It is the measure, the ideal, by which we judge how praise or blame is to be meted out.

If we record this in our history books as a fact in our day and as the decisive thing in our progress, I do not think we shall have to correct it later on.

Twenty-five Years

> Thoughts on some photos in a Soviet front-line illustrated magazine published during the war, in 1941, showing men and women, partisans and soldiers, defending their country.

At whom is this young woman shooting? Whom has she there in the sights of her gun—a couple of hundred yards away from her and twenty-five years away from us?

And the next picture: three girls. The sky, nowhere so lofty as in August in Russia, hangs over their bayonets this summer. Already behind them the horror that the solid, safe sky can be wounded, shot through, torn apart; the soul-searing shock when they realize that it is they, and only they who must stand guard before their country. Behind them the farewells, the departure. They will fire at the enemy that marched through their defenceless village, singing, laughing, hen-chasing. There was no time to change, not enough uniforms to go round; their harvesting clothes will do just as well. Cartridge belts resting firmly on their hips with the unaccustomed weight. Orders issued in unaccustomed words in their own language.

Still the same country, but the shouldered gun has changed everything. The wooded hills that were once, an infinite six weeks ago, the frontier to their fields and the place where they went for walks on Sundays—now a refuge, or a first line of defence. Still a trace of surprise in the eye for the young man who yesterday distributed the work amongst his kolkhoz team and today issues military orders. He will not have to repeat a single word.

Everything changed, even the face. The other two faces already begin to look alike, and also like the face of the woman on air raid alarm duty at night in Leningrad, hundreds of miles away, and like the faces of the girls bringing baskets of eggs to the collecting center. And they still have the great changes before them. What will they not have to see, what will they not be forced to do! Time will break apart into "before" and "after," and no one should harbor illusions about the possibility of healing this gap. Nothing will ever be as it was before. The last remnants of softness will disappear with this hope.

If these women are still alive (how much one wishes it and how unlikely it is) they will not remember the summer sky of 1941. It won't have existed. Nothing will be left of what this summer owed them. No one should think that any part of it can be repeated: a single song, a working day, a dream, a love. Shot to pieces, bombed to bits. Life narrowed down to the zone of fire, to a spot, that white spot in front, the hated face of the enemy.

> *Doch als wir vor das rote Moskau kamen*
> *Stand vor uns Volk von Acker und Betrieb*
> *Und es besiegte uns in aller Völker Namen*
> *auch jenes Volks, das sich das deutsche schrieb.*

(But when we got to Moscow the red city / Men from the farms and factories confronted us. / And we were beaten in the name of all nations / Including that nation which calls itself German.)

Yes, the enemy is there. You can see it in the faces of these men and women, already defeated. How is it that no aggressor can ever see this in the faces of those he attacks, that he never recoils before its calm steadfastness, that he pays so lightly the price to the school of aggression—contempt for human life—again and again? Blind worship of the machinery of war which does, in fact, seem to be capable of endless improvement. That is what they call "progress." And behind the steel walls stands the man, more and more despicable, who presses the button when he gets his orders.

On the other hand, human beings. Photos from the Moscow archives. The opponents of German fascism in the summer of the year nineteen hundred and forty-one.

Twenty-five years. At whom is the young woman shooting? No longer at us. Discharged, forever discharged from the compulsory school of aggression.

That is what we call liberation.

Raymond Williams
from Culture Is Ordinary (1958)

The bus stop was outside the cathedral. I had been looking at the Mappa Mundi, with its rivers out of Paradise, and at the chained library, where a party of clergymen had got in easily, but where I had waited an hour and cajoled a verger before I even saw the chains. Now, across the street, a cinema advertised the *Six-Five Special* and a cartoon version of *Gulliver's Travels*. The bus arrived, with a driver and a conductress deeply absorbed in each other. We went out of the city, over the old bridge, and on through the orchards and the green meadows and the fields red under the plough. Ahead were the Black Mountains, and we climbed among them, watching the steep fields end at the grey walls, beyond which the bracken and heather and whin had not yet been driven back. To the east, along the ridge, stood the line of grey Norman castles; to the west, the fortress wall of the mountains. Then, as we still climbed, the rock changed under us. Here, now, was limestone, and the line of the early iron workings along the scarp. The farming valleys, with their scattered white houses, fell away behind. Ahead of us were the narrower valleys: the steel-rolling mill, the gasworks, the grey terraces, the pitheads. The bus stopped, and the driver and conductress got out, still absorbed. They had done this journey so often, and seen all its stages. It is a journey, in fact, that in one form or another we have all made.

I was born and grew up halfway along that bus journey. Where I lived is still a farming valley, though the road through it is being widened and straightened, to carry the heavy lorries to the north. Not far away, my grandfather, and so back through the generations, worked as a farm labourer until he was turned out of his cottage and, in his fifties, became a roadman. His sons went at thirteen or fourteen on to the farms, his daughters into service. My father, his third son, left the farm at fifteen to be a boy porter on the railway, and later became a signalman, working in a box in this valley until he died. I went up the road to the village school, where a curtain divided the two classes—Second to eight or nine, First to fourteen. At eleven I went to the local grammar school, and later to Cambridge.

Culture is ordinary: that is where we must start. To grow up in that country was to see the shape of a culture, and its modes of change. I could stand on the mountains and look north to the farms and the cathedral, or south to the smoke and the flare of the blast furnace making a second sunset. To grow up in that family was to see the shaping of minds: the learning of new skills, the shifting of relationships, the emergence of different language and ideas. My grandfather, a big hard labourer, wept while he spoke, finely and excitedly, at the parish meeting, of being turned out of his cottage. My father, not long before he died, spoke quietly and happily of when he had started a trade-union branch and a Labour Party group in the village, and, without bitterness, of the 'kept men' of the new politics. I speak a different idiom, but I think of these same things.

Culture is ordinary: that is the first fact. Every human society has its own shape, its own purposes, its own meanings. Every human society expresses these, in institutions, and in arts and learning. The making of a society is the finding of common meanings and directions, and its growth is an active debate and amendment under the pressures of experience, contact, and discovery, writing themselves into the land. The growing society is there, yet it is also made and remade in every individual mind. The making of a mind is, first, the slow learning of shapes, purposes, and meanings, so that work, observation and communication are possible. Then, second, but equal in importance, is the testing of these in experience, the making of new observations, comparisons, and meanings. A culture has two aspects: the known meanings and directions, which its members are trained to; the new observations and meanings, which are offered and tested. These are the ordinary processes of human societies and human minds, and we see through them the nature of a culture: that it is always both traditional and creative; that it is both the most ordinary common meanings and the finest individual meanings. We use the word culture in these two senses: to mean a whole way of life—the common meanings; to mean the arts and learning—the special processes of discovery and creative effort. Some writers reserve the word for one or the other of these senses; I insist on both, and on the significance of their conjunction. The questions I ask about our culture are questions about our general and common purposes, yet also questions about deep personal meanings. Culture is ordinary, in every society and in every mind.

. . . There is an English bourgeois culture, with its powerful educational, literary and social institutions, in close contact with the actual centres of power. To say that most working people are excluded from these is self-evident, though the doors, under sustained pressure, are slowly opening. But to go on to say that working people are excluded from English culture is nonsense; they have their own growing institutions, and much of the strictly bourgeois culture they would in any case not want. A great part of the English way of life, and of its arts and learning, is not bourgeois in any discoverable sense. There are institutions, and common meanings, which are in no sense the sole product of the commercial middle class; and there are art and learning, a common English inheritance, produced by many kinds of men, including many who hated the very class and system which now take pride in consuming it. The bourgeoisie has given us much, including a narrow but real system of morality; that is at least better than its court predecessors. The leisure which the bourgeoisie attained has given us much of cultural value. But this is not to say that contemporary culture is bourgeois culture: a mistake that everyone, from Conservatives to Marxists, seems to make. There is a distinct working-class way of life, which I for one value—not only because I was bred in it, for I now, in certain respects, live differently. I think this way of life, with its emphases of neighbourhood, mutual obligation, and common betterment, as expressed in the great working-class political and industrial institutions, is in fact the best basis for any future English society. As for the arts and learning, they are in a real sense a national inheritance which is, or should be, available to everyone.

Ngũgĩ wa Thiong'o

from Decolonising the Mind: The Politics of Language in African Literature (1985)

. . . So what was the colonialist imposition of a foreign language doing to us children?

The real aim of colonialism was to control the people's wealth: what they produced, how they produced it, and how it was distributed; to control, in other words, the entire realm of the language of real life. Colonialism imposed its control of the social production of wealth through military conquest and subsequent political dictatorship. But its most important area of domination was the mental universe of the colonised, the control, through culture, of how people perceived themselves and their relationship to the world. Economic and political control can never be complete or effective without mental control. To control a people's culture is to control their tools of self-definition in relationship to others.

For colonialism this involved two aspects of the same process: the destruction or the deliberate undervaluing of people's culture, their art, dances, religions, history, geography, education, orature and literature, and the conscious elevation of the language of the coloniser. The domination of a people's language by the languages of the colonising nations was crucial to the domination of the mental universe of the colonised.

Take language as communication. Imposing a foreign language, and suppressing the native languages as spoken and written, were already breaking the harmony previously existing between the African child and the three aspects of language. Since the new language as a means of communication was a product of and was reflecting the 'real language of life' elsewhere, it could never as spoken or written properly reflect or imitate the real life of that community. This may in part explain why technology always appears to us as slightly external, *their* product and not *ours*. The word 'missile' used to hold an alien far-away sound until I recently learnt its equivalent in Gikuyu, *ngurukuhi*, and it made me apprehend it differently. Learning, for a colonial child, became a cerebral activity and not an emotionally felt experience.

But since the new, imposed languages could never completely break the native languages as spoken, their most effective area of domination was the third aspect of language as a communication, the written. The language of an African child's formal education was foreign. The language of the books he read was foreign. The language of his conceptualisation was foreign. Thought, in him, took the visible form of a foreign language. So the written language of a child's upbringing in the school (even his spoken language within the school compound) became divorced from his spoken language at home. There was often not the slightest relationship between the child's written world, which was also the language of his schooling, and the world of his immediate environment in the family and the community. For a colonial child, the harmony existing between the three aspects of language as communication was irrevocably broken. This resulted in the disassociation of the sensibility of that child from his natural and social environment, which we might call colonial alienation. The alienation became reinforced in the teaching of history, geography, music, where bourgeois Europe was always the centre of the universe.

This disassociation, divorce, or alienation from the immediate environment becomes clearer when you look at colonial language as a carrier of culture.

Since culture is a product of the history of a people which it in turn reflects, the child was now being exposed exclusively to a culture that was a product of a world external to himself. He was being made to stand outside himself to look at himself. *Catching Them Young* is the title of a book on racism, class, sex, and politics in children's literature by Bob Dixon. 'Catching them young' as an aim was even more true of a colonial child. The images of this world and his place in it implanted in a child take years to eradicate, if they ever can be.

Since culture does not just reflect the world in images but actually, through those very images, conditions a child to see that world in a certain way, the colonial child was made to see the world and where he stands in it as seen and defined by or reflected in the culture of the language of imposition.

And since those images are mostly passed on through orature and literature it meant the child would now only see the world as seen in the literature of his language of adoption. From the point of view of alienation, that is of seeing oneself from outside oneself as if one was another self, it does not matter that the imported literature carried the great humanist tradition of the best in Shakespeare, Goethe, Balzac, Tolstoy, Gorky, Brecht, Sholokhov, Dickens. The location of this great mirror of imagination was necessarily Europe and its history and culture and the rest of the universe was seen from that centre.

But obviously it was worse when the colonial child was exposed to images of his world as mirrored in the written languages of his coloniser. Where his own native languages were associated in his impressionable mind with low status, humiliation, corporal punishment, slow-footed intelligence and ability or downright stupidity, non-intelligibility and barbarism, this was reinforced by the world he met in the works of such geniuses of racism as a Rider Haggard or a Nicholas Monsarrat; not to mention the pronouncement of some of the giants of western intellectual and political establishment, such as Hume ('. . . the negro is naturally inferior to the whites . . .'), Thomas Jefferson ('. . . the blacks . . . are inferior to the whites on the endowments of both body and mind . . .'), or Hegel with his Africa comparable to a land of childhood still enveloped in the dark mantle of the night as far as the development of self-conscious history was concerned. Hegel's statement that there was nothing harmonious with humanity to be found in the African character is representative of the racist images of Africans and Africa such a colonial child was bound to encounter in the literature of the colonial languages. The results could be disastrous.

In her paper read to the conference on the teaching of African literature in schools held in Nairobi in 1973, entitled 'Written Literature and Black Images', the Kenyan writer and scholar Professor Micere Mugo related how a reading of the description of Gagool as an old African woman in Rider Haggard's *King Solomon's Mines* had for a long time made her feel mortal terror whenever she encountered old African women. In his autobiography *This Life* Sydney Poitier describes how, as a result of the literature he had read, he had come to associate Africa with snakes. So on arrival in Africa and being put up in a modern hotel in a modern city, he could not sleep because he kept looking for snakes everywhere, even under the bed. These two have been able to pinpoint the origins of their fears. But for most others the negative image becomes internalised and it affects their cultural and even political choices in ordinary life.

Thus Léopold Sédar Senghor has said very clearly that although the colonial language had been forced upon him, if he had been given the choice he would still have opted for French. He becomes lyrical in his subservience to French:

> We express ourselves in French since French has a universal vocation and since our message is also addressed to French people and others. In our languages [i.e., African languages] the halo that surrounds the words is by nature merely that of sap and blood; French words send out thousands of rays like diamonds.

Senghor has now been rewarded by being anointed to an honoured place in the French Academy—that institution for safe-guarding the purity of the French language.

In Malawi, Banda has erected his own monument by way of an institution, The Kamuzu Academy, designed to aid the brightest pupils of Malawi in their mastery of English.

> It is a grammar school designed to produce boys and girls who will be sent to universities like Harvard, Chicago, Oxford, Cambridge and Edinburgh and be able to compete on equal terms with others elsewhere.

> The President has instructed that Latin should occupy a central place in the curriculum. All teachers must have had at least some Latin in their academic background. Dr. Banda has often said that no one can fully master English without knowledge of languages such as Latin and French . . .

For good measure no Malawian is allowed to teach at the academy—none is good enough—and all the teaching staff has been recruited from Britain. A Malawian might lower the standards, or rather, the purity of the English language. Can you get a more telling example of hatred of what is national, and a servile worship of what is foreign even though dead?

In history books and popular commentaries on Africa, too much has been made of the supposed differences in the policies of the various colonial powers, the British indirect rule (or the pragmatism of the British in their lack of a cultural programme!) and the French and Portuguese conscious programme of cultural assimilation. These are a matter of detail and emphasis. The final effect was the same: Senghor's embrace of French as this language with a universal vocation is not so different from Chinua Achebe's gratitude in 1964 to English—'those of us who have inherited the English language may not be in a position to appreciate the value of the inheritance'. The assumptions behind the practice of those of us who have abandoned our mother-tongues and adopted European ones as the creative vehicles of our imagination, are not different either.

Thus the 1962 conference of 'African Writers of English expression' was only recognising, with approval and pride of course, what through all the years of selective education and rigorous tutelage, we had already been led to accept: the 'fatalistic logic of the unassailable position of English in our literature'. The logic was embodied deep in imperialism; and it was imperialism and its effects that we did not examine at Makerere. It is the final triumph of a system of domination when the dominated start singing its virtues.

UMBERTO ECO

from Postscript *to* The Name of the Rose (1983)

Actually, I believe that postmodernism is not a trend to be chronologically defined, but, rather, an ideal category—or, better still, a *Kunstwollen*, a way of operating. We could say that every period has its own postmodernism, just as every period would have its own mannerism (and, in fact, I wonder if postmodernism is not the modern name for mannerism as metahistorical category). I believe that in every period there are moments of crisis like those, described by Nietzsche in his *Thoughts Out of Season*, in which he wrote about the harm done by historical studies. The past conditions us, harries us, blackmails us. The historic avant-garde (but here I would also consider avant-garde a metahistorical category) tries to settle scores with the past. "Down with moonlight"—a futurist slogan—is a platform typical of every avant-garde; you have only to replace "moonlight" with whatever noun suitable. The avant-garde destroys, defaces the past: *Les Demoiselles d'Avignon* is a typical avant-garde act. Then the avant-garde goes further, destroys the figure, cancels it, arrives at the abstract, the informal, the white canvas, the slashed canvas, the charred canvas. In architecture and the visual arts, it will be the curtain wall, the building as stele, pure parallelepiped, minimal art; in literature, the destruction of the flow of discourse, the Burroughs-like collage, silence, the white page; in music, the passage from atonality to noise to absolute silence (in this sense, the early Cage is modern).

But the moment comes when the avant-garde (the modern) can go no further, because it has produced a metalanguage that speaks of its impossible texts (conceptual art). The postmodern reply to the modern consists of recognizing that the past, since it cannot really be destroyed, because its destruction leads to silence, must be revisited: but with irony, not innocently. I think of the postmodern attitude as that of a man who loves a very cultivated woman and knows he cannot say to her, "I love you madly," because he knows that she knows (and that she knows that he knows) that these words have already been written by Barbara Cartland. Still, there is a solution. He can say, "As Barbara Cartland would put it, I love you madly." At this point, having avoided false innocence, having said clearly that it is no longer possible to speak innocently, he will nevertheless have said what he wanted to say to the woman: that he loves her, but he loves her in an age of lost innocence. If the woman goes along with this, she will have received a declaration of love all the same. Neither of the two speakers will feel innocent, both will have accepted the challenge of the past, of the already said, which cannot be eliminated; both will consciously and with pleasure play the game of irony. . . . But both will have succeeded, once again, in speaking of love.

Irony, metalinguistic play, enunciation squared. Thus, with the modern, anyone who does not understand the game can only reject it, but with the postmodern, it is possible not to understand the game and yet to take it seriously. Which is, after all, the quality (the risk) of irony.